*THE
STRUGGLE
FOR
WORLD
POWER*

© GEORGE KNUPFFER 1971

1st Edition 1958
2nd Edition 1963
3rd Fully Revised Edition 1971

Paper ISBN 0–85172–703–4

Cloth ISBN 0–85172–705–0

GEORGE KNUPFFER

THE STRUGGLE FOR WORLD POWER

REVOLUTION AND
COUNTER-REVOLUTION

LONDON
THE PLAIN-SPEAKER PUBLISHING COMPANY
1971

Published by the
Plain-Speaker Publishing Company,
43 Bath Road, London W4 1LJ, England

Printed in Great Britain in
10 on 11 pt. Juliana on Antique Wove paper
by the B.P.S. Printing Company
Chawleigh, Chulmleigh, Devon EX18 7HL

Contents

		Page
	Foreword to the Third Edition	7

Chapter

1.	The Three-Card Trick	9
2.	Towards Widespread Power	18
3.	Economic Roots of Power	28
4.	The Political Consequences of Economic Power	36
5.	The Nature of Capitalism and Banking	40
6.	The Nature of Socialism	46
7.	Making Sure of Borrowers	58
8.	Unemployment	64
9.	The Essence of Financial Capital	68
10.	The Solution of the Economic Problem	77
11.	The Role of the Banks under a New Dispensation	86
12.	The Political Attack of the Usurers	97
13.	The Foreign Policy of the Financiers	111
14.	Some Historical Illustrations	121
15.	The True Russia	128
16.	Some Details about Russia	138
17.	The Background of the Revolution	147
18.	The "Case" against Russia	153
19.	Policies which Mislead	160
20.	Russia's Struggle with Communism	167
21.	Allied Mistakes Towards Russia	180
22.	The Motives of the World Struggle	184
23.	The Plan of Counter-Revolution	190
24.	The Russian Émigrés	197
25.	Conclusions	203
	Appendix	213
	Index	233

DEDICATION

The writing of this book was suggested to me in 1955 by my old friend and collaborator in several important fields of over thirty years, Captain Henry Kerby, Member of Parliament, 1954 until his death in January 1971, and the third edition of *The Struggle for World Power* is dedicated to the memory of a deeply-informed and tough fighter for the right principles.

GEORGE KNUPFFER

Foreword to the Third Edition

The First Edition of this book was published in 1958, the Second in 1963, and that, too, is now exhausted. At the same time as the last edition this work was also published in Spain as "La Lucha por el Poder Mundial". The book has been read in all countries not only of the "free" world, but also orders had been received even for the First Edition from every one of the countries behind the Iron and Bamboo Curtains, though, of course, there it will have been read only by persons in authority, since the mass of the people are not free to read the truth.

And I can vouch for the fact that this book is true. The MS was ready in 1956 and I shewed it to top-level experts here and in the USA, asking them to point out any possible errors in fact or deduction. I was told by all that there were no mistakes. And since then, in almost 15 years, nobody has even attempted to prove that this book is in any respect mistaken.

But it is not merely the dissemination of very important truths bearing on political and economic practice against a background of a tremendous spiritual struggle for the possession of the souls and bodies of all humanity which comes into question. We must concern ourselves with the essential counter-revolutionary fight, to preserve our freedom and the possibility of working not merely for well-being on earth, but more especially for eternal salvation which is the most important aim of life.

We are living in very dangerous times. The enemy is close to final victory. He controls almost everything in the West and the East, under Capitalism and Democracy and under its product—Communism. The aim of the Revolution is World Government, the absolute and universal enslavement of everyone everywhere. And the protagonists of this plan are conscious, ruthless fighters for power. Therefore, if we are to survive, we, too, must be ready to fight for power in the service of the highest ideals, of the Church of Christ. Passive protest and rejection are not enough; we must be ready to organize to expose the dangers, to specify the weaknesses of the opponents, and then to organize to remove the enemy from the seats of power and replace his tools by men of faith, sense of duty and determination. For this purpose we are working to create the necessary organizations and to disseminate the required knowledge. All men and women who are not yet poisoned by materialism, pornography, liberalism and godlessness must join the struggle, before it is too late.

This book serves no other purpose than to inform and to call to action. There are other works, too, on these subjects, and those who care to do so should be encouraged to study the whole problem widely. But ultimately, if we are to win, we must come together in a global united front. Contact us if you are interested. Make the subject known to all your friends. Encourage them to study it. Fight while you still can. Both self-interest and a sense of duty towards others demand it. Raise the standard of the progressive and constructive Counter-Revolution, the fight for the new age of Faith and Freedom.

London, June 1971

GEORGE KNUPFFER

I

The Three-Card Trick

We are all now approaching the climax of the struggle for world power, which has been going on for centuries. This problem concerns each of us intimately. The author is a Russian but that which follows is not written predominantly from a Russian point of view, indeed it is not even written in Russian. An attempt is made to draw attention to a question of immense importance, and one which may be solved, one way or the other, within the lifetime of most people who are likely to glance at these pages. It follows that those who read them should, if they agree with the conclusions here set out, consider carefully and urgently what each of them can and must do, if certain eventualities are to be averted. Are we to be free men, serving our God and our fellow creatures, or are we to be slaves, deprived even of the right to worship the Almighty each in our own way? That is the question, and it involves also the survival of our nations and States, our culture and even racial survivals. Everything is at stake, including in many cases our very lives.

In this atomic age the potentialities of world-wide power are immense. Clearly those who control atomic power and nuclear weapons, either nationally or internationally, will wield such power as to be almost irresistible. Therefore the moral, social, political, economic and technical consequences of authority today are such that we must make ourselves aware of them at once and before it is too late. But first of all it is necessary to realize that most of us have almost no knowledge and understanding of the methods and technique by means of which power is obtained and used. Here we will try to illuminate some of the basic essentials, and we hope that our readers will then be encouraged to pursue the question further. The choice now for all of us everywhere is between utter slavery and an unprecedented prosperity with true liberty.

If some may think these propositions are too extreme, let them consider the fate of the lands behind the "Iron Curtain"; let them contemplate the utter slavery of hundreds of millions of people and the slaughter of scores of millions; let them remember the ruthless attempts to annihilate all faiths. And that is only a first round, a preliminary stage. The men who perpetrate every crime against God and man which a diabolical consciencelessness can suggest to them, are in control of only one third of the dry surface of the globe and one half its population. What must we expect if and when they have achieved power over all the earth? Let us never delude ourselves with the thought that such terrible things are too unlikely to be worth considering, or that they happen only to second-rate peoples. Not all those who may think themselves first-rate or immune are in reality so far from catastrophe.

Most of us, in all lands, have assumed for over fifty years, that by and large, the world is politically divided into two camps—the Reds and anti-Reds. We assume that the free and Democratic world is being threatened by Communism, and is resisting.

In fact that situation did apply in the earlier phases of the historical epoch which began with the Russian revolution of 1917, but it exists no longer.

There are now three camps in the world which are of major historical and political importance, and these camps are not, (as is sometimes superficially assumed) determined by national boundaries. They are three factors which are involved in a struggle for world power.

The fate of all humanity depends on a correct understanding of the issue and the proper actions.

Fundamentally, the world has been the scene of a deep struggle of ultimate significance—the struggle between the two Messianisms: that of the moral world and the world beyond the grave, of the life everlasting, and that of this world of material power and possessions. This struggle began two thousand years ago, and it is still the dominant theme of events.

It is, consequently, not surprising, that various philosophical and political teachings and movements have given expression to this theme for centuries. It is not surprising, in particular that approximately one hundred years ago there came into being the Marxist Socialist-Communist conspiracy to overthrow all existing states, governments, social and economic structures, and especially all faiths, so as to establish on earth the one rule of the materialistic anti-faith.

To the founders of this phase of the conspiracy it was clear from the start that Russia was a major obstacle to their plans, and later they also realized that, if it could be seized by the conspirators, it would provide a major base for further expansion throughout the globe. Though the Imperial régime was deeply rooted and accepted by the mass of the people, yet there were certain weaknesses which made the realization of the first stage of the world-revolutionary plan possible and Russia became, for the time being, the base and the tool of the conspirators.

However, it should never be forgotten that the origins of Marxism are Western and not Russian and that the roots of the revolutionary activity were outside Russia. The revolution, as is well known, was heavily subsidized during the decades preceding it, and more especially during the First World War. Most of the money came from two sources: New York and Berlin. This may seem somewhat strange to the uninitiated, as in the last period of the war Germany and America were enemies. Nevertheless the truth is simple: in New York the money was given by such as the banking firm of Kuhn, Loeb & Co., whose directors included Mr. J. Schiff and Mr. Warburg, founder of the Federal Reserve System, related by marriage, while in Berlin the financing of the revolution was handled by the German Imperial General Staff, working in conjunction with a German banker who was a brother of the New-York Warburg. So it will be seen the monetary support of the Russian revolution was only by chance also a matter of a German war policy; the main point was that this revolution was supported first and foremost by certain circles to whom national boundaries were a matter of no importance and who thought and acted internationally at all times.

The Bolshevik Communists set up the Third International as the body which was to handle and co-ordinate activity throughout the world. At first it was an organ to which even the Soviet-Government of the U.S.S.R. was subjected, and it was, indeed, the potential Government of the World. And it must never be forgotten that the Soviets are not the enemies of those circles, capitalistic though they were, which had supported them and made their victory possible. In fact Mr. Aschberg, the representative of the bankers who had made the revolution possible and had sustained it at its most difficult periods, remained in Moscow, close to the régime, until quite recently.

At first it was assumed by the backers of the Russian Revolution, both phases of which (February and October) were in reality interlinked, that the rest of the world would soon succumb to the charms and the threats of Communism. But these hopes were soon dashed. And worse was to follow: the Russians themselves were unwilling to submit and to let themselves be moulded into a brainwashed, terrorized and controlled instrument of world domination. Years of Civil War were followed by sustained risings in all parts of that huge country. The recent war brought about events which shook the régime even more. The terror, great and sustained though it is, and it has cost Russia tens of millions of lives and there are, at any given time, some twenty million people in prisons and concentration camps for political reasons, that terror has not broken Russia. On the contrary, the régime is being forced, slowly but surely, to adjust itself to the wishes and needs of the Russian nation. To sum up: the

Soviet régime is no longer the sole effective tool for the achievement of world domination by the materialistic messianists.

It is true the Soviet dictators still proclaim their old aims and still act so as to attain world power. They, are, in fact, already in control of almost half the world, the rest being weak, irresolute, blind and ineffective. It is now nearly ready for the kill. But the question arises: are the Soviets the only factor which is now aiming at world power?

The Soviet tyrants are riding the proverbial tiger: they cannot dismount. But also they are deeply involved in a game for the highest stakes; it is not alone a question of their personal survival, which would be unlikely if they retreat, but also of the alternative of complete assurance of safety and the greatest possible power and its fruits if they carry the old plans of world domination to an end. Feeling themselves close to ultimate success, they are unwilling to give up now. If they have had to retreat in very many respects inside Russia, they always know that that is precisely what they were taught—that it is well to be flexible and to allow temporary retreats.

Yet to their original backers, indeed begetters, the Soviets are no longer the only tool with which the world is to be conquered. They are no longer the sword of World Government. And this is by no means the case because they are undemocratic or cruel. All that has been forgiven in the past a thousand times every day. In fact when the Soviets were fully at the mercy of the West just after the recent war, being exhausted and having no atomic bombs, while the West was fresh and had the bombs, and much else, to say nothing of the internal Russian situation being fully ripe for a political explosion, while millions of violently anti-Communist Russians were available to the West, the West did nothing to overthrow or even to hinder the progress of the Kremlin clique. The secret of the bombs was passed to the Communists by many willing intermediaries. The Russian anti-Communists, a part of the nation which is and always has been anti-Soviet, were handed over by the million to the Bolsheviks to be slaughtered, and half the world was then tamely yielded to the declared enemy of the free peoples. In fact the war was lost. It had been ostensibly declared to rid the world of a dictator who wanted to spread his rule far and wide, and it ended with a dictator far worse and with ambitions not merely wide, but universal, firmly established. This paradox, which smells of treason and collusion between alleged opponents, can be understood only if it is realized that those who largely dominate the West, i.e., those who financed the Russian Revolution, could not allow their own creation to fall in circumstances in which it would have been replaced by that former dispensation in Russia which had been the main stumbling block to their aims. And this despite the fact that their own creation was no longer the only moral and political battering ram for the overthrow of the old order everywhere.

Bolshevism had proved to its sponsors that it was not an efficient instrument. It could not overcome certain resistances in Russia and elsewhere and even provoked certain anti-toxins. Also it had become unmanageable and disobedient. It had to go. But this decision called for two acts of policy: there had to be a ready alternative both for Russia and the satellites, and for the rest of the world. Meanwhile there had to be temporary and qualified support for the Soviets. That conditional support is still being given to prevent their premature elimination and the appearance of a far "worse" alternative. Nothing which is really dangerous to the Soviet receives encouragement or support, while the Communist régime has been subsidized for over 50 years.

In the meantime the alternative dispensation for Russia, for other Communist-dominated countries and for the whole world, is being actively and energetically prepared, with the expenditure of huge sums, mostly of American money. The raw materials are recent Communist collaborators. For Russia there is being built up an organization with certain attached groups with real aims largely hidden from Russians and others and known only to leaders and a relatively small number of well-informed people. The apparent policy is one of anti-Communism, democratic freedom, respect for national aspirations and full freedom for the Church. The actual policy is one of a modified Socialism, providing full control of economic and social life, laicism in the realm of education and thought, complete internationalism, with acceptance of World Government and World Federation, and finally, as a part of that scheme, the splitting up of Russia into its alleged component parts. Incidentally, this policy will fail, as it will drive the unwilling nation into the arms of the Soviets, as Hitler did, by his attack on Russia, and not on Communism.

We see that if once the centre, the focal point, of the conspiracy to attain materialistic world power seemed to be in Moscow, its leadership being symbolically vested in the Third International, now the centre, and focal point, of the same struggle for global domination, backed by the same people as before, is not in Moscow, but remains in Washington and New York, the place of the Third International having been taken by the United Nations. If the old League of Nations had been intended as a training unit and an example, to accustom people to the idea of internationalism and the abandonment of state sovereignty in favour of an anonymous international power which is not even declared to be Christian, the

United Nations is meant quite seriously; it is the final expression of the plan to set up the materialistic messianism.

In this light we can understand why in recent years such large numbers of open and hidden Communists have become leading and, indeed, sincere anti-Communists. We may think, at first glance, that they have become reformed characters. Nothing of the sort: they are quite logical and consistent, fighting for the same objectives as before, but in a new and "better" form. They have not abandoned their ultimate aim, but only the tools which have proved to be ineffective.

But to us, the huge majority of ordinary, decent, God-fearing people in all lands, including those behind the Iron Curtain, all these conspiracies are repellent, if only we realize their aims. We are the proposed victims—the third factor. It is for us to defend ourselves. We may have very little time left. We must act now.

Whoever you are, wherever you may be, do your part. Do not be misled by those who tell you that the enemy is only in Moscow. It is quite true that one of the enemies is there, and it is an enemy of a kind with whom there can never be compromise of any sort. But we must realize that if we continue to see the enemy only in Moscow, we will be stabbed in the back by the enemy in New-York, who wants to lead us. But that enemy, like the one in Russia, is only using America as a base. The American nation is no more guilty than the Russians. Both are victims of a subtle and powerful subversive force which they have not recognized in time.

More than that. It follows quite logically that the Russians, the Americans, the British and all others must unite to resist the dangers which face them all. There must be a nationalist and patriotic international, an international organization whose object is not to foist World Government on us all, but to defend independence because that is at the moment the only way in which we can defend true liberties, principles and faith.

It does not follow that world wide co-operation is not desirable and possible, but it is not the immediate problem. First of all we must survive as free men, before we can think in the future of free collaboration between ourselves on a permanent basis. Today we must close the ranks to resist the conspirators. We must take advantage of the fact that in their camp there is a deep and serious rift. We must be ready to intervene in our interests.

We use the term "materialistic-messianists" to describe what has become in the course of centuries a very well defined set of people, with a clear and consciously pursued policy and method. With the beginning of the Christian era there entered into our lives certain fundamental religious and philosophical conceptions, and a set of active policies in all spheres of human activity, which are the natural results of the Christian influence on human affairs. If the pre-Christian Old Testament Jewish teaching, which has become an integral part of our religious and cultural heritage, taught us monotheism and much else of fundamental value, and the prophets of Israel prepared the way for the Saviour, then the main theme of our present faith and culture, in so far as they are still accepted, are the teachings of the Messiah, the Son of God, who came to save us, to assure the life everlasting, to establish the Kingdom of God.

But Satan was not content to leave it at that. He immediately began to oppose the teaching and the work of the newly-established Christian Church, founded by Christ Himself. The Tempter has ever since tried to crucify every Christian, as he had crucified our Lord, and to oppose and prevent all the teachings of our Faith. In the place of the true spiritual messianism, which is concerned with the spiritual Kingdom of God, the Devil is striving to put the false messianism of the kingdom of this earth. He asserts that the ultimate aim of human life should not be the preparation for the life everlasting, but only a struggle for worldly power and possessions. And in this work the evil one has many adepts, active and often conscious, who are led by a small clique of entirely conscious world conquerors, whose aim is to seize control over all humanity by methods which we will set out below in outline.

The strength of the materialistic-messianists arises from their being concerned with the most important and fundamental issues which affect humanity. Their motives and their methods are in tune with deep forces and desires, present in everyone, and they are led by a fallen angel, a leader of supernatural ability. It is not the desires and calculations of humans alone which come into question, but also forces of a more powerful order. Only shallow and stupid materialists can deny these things.

But the weakness of the enemy is that, in the end, evil and the lie will not triumph. Good and truth will win the struggle which is the dominant motive of all history. But the struggle will be won only if we first understand the issues involved, and then decide with complete determination to leave nothing undone until evil has been defeated. Those who may care to glance at these pages will, perhaps, discover some practical information which may be useful and some of which has never been given before, especially in a form which shows the interrelation between a number of very important factors. No attempt will be made here to deal with the spiritual foundation of the struggle. It is assumed that those who will find the facts here stated useful, will also understand that they are intended primarily for the information of those to whom the fundamental theological and philosophical thesis is acceptable as the starting point of the whole discussion. Without that postulate, it would be difficult to draw all proper conclusions from the practical matters here set out.

An important aspect of the "three-card trick", which has a concrete bearing on present world events and explains many of its characteristics and details, is that we must bear in mind the existence, as it were, of two Bolshevisms: the "White Bolshevism" with its focal point and chief base in America, and the "Red Bolshevism" with its centre in Russia. In this context we would assume that Bolshevism is the expression of that state of mind and way of life which is induced by the materialistic messianists, irrespective of whether the technique of government in any given instance is that of parliamentary democracy or of open and ruthless terror. Of course we know and admit that life in countries which have been subjected to White Bolshevism is far better in every way, than that under the Red variety, but in their ultimate spirit and aim the two Bolshevisms are related.

Indeed, as we know, it was the White variety, or rather its sponsors, which gave birth to the Red one, and we repeat again that the Americans, the Russians and all the others are by no means themselves directly responsible for the systems which oppress or at least debauch them.

But those who intend to rule the globe cannot leave the world divided, even nominally, between the "white" and the "red" camp, between "democracy" and "socialism"; they must be brought together under "Social-democracy", as the jargon has it. To achieve this aim, the protagonists of "White Bolshevism" will come forward, now that Red Communism has become so odious, an attitude which has been consciously encouraged at the proper time, as the Liberators of the world. The "Whites" will save us all from the "Reds", substituting one variation of the same theme for another, and thus retaining the initiative and assuring for themselves very widespread support. And thus the final universal dispensation is to be achieved. This is certain unless we all take the trouble to understand the issues involved and undertake the actions for which they call.

For some years now, in Czechoslovakia and especially in Soviet Russia, we have observed the performance of political theatre, at which the Communists are masters, designed to deceive us. Various political leaders, writers, retired generals, scientists and others, receive immense and world-wide notoriety from time to time as "fighters for freedom". They write "daring" novels which always and for years manage somehow "to find their way to the West", there to be published at a huge profit by capitalistic publishers known to be Communist sympathizers. At the same time these actors, be they a

Dubcek or a Pasternak, "demand" that the norms and precepts of "socialist legality", of the "constitution", be enforced as they allegedly guarantee free speech, the Rights of man (whatever that may be) and "democracy" (which must remain undefined). Yet all these "liberals" and "protesters" declare that they are all Marxists and are not opposed to the existing Communist régimes, and most of them are also Jews. Yet these people know perfectly well that Lenin had stated clearly and repeatedly that "that is law under Bolshevism which suits the Communist revolution at any given time", in short there is no socialist law at all in theory or in practice.

Naturally all these fighters for democracy are "persecuted" and "prosecuted" by the Communist authorities, to make things look convincing. And the mass of the unthinking free peoples are fully convinced that there is, as they are being told, no alternative to Communism, but that it can be made very pleasant.

Meanwhile nothing at all is said about the very widespread real resistance to Communism, religious, intellectual and practical. Yet that is where we can find the true pointers to the future, the real guarantee of universal freedom.

2

Towards Widespread Power

There are two opposed schools of history. One, the school which is taught almost everywhere, and which is deliberately false, is that historical events happen solely for reasons which operate at the given moment and these events are only loosely connected with each other and there is no dominant motive or guiding force. The other school states correctly that for centuries past history has been a process subjected to a definite plan, aim and dominant influence, that there is, as it were, a great conspiracy which is leading the whole world towards total subjugation in a slave state ruled by a limitless terror.

The evidence to sustain this assertion is not merely adequate, but overwhelming. To attempt to quote it all would fill a large volume. We shall limit ourselves to a few incontrovertible pieces of evidence. Readers who wish to study all the questions raised in this book will soon discover how much more proof there is.

In 1844 there first appeared the political novel "Coningsby" by Benjamin Disraeli, Earl of Beaconsfield, b. London 1804, d. 1881, Leader of the Conservative Party and Prime Minister of Britain in 1868 and from 1874 to 1880.

We quote from Book Four, Chapter XV; it is Sidonia speaking to Coningsby, the former symbolically the type of a Rothschild, the latter a young English aristocrat, interested in politics:

"... My letters this morning demand me.... The minister cannot pay the interest on the national debt; not an unprecedented circumstance, and he has applied to us: I never permit any business of State to be transacted without my personal interposition; and so I must go up to town...."

"Suppose you don't pay it," said Coningsby smiling.

"... Can anything be more absurd than that a nation should apply to an individual to maintain its credit, and, with its credit, its existence as an empire, and its comfort as a people; ..."

"You never observe a great intellectual movement in Europe in which the Jews do not greatly participate. The first Jesuits were Jews; that mysterious Russian Diplomacy which so alarms Western Europe is organized and principally carried on by Jews; that mighty revolution which is at this moment preparing in Germany, (here

Disraeli forecasts the widespread European revolutionary movement of 1848 four years before the event—GK), and which will be, in fact, a second and greater Reformation, and of which so little is as yet known in England, is entirely developing under the auspices of Jews...."

"I told you just now that I was going up to town tomorrow, because I always made it a rule to interpose when affairs of State were on the carpet. Otherwise I never interfere. I hear of peace and war in newspapers, but I am never alarmed, except when I am informed that the Sovereign wants treasure; then I know that monarchs are serious."

After describing his meetings with the leading finance ministers of Europe, all Jews, Sidonia goes on:

"... So you see, my dear Coningsby, that the world is governed by very different personages from what is imagined by those who are not behind the scenes."

After this Sidonia discusses the great powers and role of the Caucasian pure race, which includes the Jews. It is obvious to the informed that Disraeli, expressing himself through the medium of a novel, stated the true facts, known to him.

In the last days of 1913, some half a year before the start of the First World War, writing in the major Vienna newspaper, "Freie Presse", Walter Rathenau wrote that "Europe (then meaning the world) is ruled by 200 men who all know each other and supplement their numbers from their own entourage".

Rathenau could be compared with today's Bernard Baruch or a Rockefeller—the top industrialist, financier and man of politics of the German Empire and the first years of the Weimar Republic, under which he was Foreign Minister. He spoke on the basis of complete and exact first-hand knowledge, as an insider.

His father, with a partner, had been the founder of the Allgemeine Elektrizitäts Gesellschaft (AEG), known also as the General Electric Company (GEC) all over the world. Old Rathenau had representatives in Russia in the decades before the revolution who were all Marxists. So when, soon after the end of the First World War, his son as foreign minister signed the Treaty of Rapallo with the USSR, leading to very close political, industrial and military collaboration between Germany and the Soviets, he was dealing with former employees of the family firm, old personal friends. It was all in the family.... And this treaty was confirmed and strengthened by the Ribbentrop-Molotov pact of August 1939, and ended only with the German attack of 1941, as a result of which Communism emerged as the sole winner of the Second World War, having obtained half Europe, half Asia and much else, with all other participants on both sides as losers. This is how things are done behind the scenes mentioned by Disraeli.

In the years of the Balfour Declaration Dr. Nahum Goldmann, President of the World Jewish Congress, explained:

"The Jews might have had Uganda, Madagascar and other places for the establishment of a Jewish 'Fatherland', but they want absolutely nothing except Palestine: not because the Dead Sea water by evaporation can produce five trillion dollars worth of metalloids and powdered metal; not because the sub-soil of Palestine contains twenty times more petroleum than all the combined reserves of the two Americas; but because Palestine is the crossroads of Europe, Asia and Africa, because Palestine constitutes the veritable centre of world political power, the strategic centre for world control."

In 1920 Dr. Chaim Weizmann, first President of Israel in 1948–52, said:

"We will establish ourselves in Palestine whether you like it or not! You can hasten our arrival, or you can equally retard it. It is, however, better for you to help us so as to avoid our constructive power being turned into a destructive power which will overthrow the world."

The Rt. Hon. Reginald McKenna had been British Chancellor of the Exchequer. He was also a professional banker, and in January 1924, as chairman of the Midland Bank, he told a meeting of its shareholders:

"I am afraid the ordinary citizen will not like to be told that the banks can, and do, create money. The amount of money in existence varies only with the action of the banks in increasing and decreasing deposits and bank purchases. Every loan, overdraft, or bank purchase creates a deposit, and every repayment of a loan, overdraft or bank sale destroys a deposit. And they who control the credit of a nation, direct the policy of governments, and hold in the hollow of their hands the destiny of the people."

Dear Reader, if, as a voter, you still imagine you matter, just give yourself a cold douche! And then, taking nothing for granted, think. We shall try to help you.

Now we shall quote from the Preface to the book *Conquest or Consent* by the eminent American author Wickliffe B. Vennard, Sr.:

"Honourable Louis T. McFadden, Chairman of the Banking and Currency Committee, made the following statement to the Congress:

"10th June 1932—'The truth is, the Federal Reserve Board has usurped the Government of the United States. It controls everything here and it controls all our foreign relations. It makes and breaks Governments at will....'"

"4th May 1933—'. . . Roosevelt . . . has brought with him from Wall Street James P. Warburg, son of Paul M. Warburg, Organizer and first Chairman of the Board of the Federal Reserve System. . . .' "

" 'This same Warburg had the audacity and arrogance to proclaim before the U.S. Senate (17th February 1950):

" 'We shall have World Government whether or not we like it. The only question is whether World Government will be achieved by Conquest or Consent'."

Thus spoke one of the chiefs of the New York Bank of Kuhn, Loeb & Co., which had been the key member of the consortium of international bankers which had financed the Russian revolution.

Yet, incidentally, because the Federal Reserve and all other banks in the USA are private, and because the US Constitution states in Art. 1, Sec. 8, Clause 5, that only Congress shall coin (issue or create) money, regulate the value thereof and of foreign coin, almost all money in all forms in America, being created by private banks, is unconstitutional. Of that more below.

The "Report of the (New Zealand) Royal Commission on Monetary, Banking and Credit Systems", 1956, states in part:

Par. 164: Creation of Money by the Trading Banks:

"The fact that a large proportion of our money supply comes into existence as a result of the operations of the trading banks obviously disturbed many witnesses. . . ."

In 1960 the Radcliffe Committee sat in London to examine the same problems by order of the Government. We quote from the evidence given by the Bank of England, Vol. 1, Memoranda of Evidence.

p. 9. 4. The Control of Bank Credit in the United Kingdom:

2. "Because an entry in the books of a bank has come to be generally acceptable in the place of cash it is possible for the banks to create the equivalent of cash (i.e. credit). Thus a bank may pay for a security purchased from a customer merely by making an entry in its books to the credit of that customer's account; or it may make an advance by means of a similar entry. In either case an increase in its deposits will occur."

In Look of the 16th January 1962, and in Life, Mr. David Ben-Gurion, first Prime Minister of Israel and then still in office, stated:

"The image of the world in 1987 as traced in my imagination: The Cold War will be a thing of the past. Internal pressure of the constantly growing intelligentsia in Russia for more freedom and the pressure of the masses for raising their living standards may lead to a gradual democratization of the Soviet Union. On the other hand, the increasing influence of the workers and farmers, and the rising political importance of men of science, may transform the United

States into a welfare state with a planned economy. Western and Eastern Europe will become a federation of autonomous states having a Socialist and democratic régime. With the exception of the USSR as a federated Eurasian state, all other continents will become united in a world alliance, at whose disposal will be an international police force. All armies will be abolished, and there will be no more wars. In Jerusalem, the United Nations (a truly *United* Nations) will build a Shrine of the Prophets to serve the federated union of all continents; this will be the seat of the Supreme Court of Mankind, to settle all controversies among the federated continents, as prophesied by Isaiah. Higher education will be the right of every person in the world. A pill to prevent pregnancy will slow down the explosive natural increase in China and India. And by 1987, the average life-span of man will reach 100 years." So now we know....

In 1955 the Christian Educational Assn., of Union, N.J., USA, published a booklet. "Facts are Facts", being the facsimile of a long and important letter of the 10th October 1954 from Mr. Benjamin H. Freedman, of New York City, a distinguished and deeply-informed American Christian Jew, to Dr. David Goldstein, Ll.D., of Boston, Mass., an American Jew converted to Catholicism, from which we quote from p.6 :

"The history of the world for the past several centuries and current events at home and abroad confirm the existence of such a conspiracy (to destroy Christianity and obtain global power). The world-wide net-work of diabolical conspirators implement this plot against the Christian faith while Christians appear to be sound asleep. The Christian clergy appear to be more ignorant or more indifferent about this conspiracy than other Christians. . . . It seems so sad."

In the examples we have given of clear evidence of the existence of an old and widespread conscious conspiracy to enslave the world, and of the roots of practical financial power which make the realization of these plans possible, there is frequent mention of Jews.

There are many students of these affairs who maintain that Jewry as such, be it by race or religion or both, is principally responsible for this attempt to subvert and enslave the world. However, while many leading Jews have frequently admitted the existence of an important Jewish problem, and there can be no doubt that it exists, it would be an error, totally unfair to the Jews, to simplify this issue and to assume that all Jews are involved.

Most of them are not involved, the great majority know little or nothing about this problem, and there are not a few leading Jews in different countries who are openly opposed to Communism, Zionism and related ideas and movements.

Similarly, too, if the roots of revolutionary power are financial, it does not follow that every banker is a leader of subversion and sedition. Indeed, as we mention below, the banks perform many important functions very well, and we need these institutions.

Consequently it follows that far from attacking all Jews and all financiers, we must distinguish clearly between the guilty and the innocent, remembering also that there are many evil men who are neither of the two. And more than that, we must hope that leaders of Finance and of Jewry will help the world to be rid of the enemies of mankind and will contribute to the establishment of a new and beneficial order, whose outlines we set out below.

If an effort to achieve the domination of the globe is today a practical possibility, that fact is clearly due to the gradual increase in the ease and speed of communications, to the effective exercise of central authority and to the interdependence of various territories in economic life.

Centuries ago the world was inhabited by tribes and nations with state organizations, each of which was not numerous by modern standards and occupied relatively small territories. But the ancient historical world already knew examples of the very considerable expansion of the political and economic power of this or that State, or at least military power. Alexander the Great, the ruler of ancient Macedonia, was, in a few years, able to extend his conquests over a great part of the world and to control large parts of India. But his empire was not stable. The Romans achieved a unification under their sway of the whole Mediterranean world, and their Empire lasted for centuries. Indeed, its influence is still felt. In Asia the Mongol Hordes attained effective power over territories larger than any in the history of the world. For hundreds of years much even of Europe, including Russia for over 200 years, was under their sway. But the factors which made the Golden Horde and its successors able to conquer and to hold their vassals exhausted them, and the Tatars reverted to their original condition of peaceful nomads.

But if the ancient empires were built up by overland conquests, in more recent centuries, with the development of sailing ships capable of undertaking long voyages and carrying cargoes of sufficient volume and value, overseas colonial empires were founded, protected by efficient navies. Sea routes proved to be in most respects better than land ones. Such were the empires of Spain, Portugal, Holland, France and Britain. But these empires too, proved unstable and disintegrated when far-away subject peoples were able to organize themselves, often with the help of not disinterested outsiders, and throw off the rule of the former conquerors.

The British Empire and Commonwealth is an exception among empires, originally built up as a consequence of conquest and colonialism beyond the seas. The outstanding genius of the British people helped them to learn from disasters, such as the War of American Independence, and to adjust their policies to the times and conditions. The idea of independent Dominions, united by the Crown, is an achievement which none of the others were able to emulate. Within the Commonwealth there remain united lands which had been conquered and others which had been colonized, thus bringing together innumerable races and religions in all parts of the globe.

However, in the founding and growth, and in the present weakening of the British Empire and the Commonwealth a predominant role has been played by an economic factor. The development of usury capitalism, the private creation of money as an interest-bearing debt, of which more below, persuaded the bankers, the chiefs of international high finance, to seek a base for their headquarters in a country which would combine comparative safety with the existence of an energetic population, including seafarers. There had to be the necessary factor to provide a minimal prosperity with the opportunity of expansion by political and economic means throughout the world, thus spreading the new money and finance dispensation.

Spain and Portugal provided these advantages for a time, but with the expulsion of the Jews, who played a dominant role in finance, a new Money-Capital had to be found. The Netherlands served the purpose of the bankers for a time, but being on the European mainland, the country was in danger of invasion. When, finally, the system approached its modern development during the seventeenth century, there suggested itself also the best solution of the question of a territorial base. Great Britain, or at first England, was the answer. An island, with a capable and reliable population, a good climate, already rich, excellent seafarers, brave fighters; good organizers and administrators, and much else recommended the country to the top usurers.

But there were, as everywhere else, considerable obstacles to be overcome. The Christian Monarchy, strong, incorruptible, in full possession of real sovereignty, including control of the issue of money, were factors which had to be eliminated by the bankers. They backed the Lenin of those days, Oliver Cromwell, they demanded and obtained the pseudo-judicial murder of King Charles I, they substituted the political power of an assembly which money could control for that of a King it could not, and after some years of struggle they consummated their plan with the installation of the Dutch King William III, pseudo-legalized by being married to the Stuart Queen Mary, his co-monarch, in 1688, and they called the revolution which deposed the lawful King James II "glorious". In 1694 the financier-revolutionaries completed the action with the founding of the Bank of England, which put the creation, lending and control of all money in their hands, and usury-capitalism, the progenitor of communism today, was established.

From that moment the development of the British Empire was the means by which this system of fraudulent exploitation was spread over the globe, but at the same time that Empire also brought its subjects many benefits which were due to the qualities of the British race; the evils of usury coincided with the good done by the true Empire builders—a duality which remained hidden for a long time.

But as the result of the First World War the centre of gravity of global high finance moved from Great Britain to an even more suitable base—the United States of America. And from that time the British Empire was doomed and its dissolution was only a question of time.

Another factor which affected that Empire during almost the whole course of its history was the so-called Eastern Policy, which meant the policy of the attempt to weaken and destroy the Russian Empire, the only major State which, until 1917, the masters of international usury did not control. When at last the combination of political, military and subversive pressures of many decades and even generations, led by usury-finance, brought about the Russian revolution and it became known that the Emperor Nicholas II had abdicated, the British Premier David Lloyd George said in Parliament of the event that through it Britain had achieved one of its major war aims. How many people in Britain or anywhere else knew that they were fighting for that, in fact for a major step towards world revolution and universal slavery?

And how many people in America or anywhere else know that the United States are the major headquarters not only of finance, but also of revolutionary subversion? But let us return to the question of power in general.

The urge to unite large areas, sustained as it is by a number of positive and useful considerations in the realms of defence, economic well-being and cultural and political integration in places which call for it, brought about the rise of land empires such as those of Austria-Hungary and Turkey. But again they proved to be unstable owing to their multi-national character and other considerations. None the less the demise of the Hapsburg Empire is genuinely regretted by many of its former subjects of all nationalities, and many arguments can be put forward in favour of its re-establishment in new forms.

Finally there are the more or less unitary empires—large states, with large populations of an almost homogenous character, or at least on the way to becoming such. These empires are, in order of territorial size, Russia, China and the United States of America. Despite all that may be said to the contrary, especially in the case of Russia, these great states and nations are not internally divided by racial or religious barriers. Each of them grew as the result of both conquests and of the colonization on almost completely empty lands. Each also had to seek expansion towards physically safe borders. Of the internal structure of Russia more will be said below in another context. Of these countries it may be said that in the foreseeable future they are likely to remain united and stable as territorial units, their populations are likely to increase and it may be assumed that they will play a very great role in the affairs of the world owing to their vast size, their numerous inhabitants and their actual and potential wealth.

But if conquest and colonization had played their part in the rise and fall of empires, there are also other factors which contribute to the unification of humanity. The role of great cultures and especially of great faiths is immense. Christianity in its early ages was usually considered a unifying force of such power that all the world should be united by it. The double-headed eagles of the Imperial arms of Russia and Austria-Hungary very largely symbolized the dual rule of the one Church and of the Emperor, its temporal protector, in the parallel conceptions of the Eastern and Western Roman Empires, the heirs of which Moscow and Vienna respectively considered themselves to be.

However, essentially Christianity was not directly concerned with the political conquest of the world, but with the conquest of each human soul. The objective was not the material well-being of humanity, but its spiritual salvation. We are clearly told that if we deal with salvation effectively, all else will follow, and our physical well-being will also be assured. But the latter is not the first and immediate objective of the Christian faith; it is its by-product.

But this conception of life, this interpretation of Christian messianism, is completely rejected by those who seek material power and possessions, who consider their messianism only in terms of political and economic rule over humanity. The materialists want to be kings of this world and they often deny the very existence of the next. Yet we know that this so often satanic materialism is by no means devoid of effective driving power and efficient ability. Indeed it is advancing.

At this point it may be well to consider the basic characteristics of this force, this materialistic messianism, which has, for the first time in the world's history, not only propounded a serious plan for world conquest, but has now come to within a very few steps of its attainment. Though the day dreams of the ancient conquerors may have extended to the idea of ruling the whole globe, yet they never even approached a method or the creation of the practical means required for this purpose. Their plans were based on military forces, and these, in turn, had to rely on a national foundation and a state of more or less limited size for their man-power and supplies. Furthermore, communications could not be over-extended without becoming too vulnerable. So, however great the ambitions, the horizon which defined their expansion was finite.

Not so in the case of the materialistic messianism. It is true that it has taken centuries for this force to grow and develop, and it is only in recent historical times that technical development has become such as to make the practical realization of these ambitions possible. But, nevertheless, we now face the fact that the force and ambition which we have in mind can, in practice, hope to seize world power very soon.

We will not here attempt a very full discussion of the philosophical and political aspects of this struggle. We prefer to leave this further development of the thesis to each of our readers, while here concentrating attention on some of the chief practical elements in the situation, and suggesting the measures for which they call.

In realistic terms the materialistic messianism does not mean a theoretical abtraction, but the reality of power and its concrete fruits —a comfortable or even luxurious life, not threatened by anyone or anything, with all that this world can give materially at one's immediate command, including the services of large numbers of other people. All else, such as social ambitions and jealousies, is entirely secondary. The aim is power, money, and that which they give.

But while that is so, the path towards the achievement of that goal is complex and long. On the way all the established ways of life, all customary conceptions and habits, all institutions and especially all faiths must be utterly destroyed. They are the products of another approach. Even those social orders which included the institution of slavery, did not provide for universal slavery for all but a very small minority and still less for the imposition of that state on the whole world. Furthermore, even slaves were able to purchase liberty, but none would have that right under the dispensation of the world masters of the future.

3

Economic Roots of Power

At this point it will be necessary for the fuller explanation of our thesis to give some general details about the history and especially the technical operation of the present "Capitalist" system of economics.

In brief outline we would try to sum up the next few chapters as an attempt to show that modern "Capitalism", which has developed during the past three centuries, should not be confused with a system based simply on the private ownership of the means of production, distribution and exchange. Private ownership has been known since time immemorial and it is by no means the distinguishing characteristic of Capitalism.

The present-day system, still in force outside the Iron Curtain, is based on usury, i.e. the lending of money at interest, the ownership of economic factors not only by individuals directly, but especially by a more or less anonymous set of ever-changing people indirectly, through shares, and by the transfer of the powers of monetary coinage, i.e. issue, from the sovereign State to private individuals and corporations, to whom both a large part of the public and even the State is indebted, in part because all money thus created comes into being as a loan at interest. The bankers are able to create money, credit, the means of exchange, out of nothing, by mere book entry. They thus control all aspects of economic and political life.

These developments are both products and the support of definite moral conditions and aims. They lead inevitably to the spread of materialism, the ever wider establishment of Socialism, and the approach of a materialistic and anti-Christian world government preceded by a "European State", with the virtual enslavement of all humanity, except a small number of bosses. Capitalism and Socialism are not opposites, but the one springs from the other. Materialism leads to both, and both encourage materialism.

It will also be seen that if materialism must inevitably lead to slavery, it is also true that Christianity is the only guarantee of true liberty. The proposition that freedom can be assured by "democracy", whatever that may mean, does not survive close scrutiny if all the facts are taken into consideration. If God is supreme then man is free; if man is deified, he becomes a slave.

These questions are of immense and urgent importance since materialism has by no means triumphed only behind the Iron Curtain. The still free West is very far from real Christianity and the future of the world may well be determined by what will happen in Russia, where the most pronounced godlessness was first established in power and where the State and society had been the most Christian not so very long ago. If Russia succumbs, the world may well be lost, and if Russia will emerge renewed and spiritually strengthened from the red cocoon, then the world may be saved. Therefore we deal also with Russia.

It was quite natural, both psychologically and in practice, that the first objective of the materialists was the acquisition of money, by trade and especially by usury, that is to say by all the various forms of money-lending at interest. In this connection it may be well to observe the fact that money is a most fundamental tester of character, quite irrespective of whether the person tested is a conscious materialist or not. It is sometimes said that alcohol will tear the veil from a man and expose him as he really is. This is not generally true. A man who has drunk too much is poisoned and not his natural self; also the psychological and physical reactions of various individuals to alcohol are very different and are not a parallel to their reactions to other factors.

But money will expose most men very deeply, if not in every respect. The degree of corruptibility of each person, or illustrations of the rare cases of true incorruptibility, the way in which a man will react to the chance of making money, or to a chance missed, to borrowing or being asked for a loan, and so on, will, if carefully watched, reveal a very great deal about almost all men and women. Even apart from the obvious fact that we need money in our daily lives, it must be admitted that it is a very considerable force, a factor of immense importance in the lives of individuals and of society and the state. It follows that those who control money, control one of the chief levers of power. All this is well known, but less well known is the process by which, in the modern world, this power has been brought under the absolute control of a small group of people. As an integral part of that seizure of power there has developed also the process of obtaining an almost complete political control of the affairs of the world. And these powers are fundamentally international and internationalist.

The mediaeval world was organized in accordance with a Christian conception of life. Manufacturers and traders were not so much competitive money-makers as they were trained and accepted experts, carrying out a service to the community for a reasonable fee, as might be expected of a doctor or clergyman. In general, competition was prohibited and, for example, the tailors in any given town, after having successfully completed their apprenticeship and having been accepted by their guild, were allotted a district in which they were able to ply their trade without fear of competition. In the circumstances any form of advertising, even a window display, was absolutely forbidden as being an attempt to deprive others of their trade and beneath the dignity of a competent man.

All undertakings were owned by individuals or partnerships directly, the owners being responsible for the quality of their goods and services and for prompt payments.

Money was, as it had been since early historical times, minted only by the State, which issued it free of debt. This function of government was carried out in a way which was calculated to serve the best interests of the state, but it was not managed by and for private groups.

In time people began to use certain documents in connection with trade. The bill of exchange and other forms of promissory notes came into customary use. They served a good purpose. It then soon followed that the promissory notes of a merchant, manufacturer or landowner of good repute were transferable instruments. A man could make a payment to another not in cash, but by giving him a letter, addressed to a debtor, whose money was due, with a request to pay it to the bearer of the note. In time this system developed in various directions.

Now, at the same time, towards the end of the Middle Ages, another process developed, which was to have immense consequences. In those days money consisted of a coinage which had a value as metal and that was the only medium of exchange. But gold and silver had to be well protected by those who possessed large quantities. The richer men kept their money in huge coffers, with many and heavy locks, which were hidden in the basements of their houses. But soon it became customary for merchants and others to ask the local goldsmiths, who had the best strong rooms and made the most effective arrangements for the protection of their valuables, to take care of their money in coin and bullion, the more so as these goldsmiths were known to be completely honest. So it was that the moneyed men in each city kept only the goldsmith's receipts at their houses, the theft of which would have benefited no burglar, as he could not have demanded the owner's money for them, being unknown to those who were taking care of it. So far, so good.

But the goldsmith soon realized that he always had considerable stocks of coin and bullion on his hands, since it never happened that all his clients would ask for all their money simultaneously. At the same time the receipts were in themselves forms of money. It was quite easy to discharge a debt to everyone's satisfaction by handing over not gold or silver coin, but a receipt for it, signed by a reputable goldsmith, since it was known that such a document could be exchanged for real money at a moment's notice. Simultaneously it was often more convenient to handle paper than to carry coin if the amounts involved were large.

It was also natural that men used what was in effect an early cheque, by giving letters to creditors, addressed to the goldsmith, with a request that the bearer be paid a given sum from the store of the customer.

All this was still no radical departure from the use of state-issued coin. Admittedly privately issued paper began to make its appearance as a medium of exchange, but these operations were still tied to the existing coinage and their total volume was very small in comparison with the amounts of the payments made in cash.

The real dividing line between the old economy and the new, the conception and embryonic growth of capitalism, was determined by the following event: the goldsmiths, realising that they held what was in effect "idle money", decided to issue their own receipts as though they were money, and, furthermore, not merely to use them for the purchase of necessities, but to lend them at interest. In earlier times the Christian attitude to money-lending had precluded such things, but in time the influence of the materialistic messianism had gradually broken down this rejection of usury. It should be noted that morally and technically the goldsmith was committing a fraudulent act. He was creating an effective form of paper money, whose value was equal to that of the coinage, being fully exchangeable for it, but he was doing so not on the basis of his own holdings of precious metals since they were only a small part of the valuables in the vaults, but he was issuing his money tokens on the security of coin belonging to his customers and held by him only for safekeeping.

But this is only half the story. If the goldsmith had limited himself to issuing paper money of a face value equivalent to the cash in hand, he would have been guilty of misusing that which had been put in his care. But he went even further and issued his certificates to a total nominal amount in excess of all his real holdings, being aware of the fact, on a basis of long experience, that all this paper would never be presented at the same time. Consequently his reputation for prompt payment on demand would remain unimpaired.

Yet while the goldsmith was lending his spurious money at interest, he was thereby acquiring real wealth, for which he paid nothing more than ink and paper. He began to hold land, houses and other valuables, and was able to increase his stocks of cash, which enabled him to expand his credit money even further. He could also borrow gold and silver at interest and lend a much larger amount in paper, at a great profit.

It will be readily understood that this discovery was bound to prove to be of world-wide and historical importance. The goldsmiths, now turned bankers, had discovered a formula by which they could acquire wealth with an ease and at a rate which no one else could match. The one condition of complete success was secrecy, and added to that there had to be the full acquiescence of the State, so that the new technique would be legalized and protected, and its monopoly maintained.

To assure the full and uninhibited development of the new economic system it was by no means enough in the long run to control only the issue of money and credit. It is in the nature of usury that it needs an ever expanding market. This parasite cannot live indefinitely on one and the same victim only. He must continually bring new ones into his net. On the other hand the old political and social orders did not suit the plans of the bankers.

Before continuing our main argument as to the foundations, levers and consequences of modern economic power, which is also the factor which controls political power, it would be well to consider some of the essentials of Marxism, as this theory has had a very great influence on the thought and actions of the present day.

However negative may be our attitude to Marxism we can not deny that it does contain some elements of truth; without that it would not have been able to influence anyone. But there are very many errors, oversimplifications and omissions. A full critical analysis of Marxism and Communism would not be possible within these lines, and we shall limit ourselves to some observations on the more important sides of the major theory of modern Socialism.

Marx's suggestions in the realms of the analysis of costs and prices are faulty, because what the entrepreneur earns (as we point out below) is not some mysterious and elusive increase, but simply his variable wage, as distinct from the fixed one of his employees. It is true, of course, that an increase of population and improvements in the methods of production will bring about the availability of additional values, but it does not follow that this economic improvement passes only into the hands of the "capitalists". We know that the material level of existence of all classes has risen steadily for decades and even generations in the more highly developed countries.

We also deal below with the basic conception of the formula which is at the root of dialectical materialism—that circumstances determine outlook. Thus it may be deduced that religion is merely a by-product of material conditions and is encouraged by the "capitalists" in order to keep the workers quiet despite their economic wants. Marx overlooked the fact that while the above-mentioned formula is partly true, it is equally true that outlook can determine circumstances and that religious faith can give direction and shape to all manifestations of practical life, as well as the contemplative and philosophical life of the mind and spirit.

But the Marxist historical teaching is more interesting, by being nearer to the truth and providing, therefore, an undoubtedly accurate explanation of some historical and social phenomena. Marx and his followers almost completely ignored the factors which we shall carefully consider: monetary issue, usury, financial control through shareholders' companies, and much else. These things are immensely important and because Marxism leaves them out of account, its picture is neither fully true, nor quite complete. However, it is not reasonable to ignore the historical theory of Socialism altogether.

Marx was largely inspired by Hegel. His key to the understanding of historical and social processes was to be found in the propositions that "each social phenomenon must be observed in the framework of its historical connexion and development" and "every form of human organization came into existence with the seeds of its own destruction within it".

Accepting this proposition, Lenin supposed, and correctly, that no successful revolution was possible without the disintegration of the ruling class. This can be illustrated with ease by glancing at the history of many countries, such as England, since mediaeval times. But of course, besides the decay of the ruling class, it was also necessary to have an energetic and intelligent leadership of the elements seeking power in its place and trying, for that purpose, to bring about social and political changes. It has often happened, in England, France, Russia and elsewhere, that the first revolutionary stage was partly led by members of the abdicating class.

In view of the persistent and loud agitation in favour of "top-level" talks with the Soviet Communists, "containment", "coexistence" and so on, it is necessary to consider the root characteristics of Marxist-Leninist tactics and strategy, which are still relentlessly pursued by the Soviets, both because they bring them ever nearer to ultimate success, and because the Soviet tyrants have such torrents of blood and suffering on their consciences that they can never stop or retreat. The West, whose leadership is egoistical, blind and irresponsible to the point of inanity, appears not to have the least conception of these Communist methods, despite the fact that they have been practised for over fifty years and had been openly proclaimed by Marx and Lenin many years before the Russian revolution.

Already in 1905 Lenin wrote "The Two Tactics of Social-Democracy", published openly in Russia in 1908. In this work he suggested that it would be wise if the Marxists were to ally themselves with the Liberal bourgeosie against Tsarism, proclaiming the former to be enemy No. 2. With Tsarism eliminated, the Bolsheviks should work with the Mensheviks and Social-Revolutionaries against the Liberal bourgeoisie, calling the former enemy No. 2. The Bolsheviks must go with the smaller farmers against the big land-owners, and then with the landless peasants against the farmers, the kulaks. He said: "Ally yourselves with one of your enemies against another, and destroy them one by one". It is not difficult to see that precisely this technique is being used by the Soviets also in international relations. It is in this light that we must see the Red Alliance with the Nazis and then the West in the Second World War.

But whereas it may be fairly convincingly demonstrated that the succession of classes brought new rulers to the top, who were able to govern effectively, the process came to a halt with the nominal triumph of the proletariat in Russia. Of course not one of the leaders of Bolshevism was a proletarian and few of them were Russians, but when in power, in the name of the working masses, they did at first try to hand economic control to the workers by instituting elected committees to run the factories, transport etc. The plan was a total failure as these people were quite unable to run anything, and Lenin openly admitted that fact. The ultimate and inevitable result was the formation of a bureaucratic and terroristic régime, run by the Communist Party. Some call it State Capitalism. But the political strategy of this régime is still essentially Marxist.

Clearly, however, the Soviet régime contained from the first day the seeds of its own destruction, and to a much greater extent than any other. Marxist arguments can be used to prove that Marxism in practice is a total failure and doomed. Instead of the liberation of the proletariat and the acquisition of power by it, the mass of the Communist-dominated nations have become total slaves and even the rulers must terrorize each other in order to maintain the system. Therefore the collapse of Communism is assured through the disintegration of the ruling class, but it does not follow that it is safe to await this event passively, as global Marxist success could come before its catastrophe. The situation calls for an active political counter-attack and in the first place an understanding of Communism in action. The decay at the top in the still free world must be repaired by the encouragement of new elements.

In conclusion we should note that both in Russia and elsewhere the Marxists have shewn not a little ability in making use of national and religious feelings. Here, too, the tactic of alliance with one factor against another is pursued. But the Communists were wrong in their original assumption that total terror and all-pervading propaganda can effectively change a nation. At the root the Russians have not changed and thus Communism is doomed in the end.

4

The Political Consequences of Economic Power

The Churches, the Crown, the landowning aristocracy, the army and civil service were often among the factors which made for stability and the maintenance of the social order, itself in many respects the product of Christianity, while making full allowance for human weakness. But it was not only classes and institutions which stood in the way of "progress", but also the laws and customs and the established practice of the courts. Indeed there was nothing either in the realm of faith and thought or in the sphere of established institutions which were not a hindrance to the ultimate plans of the bankers, the money-lenders, the materialistic messianists. Even the very existence of separate and independent states, with their boundaries, their customs and tariffs, their differing legal systems, their wish to maintain their own ways of life, was intolerable to those who had discovered the key to world power and wanted to make full use of their opportunities.

But naturally it was not wise to let the intended victims of this immense conspiracy know just what was in mind. Yet their cooperation had to be mobilized. The necessary formula soon suggested itself: if the plans of the bankers were progressive, then, conversely, the actions and the existence of all that represented the old order was regressive; if the men who wanted to be the new masters were not free to proceed unhindered, then the old régimes were the enemies of freedom. If the Christian faith taught men to obey moral laws incompatible with the wishes of the usurers, then every belief in God had to be eliminated and suppressed. The aim of material enrichment had to be proclaimed as the only worth-while idea. Where reforms were necessary, they were mis-directed.

Yet is must be said at once that the plans of the financiers were by no means devoid of a practical reality. As we have seen already, the schemes, of the goldsmiths, who were to become the first private organs for the emission of money, paid extremely well. It is just this fact that the plans are extremely profitable which makes them so effective.

Soon the discovery of American and other distant lands, and then, later, the Industrial Revolution in England were to provide new opportunities. An immense increase in the wealth of all nations became possible and the new financial techniques not only adapted

themselves with ease to the new situation, but in some respects, by
making plentiful credit available, they were a useful factor. As it
developed, together with industry, capitalism worked effectively, if
not perfectly. It still does, being an organic growth, though encouraged by motives we shall partly describe.

The schemes of the bankers had at all times to be carried out so as
both to take advantage of political changes and opportunities and to
bring about those adjustments and even violent events which paved
the way for the next phase. A very typical early example is provided
by the history of England during the seventeenth century. Every
encouragement was given to the rising Liberalism of the time and to
all that which tended to weaken and eliminate the influence of the
Christian Monarchy. Eventually King Charles the Martyr was
violently overthrown and killed after a pretence of a trial, and the
rule of Cromwell, progressive according to the jargon of more recent
times, was also the period of opportunity for the bankers. Cromwell
had been in close touch with their representatives in the Netherlands
and had received support from them. He opened the doors of England
to them.

But the complete elimination of all that Charles I had stood for
was not yet possible. The mood of the country changed and, in part,
returned to its old paths. The murdered King was succeeded by his
son, who returned from exile in triumph. But Charles II did not
eliminate the essentials of the "progressive achievements" of the
upstart bankers. However, the struggle, largely unconscious, between the old order and the new in this particular issue, went on,
with the bankers having occasionally to retreat for a while. The
reign of King James II saw a final attempt to stem the tide, but the
enemy was too strong and the old order too unaware of the real
issues which were involved. The King went into exile, to be replaced by a nominee of the bankers, William III, backed by their
associates, largely drawn from that class which benefited materially from the Reformation under Henry VIII. The usurers were now
in the saddle in England and Scotland.

It was thus quite natural that the establishment of the Bank of
England followed soon after the forcible departure of King James II.
In terms of the jargon, which was gradually to become so all-embracing and habitual and which was designed to hide from the uninitiated
the true nature of political, social and economic events, the fall of
the King was described as a "Glorious Revolution".

While, during the Renaissance period, there had arisen a number
of banks in Italy and elsewhere, these institutions were not at first
engaged in the issue of new money in any form. They lent what they
had or what they had, in turn, borrowed themselves. But the Bank

of England, set up in the last years of the seventeenth century, was the first private institution which was legally empowered to issue State-authorised paper currency and, furthermore, the Government itself became its debtor. Thus the State not only renounced its monopoly of monetary emission, but it also agreed to borrow the privately created money from the bankers, though in the first instance it was lent real money; it accepted a bribe once, in order to burden the nation forever with an atrocious hoax, the full nature of which will be described below.

The eighteenth century saw both the beginning of the Industrial Revolution in Great Britain and the rise of the House of Rothschild in Germany, which was later to set up branches in many of the chief centres of Europe. The development of industry and the growth of trade called for great financial expansion and the bankers rose fully to the occasion. But at the same time they were not prepared to enable trade and industry to flourish while missing the chance to extend their political power. This line was dictated not merely by excessive ambition, but by the realization that eventually the power of the usurer will weaken unless he has obtained control of the State. This will lead, as we shall see below, to the encouragement of Socialism. But for that the time had not yet come.

The first stage in the subversion of Government was carried out with the help of open and secret "progressive" and revolutionary societies. The important role of certain forms of freemasonry must not be overlooked in this connexion. The most extreme and daring ideas were formulated and fostered and the aims which they put forward were gradually attained. Almost exactly one hundred years after the "Glorious Revolution" in England, the same forces succeeded in organizing another "Glorious Revolution", this time in France. Outwardly the slogans of liberty, fraternity and equality, these factors which can never be truly reconciled, were the aim. In practice subversive forms or freemasonry led the middle classes to power. This time the attack on the Faith was more open and intense. And again the result was that the usurers were in the saddle.

It would be idle to deny that such revolutions foster and release many impulses and ideas and become a complex process. It would be easy to find many other factors in this period of French history. But the basic essentials are those we have indicated. The essence is that the Christian culture and way of life has been largely replaced by the rule and methods of the materialistic messianists. In France their fight against the Church, for example, is still a major element in French political and intellectual life. The conquests of Napoleon are gone, and much else, but the rule of the bankers, and of their philosophy, remains.

Indeed the French revolutionary wars and especially the campaigns of Napoleon, which involved the whole European continent in war during many years, gave the bankers, and in the first place the brilliant Rothschilds, their greatest opportunity. The family of Rothschild was represented in the chief western capitals and it was thus able to lend to all sides simultaneously. Furthermore, an extremely well organized information service enabled the Rothschilds to gamble successfully on the Stock Exchanges with the help of exact advance information. The beginnings of a massive National Debt were laid. For example, the sums lent by these bankers during the Napoleonic wars have not yet been repaid and are still a part of the public debt of Great Brtain, and they still yield an interest income and will do so, theoretically, forever.

Before we come to a more detailed technical discussion of the working of usury capitalism, it may be well to glance at the history of another aspect of this system. If the chief basis is the banking system and the issue of the means of exchange as a debt at interest, both to private individuals and to the State, a very important addition to the scheme is the institution of trading and manufacturing companies which are owned not by individuals or partnerships, but by stockholders and shareholders.

In the Middle Ages it had been a well-established principle that a business should be owned by identifiable persons, who were fully responsible for everything and who were not empowered to sell their share of the business, that is to say to allow others to take their place in a partnership, unless all the other partners agreed. When later the various joint stock and chartered companies appeared, this rule applied. But gradually the conception was encouraged to gain ground that a share in a business, a claim to a fixed rate of interest on a nominal sum, or a claim to a participation in the profits of the undertaking, was a saleable commodity, to be transferred at will by the owner. It was this conception, once established, which led to the foundation of the Stock Exchanges, whose role became more important than that of the old Exchanges, where trade was done in goods or bills of exchange which were the direct result of trade. And thus there came into business an element of speculation, of anonymity, of instability and of irresponsibility: Above all, there came about the control of all business by the financiers. The legalization a hundred years ago of the limited liability company completed this process. Of this particular matter more will be said below.

At this stage it will be well to examine in greater detail the present state of the technique of financial capitalism, under the two main headings of banking and credit, and of the organization and functioning of companies.

5

The Nature of Capitalism and Banking

There is a widespread misconception regarding the true nature of capitalism, which has been largely brought about by an uncritical acceptance of Marxist Socialist terminology, itself not only basically untrue, but intended to be misleading. The essential characteristic of capitalism is not that it permits the private ownership of the means of production, distribution and exchange, be they land, buildings, machinery or personal credit and ability. The personal ownership of all these factors had been since the beginning of mankind a part of the natural law. Even the earliest barbarians who owned a stone axe and a bow and arrows, or the most primitive plough and other tools, or dug-out canoes, horses and other domestic animals were not capitalists. Neither were the men of feudal times capitalists even if they were great lords. And not even the miser who had accumulated a hoard of gold was a capitalist. They were, and in similar circumstances still are, owners of property.

The distinguishing characteristic of capitalism is that it is concerned with the means of exchange, that it is a system in which usury—the lending of money at interest—plays a leading role; it is the essence of capitalism, in addition to the private issue of money. Capital is not land, or money as such, or a factory, if we consider it under the heading of capitalism. Under that heading capital is not an asset, but a liability; it is not property, but a debt burdened by interest payments. The capital of a company is not what it owns, but what it owes. Capitalism is the system which has been created by the moneylenders, by the parasites. It is not the system of the constructive owners, the true creators of wealth by work and invention. It is the system of those who "use idle money and put it to work for them", to use a piece of typical capitalistic jargon. It follows that most of the attacks of the Socialists are entirely misdirected; as we shall see, this is a part of overall plans. It is true that most people also think of real values as capital (which is a proper description), but in order to avoid the usual confusion we should understand clearly that there are two entirely different kinds of capital.

As we have noted, the early bankers were a development of certain operations undertaken by such as the goldsmiths, when they had become depositories of coin and precious metals. They assumed the functions of monetary emission, usurping them from the State, and they also indulged in large-scale usury, although money-lending was forbidden both by Christianity and Mohammedanism, especially if loans were for unproductive purposes.

Most people, even those with much experience of business, assume that when they approach a bank for a loan or overdraft, they are asked for complete security because the bank risks either a part of its own capital and accumulated savings, or money lent to it by investors. It is assumed that when the loan has been granted, money is transferred from some existing account to that of the borrower, who is called upon to pay interest quite properly for the sacrifice made by the lender. This, however, is not the case at all. The bank creates money out of nothing when granting accommodation. And these loans are called "deposits" in the balance sheet of the bank, though they are monetary creations.

As a matter of history it may be noted that until just before the middle of the last century the banks were mostly concerned with the issue of their own banknotes, i.e. paper money. But after there had been British legislation which limited these operations, the banks began to devote their attention in the sphere of monetary emission predominantly to the encouragement of the use of cheque-money, which served their purpose even better than banknotes, the issue of which is now usually in the hands of the central bank.

If the general policy of the bankers is to expand credit, if the given customer is known to be reliable, and if security is offered, in the form of stocks and shares or Government loans, or guarantees, or the deeds to buildings or land, or any other easily realizable valuables, the bank merely makes an entry in its books, crediting the customer with the amount agreed. The borrower is then free to draw on this sum, and it is known on the basis of long experience that average business men make over ten elevenths of all payments by cheque, and only one eleventh or less of the amount they spend, in business or privately, is in cash or coin, the latter being about 1 per cent of the total turnover of the means of exchange.

By having thus created new money out of nothing, and put it into circulation burdened with an interest charge which is a real charge on the productive life of the community, the banker has increased the total amount of money in circulation. Conversely, if the customer repays the debt, the amount of money in the land will have been reduced by the given sum. The bank takes no risk of not being repaid, as it always has full security.

Now this fact is absolutely fundamental and is the chief key to the understanding of the modern economic system which we usually call Capitalism. It does not apply under Communism, though we shall see below that the latter system is an organic development, derived from capitalism. This basic fact of capitalism means that those who control the banks of the world, and they have all been interlinked for a long time, even in conditions of war, control all wealth and, therefore, most of the world's activities. The means and possibilities of the financiers are only limited by the productivity and gullibility of humanity.

Technically and theoretically the only factor which limits the issue of money by the banks is the fact that in the highly developed countries five to ten per cent of all payments are made in cash—paper or coin—and the banks must always hold enough in order to meet demands. Consequently a bank can issue credits (in practice cheque money) exceeding by ten or even twenty times its cash holdings. It follows, to make the position quite clear, that 80 per cent to 95 per cent of all the means of exchange in any modern country have been issued as a loan at interest by private banks on a basis of small cash holdings and against full security, while taking no risks. Cheques are money and they are all the results of usury operations by the banks, and all money is thus burdened with interest payments instead of being issued free by the State.

Clearly that alone would provide the financiers with immense profits. They would not only enjoy the profits of the issue, since all the money which they in fact coin, just like any forger of banknotes, only with much greater ease and while protected by the legislation which they so largely influence, is a clear profit, but they also collect interest on all this money, all but the ten per cent or less of paper and coin. But this is only a part of the picture. Since the banks control the volume of money in circulation, as it is they who determine how much is to be lent or withdrawn, it follows that the financiers can predetermine prices, production and employment levels, etc. This, too, can be the source of immense profit. Obviously the ability to predetermine the value of money implies the ability to decide in advance changes in the prices of all goods, services and stock exchange paper. In the circumstances the controllers of money can indulge in massive speculations without any risk of loss. In addition to huge profits, this fact also increases the power of finance.

Here it should be explained that if there is more money in circulation, while the amount of goods remains the same, then prices will rise and, on the contrary, if there is less money with the same amount of goods, prices will fall. Conversely, if the amount of goods increases, but the volume of the means of exchange does not, then prices will fall, and, naturally, if there are fewer goods but the same total amount of money in the country, prices will rise. But the issue of money and the control of its amount, profitable though it is, is not all.

There is yet more to follow. The banks are not even bound by the limits within which credit can be issued which are set by the cash holdings, since the banks can, in practice, get as much cash as they require from the State or central bank by means of a simple operation called "open market operations". It should be noted that all the activities of the banks and financiers have always been hidden by a completely impenetrable jargon, whose verbiage has no relation to the facts at all. The "open market" operation amounts to the purchase by the banks, with money created by them out of nothing, of Government or other securities, which are exchanged for cash. Thus the only consideration which remains is the value which money is to be given at any time, by means of the control of its total amount, which, as we have seen, is arranged by either lending money or demanding its repayment. In theory the purchasing power of the currency is supposed to be determined by the Government, by the Chancellor of the Exchequer or the Minister of Finance. In the United States of America this fact is embodied in the Constitution, which is, however, flouted in practice.

For generations the State has not only yielded its power of coinage to the usurers, but has borrowed heavily from them, paying interest on the money the bankers make by means of book entries. It is phantastic, grotesque, unbelievable, but nevertheless true. It may seem the biggest hoax by the collusion of two partners to the game which has ever been perpetrated on humanity. In practical terms it follows inevitably that the Governments are all too strongly influenced by the so excessively powerful financiers. They, as well as political parties, individual politicians and newspapers, are held in pawn by the bankers.

It is well known that His enemies wanted to trap Christ into a statement aimed against the Roman authorities when they asked Him if it is lawful to pay taxes. Jesus replied by asking for a coin, and then enquiring, whose image was on it. When told that it was Caesar's, He said that one should give to Ceasar, i.e. to the State, that which is Ceasar's, and to God that which belongs to God. It is important to note that Christ here not only stated that taxes were lawful, but also, and this fact is always overlooked, that it is proper that Ceasar, i.e. the State, should coin the money. And it was also Christ who chased the financiers out of the Temple. The lesson of these events is absolutely clear.

The usurers must always have an expanding internal and external market at their disposal. You cannot go on for ever collecting interest on the same debt from the same people unless they are persuaded that they will again need the lender. But even more dangerous for the lenders is the fact that their system inevitably leads to an ever growing debt structure, and, sooner or later, the given victim of the parasite can no longer feed him. A clear example is the National Debt, which has been growing in most countries for nearly two hundred years. Already Income Tax has reached so high a level as to be also incapable of further extension, and the same applies to death duties and other direct and indirect taxes, yet a very large part of the sums collected goes towards the "servicing" (i.e. interest payments) of the Debt. There must come a day, quite soon, when no further loans to the State will be possible, unless some of the old ones are crossed off or the rate of interest is drastically reduced. The position is foreseeable when that rate would have to be almost infinitesimal; in short the whole system already faces collapse in a foreseeable future. Parallel conditions exist in private business. Yet the bankers must not be found out; they must not seem to be a burden, an exploiter who gives nothing useful in return for all he takes. On the contrary, the banks must at all times be considered as institutions performing most useful functions, as a friend in need. And in fact it is clearly undeniable that in practice the banks do perform a large number of very useful and essential functions, and perform them very well. Indeed, it must be said of the whole capitalistic system that so much of its strength lies in the fact that, as had been written by the late Henry Ford, it works. And it works not only from the point of view of a Mr. Ford, but it has in general been the accompaniment of the period of the world's greatest material development so far. It is a system which contains elements of undoubted value, and it is not possible to think seriously at the present time on the lines of the complete elimination of all aspects of the capitalistic technique. Sweeping and deep reforms are needed, but not a destructive revolution. If we must say that the economic system we are considering is in some respects a huge hoax, its strength lies, none the less, in the fact that it has solved many problems in so successful a manner as to have not only survived for many generations, but to have at least not retarded to the point of elimination a very great deal of real human progress in the technical and material sphere. Yet we will shew that the reforms which come into question will not only eliminate certain shortcomings of the present structure and some of the dangers which face us as a result, but will also make possible an even greater development of humanity's practical possibilities, providing only that the spiritual powers of the world will not continue to decay. If they do, and if there is no spiritual revival no new formula will help.

In part the spiritual decadence of humanity has been encouraged by the gross materialism of the usury system. And it must also be noted that Capitalism is potentially monopolistic; it is the ambition of every capitalist to control everything and eliminate every competitor, and that is the trend of the whole. The only values which count are material ones, and they count proportionately to their size, not quality. The acquisition of wealth is the only criterion of success. It is said to be the key to happiness and the only thing which matters. It is, therefore, not surprising to find it stated again and again, even by bishops, that in order to stem the tide of Communism, one must raise the standard of living, especially in the "underdeveloped areas" of the world. This is the formula of Marxist dialectical materialism—that conditions determine outlook. The statement is partly true but to a much greater extent it is untrue, since it is outlook which determines conditions and the spirit which is stronger than the flesh. Yet the usurers need this piece of Marxism, since it helps them to spread their net. So we see the two allegedly opposed camps, that of Capitalism and that of Communism, in fact driving the game towards each other. The threat of Communism helps the "investors" to place their money, and ultimately it is Socialism which is the aim of the Capitalists.

6

The Nature of Socialism

It is one of the stock misconceptions which have been fostered for generations, that Socialism is nothing but a protest against the evils of Capitalism and the latter's enemy. Of course it is true that many, indeed most, rank and file Socialists in all lands, and even some of the uninitiated leaders, are inspired not merely by jealousy and a class-conscious inferiority complex. They are often inspired by a very proper unwillingness to accept the shortcomings of Capitalism. Such Socialists are right. It follows quite naturally that so many of them are obviously good men, and it is not surprising that Socialism has attracted so much support during so long a time.

But the true nature of Socialism is not expressed by its milder and certainly not anti-religious forms. The "Democrats" and "gradualists" in their camp are useful to it, but they are not of decisive importance. The key to Socialism of the uninhibited and undiluted kind is not simply its materialism, which brings it close to Capitalism, but more especially the fact that, as we have already indicated, usury-Capitalism cannot hope to exist for ever in its present fluid and expanding forms. There must soon come a time when every State, every firm and every individual is paying the greater part of his income in tribute to the moneylenders, and then the system will collapse by having become an unbearable and unworkable scandal. However accustomed people are now to the acceptance of the usury parasites, they will revolt if and when the monster gets too large and too greedy. Also the constant need for creating new loans so as to sustain the structure, as well as the political need for avoiding excessive unemployment, which is no longer acceptable as inevitable, lead irresistibly to a growing inflation everywhere. Sooner or later money will fall in value to such an extent as to make the system of exchange of goods and services and the accumulation of sums for the capitalization of business impossible. In short, for these and many other reasons, Capitalism is doomed.

This has been understood by its leaders for a long time past. Moreover they are not really interested in an everlasting struggle for survival. Having achieved so much already, in having obtained control of the world by means of their quite amazing economic discoveries, the usurers are bound to think on the lines of the establishment of their absolute and undisputed rule throughout the globe by means of the creation of the requisite political machine. Furthermore, it cannot be denied that such plans are realizable and by no means fantastic.

If the growth and development of Capitalism had been, so to say, a process of the gradual clarification and definition of a picture on the surface of the globe, the picture of the present-day scheme of things, the managers of this process had to treat it as they would a developing photograph in its chemical bath in the darkroom. There comes a moment when the picture is ready and further procrastination will ruin it irretrievably. At this point the operator stops the process of development and fixes the image by plunging the photo into another bath, with another mixture in it. He will then have what he ultimately wants in a permanent form.

Approximately this tendency has been apparent with regard to the money-lenders. They, too, had to have a fixative ready for their developing world-picture. And that fixative of their scheme, their rule, is true and ultimate Socialism, irrespective of whether it is approached by direct and open declaration or by sly and insidious Fabianism. It is not surprising that the "Capitalist" Engels, owner of factories in Germany and England where labour was sweated, as it was in all others at that time, used a part of the relatively easy profits of his trade to support Marx, who, in turn, propounded the basis of present-day Socialism. It is not surprising that it were leading bankers who financed the establishment of Marxism in Russia. It is not surprising that, ever since, the Capitalists have ultimately sustained the Soviets, politically and economically though sometimes going through the motions of seeming to oppose them.

Conversely, too, Socialism has never seriously attacked Capitalism, it has never dealt with its root characteristic of usury. Attention has always been diverted by the Socialists from the basic essentials, from the private issue of money and its loaning at interest, to the question of the private ownership of the means of production, distribution and exchange. The Socialists claim that it is the so-called "nationalization" of property which is a cure for all ills. The reason for this formula is obvious: to attack usury would be to attack the true bosses, while to preach confiscation is to assure the transfer of all that we own to the control of the materialistic messianists. Such intermediate measures as the nationalization of central banks as an allegedly Socialist measure are devoid of any practical significance and a mere sop to the people who have fallen into the socialistic trap and must be given some outward political encouragement. Whether a central bank of issue is nominally controlled by shareholders or by the government is quite unimportant; the shareholders are bankers, and the government is controlled by bankers. Capitalism is the father of its intended heir: Socialism.

Was it not Mr. Henry Ford's great automobile business which gave expert advice and help during a long time in order to enable the Soviets to build and work their first big mass-production plant for motor cars and tractors at Nizhny Novgorod (now Gorky)? Was it not a Mr. Campbell, who owns some 100,000 acres in Montana, U.S.A., who was Stalin's chief adviser on the formulation and execution of the collectivization of the farms in Russia, which cost the country many millions of lives and led to the moral and material ruin of the Russian peasants? Has it not been the alleged reason for recognising the Soviets that good business can be done in the USSR and that the cheap purchase of the products of slave labour can yield good profits? Indeed, has there ever been such morality, or principle, or even what would seem to be normal self-interest in the dealings of the big capitalists with the Communist Soviets?

The action of Fords in the very early years of Soviet Communism has been followed more recently by Fiat and others, in building new motor car factories and others in Russia. It is the result not of Russian, but of Communist failure. In over 50 years the system of slavery has proved to be totally inefficient and unproductive, and therefore dependent on Capitalistic subsidies and technical assistance on a huge and permanent scale.

Trade between the major countries and the USSR is such as to provide a perpetual but hidden subsidy, as there are recurring losses for the Western countries, though individual firms make very adequate profits and are usually promptly paid by the Soviets.

The ultimate real aims of Capitalism and Socialism are identical: the centralized rule of a political group, which owns all the means of production, to say nothing of controlling all money, and which thus achieves the ideal of the materialistic messianism. It is a natural attribute of this conception of power that it must be international, worldwide. And it is not so much the case that Socialism cannot survive in one, or a few, countries. Stalin said it could, and he was right. The real trouble is that Capitalism cannot survive at all, either in one country, a group of countries, or in the whole world. If the Soviets are alleged to be sitting back now, and waiting for the collapse of Capitalism, they are right. But we must not fall into the trap of assuming that the Soviet tyranny is Capitalism's enemy and alternative; it is its product and its completion. However, as we shall see below, there are also some real struggles within the Capitalist-Socialist bloc, but they are not concerned with aims such as most normal people would wish to pursue. In this connexion we should remind our readers that the huge majority of constructive workers, be they owners and managers of factories, transport companies, farms, insurance offices, and, in fact, almost every possible profession, or employees, are by no means involved in this Capitalist-Communist conspiracy, not being capitalists in the sense here implied, but merely owners of property or paid workers. The majority of us are the intended victims of the plot.

Let us note also that the financiers who have wielded so much power in the world for so long and who are able to do much towards keeping those of whom they disapprove short of funds, while lavishly helping those who serve them, have never kept the Socialists short of cash in any country. And in how many Parliaments, in which there are many parties, do we find that effective, but unadvertised, hand pushing Socialists into many key jobs, such as chairman or even Premier or President, when there is no Socialist majority.

And there is yet another method by which the capitalists further their ultimate Socialistic objectives. They not only encourage Socialism as an alternative form of their own power, but at the same time they use it as an opposition controlled by themselves. By this means they try to assure that no real opposition to usury capitalism will appear, as all dissatisfaction will be safely canalized into controlled channels and either used, or neutralized, as circumstances dictate. Of course the technique of controlled opposition of bogus competitors, created by those whom they are supposed to eliminate, is not new, but it is not generally realized that that is one of the chief characteristics of all forms of Socialism.

There are also other approaches to the same end. Among these an important place is occupied by the various efforts which, with varying degrees of success, are being made to establish this or that form of a controlled or managed economic structure. Even many ostensible Conservatives are open exponents of the different forms of controlled economy. Among the expressions of these trends are to be found P.E.P. (Political and Economic Planning) in England, and the Rooseveltian New Deal in the United States. Such plans are intermediate forms between Capitalism and Socialism, and are, as such, naturally unstable and temporary expedients. Socialism remains the true ultimate purpose.

It is true that there are very many people, in most countries, who well understand that any form of more or less camouflaged modified Socialism ultimately leads to Communism, but there are too many, who, having seen that point, come to the conclusion that the proper answer is a defence of Capitalism. If the true facts are known, it will be seen that, it is by no means an answer to the problem. An outline of the true solution is indicated below, in ch. 10 and ch. 11.

There is an additional phenomenon, closely connected with the fostering of Socialism by its alleged opponents, which usually escapes notice. It is the fact that Socialism takes on differing forms and more especially differing degrees in the various countries in which it is a more or less important and active political factor, irrespective of whether it is in power or in opposition.

It is, of course, undeniable that all social and political phenomena in each country are affected by that country's traditions and national character. But on the other hand Socialism is never a local growth, the product of local thought and initiative. It is always the product of the thought, initiative and support of the whole international complex of the materialistic messianists. It is their tool.

Consequently it follows that this political trend is by no means to be allowed to take its own course. It must be strictly controlled, as all the other activities of the same masters. In each country its true aims, as distinct from those for which it pretends to work, are attuned to the overall plan.

Therefore in a land which in any event cannot display any effective resistance to be coming universal dispensation, or one whose role in world affairs is slight, or again a State whose people are more or less passive and pliable and content to live from day to day for their smaller pleasures, will have only a mild Socialism imposed on it. Such in general is all Western Europe and in particular Scandinavia, where the Social Democratic parties have been in power for over 40 years without having brought about a really fundamental revolution.

On the other hand the United States of America are still not ripe for the slaughter, because they are needed as the base for operations during the Capitalistic phase of the overall plan. But should the time come when Socialistic World Government will be imposed on us all, then, because Americans would offer tough resistance, America, like Russia, may be forcibly subjected to extreme Socialism. Let none say "it cannot happen here"; it has happened in too many places already. Be warned, and be prepared.

It is in this light that we must consider the Socialist-Communist Revolution in Russia. That country was the chief obstacle, as we have noted elsewhere, and also the potential chief base for subsequent operations. Russia, and its neighbours—China, Poland and the others—had to be subjected to the most extreme form of Socialism. That there were some elements in the Russian situation which made such extremes somewhat easier, is quite subsidiary. It is largely accidental. In this connexion it could be observed that, since time immemorial, red has been the favourite colour of the Russians and in the Russian language the words for red and beautiful are almost identical. Red Square in Moscow had always borne that name and it also means "Beautiful Square", In this sense the revolutionaries were fortunate in Russia in having chosen the red colour—that of the blood of their intended victims—as that of their movement. Chance does play a role in human affairs, but essentially it is not accident but the ability to use opportunities, in the desired direction which is decisive; there is an overall plan for world subjugation, and this or that more or less accidental factor which may help is not, in itself, the thing that really matters.

If we are to have a correct picture of the aims and activities of the Socialist aspect of the world conspiracy, we must bear in mind the specific purposes which it serves in general and in each country in particular.

There are two factors appertaining to Socialism which may be regarded as somewhat debatable: on the one hand, when we contemplate the undoubted achievements of Socialism in the USSR and elsewhere, and the fact that this system has been able to achieve a stability and attain even a driving force which provide a real threat to the rest of the world, we may wonder if this system may not, when it has been improved by experience, be the dispensation of the future. Surely, we might say, the world is becoming more integrated, more organized, more closely controlled as the result of a denser population and technical progress, without which that population could not survive. On the other hand we might then assume that if that is so, then we must reconcile ourselves to a loss of freedom, with the inevitable growth of controls and management of economic and social life.

But this line of argument in favour of the apparent inevitability of Socialism is faulty. Firstly it is quite clear on the basis of long and extended experience, that liberty in practical life leads to greater efficiency, and we can justly claim that it always will. Regimentation is not something which fosters and encourages progress and even productivity. Human nature is such that it flourishes best in freedom, though some organization is, of course, essential. Some of the arguments which suggest themselves in favour of a different view are true only if we consider present-day capitalism, and not a system of true freedom and balance, as will be outlined below.

Secondly, the driving force of Socialism does not lie in the truth of its ideas, but in the fact that it is a method by which ambitious men can achieve power and possessions. It is merely another path and area of great adventure and achievement. The men who lead Socialism are by no means self-effacing idealists, serving an exalted cause. They are tough fighters for a position of power and for its fruits. And being in the same class as the capitalists, being also materialists, they are far from any vestige of an interest in the welfare of the people. On the contrary, the financiers and the Socialists who are their creation are both concerned essentially with the exploitation of the masses. To relieve the more or less wealthy classes of their possessions, by financial or political means, is a trifle and a process which does not last long; the riches are soon gone. It is only the exploitation of the working masses which can provide a large and permanent source of income to the bosses. The workers themselves are, in the first place, caught in the net by slogans which are attractive, especially when the moral atmosphere is already poisoned by long years of materialistic preparation, and then they are the chief victims of the plot. There is no master so heartless as that class which is the product of materialism, but under the first phase of capitalism the yoke is softened because so much still remains of Christianity in practice and consciousness.

Thus only a return to a dispensation which is based on moral foundations and conceived with scientific accuracy can assure the people a free and prosperous life, under the leadership of people who, while not devoid of some personal ambitions and the wish to provide for themselves, are essentially active in an atmosphere of public service and not private gain. We can not assume that human nature would ever make an ideal possible, but we can certainly say that immense improvements are possible. In this light it is necessary to provide the working peoples of the world and their leaders with a new conception of their own interests and a new plan for the attainment of progress. The scheme, based on old truths and tried traditions, can and must be devised and stated. We hope here to provide some material for this essential and urgent work.

If we are to consider in somewhat greater detail the situation in which Socialism, i.e. total slavery, can be eliminated and the measures which must be taken for the purpose, it may be well to consider the stages of historical development which have led from the natural dispensation, when the private ownership of the means of production and distribution and the State issue of the means of exchange were the basic rule, whatever might have been the political and social superstructures.

We might make use, without stretching the parallel too far, of the example of the life-cycle of the moth or butterfly. First there is hatched the egg, which grows into an energetically feeding caterpillar. The egg and caterpillar are the beginning and developed structure of usury-capitalism, feeding on the vegetation and body of the natural system of free men, free enterprise, free ownership. In the process of feeding, the caterpillars gradually modify the system which sustains them, they poison and change it.

Also there takes place, at the end of the capitalistic phase, the development of the red cocoon, the structure of the democratic, often republican, laic or anti-religious and increasingly planned and centrally controlled State and social and economic dispensation. We see the appearance of huge monopolies, combines and financial controllers run by men who are in no way personal owners, but are mere managerial employees of owners who are impersonal, if not in many cases also representative of the State. These forms develop not only within each country, but also internationally.

It may be claimed that the process is inevitable because large undertakings can run productive processes which are beyond the powers of small firms, and that these big structures must necessarily obtain the funds for development from the money market, and cannot grow from small beginnings. However, this argument is contradicted by the existence of such huge industrial enterprises as Krupp in Germany, the Morris motor car works of Lord Nuffield in England and, until recently, the Ford motor car factories in America, which are or were until very recently owned by single individuals or families, and had grown from small beginnings. Furthermore, even if finance is borrowed, it does not follow that it must necessarily become the means of displacing the control of the founders. This happens only under Capitalism with its system of unrepayable debts in the form of stock and shares, whereas all debts ought to be repaid in instalments and not remain a permanent burden on industry.

Within this cocoon of planning and impersonal control, of deceptive voting both in business and the State, deceptive because the candidates and the policies are pre-determined by the "planners", there develops finally the poisonous moth of socialism-communism, the final enslaver of all mankind. In all these phases of the process there is an apparent inevitability, a seeming naturalness yet all is determined by the basic falsity of the whole capitalist-socialist system.

However, given the facts and circumstances we know, there does emerge the Socialist Global Republic, the godless world state, in which all men, deprived of reason and with their souls deadened by irreligion, are completely enslaved. It can not be stressed too strongly that when all terminology has been reduced to essentials, that is the situation: Socialism is total slavery and nothing else at all.

The case of Franklin D. Roosevelt, one of the world's greatest traitors and war criminals, illustrates well the essence of the last stage in the development of Capitalism. It was Roosevelt who said: "Things do not just happen; they are planned that way". He meant it; he knew. In that sense his crimes were so natural, so a part of himself and his surroundings, that morally it is impossible to judge him too strongly. It has been said of Roosevelt that he was a "total politician" in the sense that he quite naturally did everything possible in order to obtain and maintain power. In the atmosphere in which he developed and worked, such an attitude was natural. Yet it can be said similarly of the gangster that he is a total businessman because he does not stop at murder to get money. Are we exaggerating? Not at all. The notorious Al Capone, who had countless murders and robberies on his conscience, was, in the conditions of late Capitalism, left untouched for many years and finally imprisoned on a charge of tax evasion on his ill-gotten gains, and quite recently the US Supreme Court gave a judgment which meant that the proceeds of robbery are taxable, almost, as it were, recognized as income in law!

Therefore it was not unnatural, not surprising that F. D. Roosevelt had an all-consuming admiration for Stalin, "dear Uncle Joe", and was not merely willing but anxious to give half the world to this super gangster for no return at all. And this Roosevelt was re-elected three times as President. Such are the leaders, such the atmosphere. Consciously and instinctively Roosevelt saw in Stalin the consummation of the policies and forms of State and life which he represented. It was thus not surprising, too, that the nearest advisers and collaborators of F.D.R. were Communists or at least Communist sympathizers. The Roosevelts are the caterpillars; the Stalins the Red moths.

It does not follow at all that Americans as such, in the mass, are guilty of the crimes of Roosevelt and so many others. On the contrary, as was the case in Russia and so many other countries, the leaders of the Red course were a dominant minority. The policies they pursue are well concealed. It follows that as soon as the Americans and all others in the still free world will begin to understand what is happening, they will speedily put an end to these plans and trends. To make them known is the most urgent matter of all.

But there still remains the problem as to what, if anything, can be done to overthrow Socialist slavery once it has been established for a number of years, the potential opposition has been "liquidated" and the masses cowed and "brainwashed". The problem cannot be shelved on the assumption that it is enough to isolate the Communist areas of the world and prevent the spread of the infection. The fact remains that the Socialist challenge is active and energetic, and it must be such since Socialism cannot exist in a world half free, without forever being in real danger. Conversely, of course, the free world is also in constant danger.

The Marxists had propounded the thesis that every political, social and economic system carried within itself the seeds of its own destruction, and there is some truth in this proposition if the system is either being actively and effectively attacked by infection by organized subversion, or if it also contains many and important factors which make the system unnatural, unbalanced and unstable. At a first glance this proposition would seem to apply also to Soviet Communism, and there are not a few who try to lull opponents into passivity by assuring them that a beneficial evolution will soon bring about great and positive changes behind the Iron Curtain.

We will certainly not go so far as to pay the Socialist servants of Capitalism the compliment of having invented and created a system which differs from all others in being unassailable from inside or outside. But also we will not be so irresponsible as to claim that the whole problem of the destruction of once established socialist slavery is easy.

If instead of the "managerial class" you have a Communist Party, consisting of hand-picked and trained thugs of the worst kind, exercizing the power of slave-drivers by unlimited brute force and equally unlimited deception, you create a vested interest in comparison with which large share holders and highly paid executives are mere babies. A director or speculator, banker or hire-purchase operator who failed in business risks at most a much reduced income; a communist boss who does not maintain himself in power is a dead man, knowing also that his family and friends will not be spared. On the other hand the power of the financier and the manager is at least theoretically unstable, whereas the power of the bosses of a communist country is theoretically unassailable. There are no obvious processes within the Red system which must predetermine its disintegration. Such speculations as that the new privileged classes will soon get soft are not really convincing, unless we consider them in the light of what may or may not happen during very long periods of time. What remains of liberty in the world has not got so much time to spare.

Consequently, if we are to survive in freedom, we must consider what can be done to eliminate Socialism everywhere, and especially behind the Iron Curtain. This is not a matter of human kindness, but one of urgent self-defence.

This is a large subject to which we may one day devote a separate work on *The Strategy Of The Counter-Attack*. But here we must nevertheless indicate some of the essentials. We can not offer the Red bosses any alternative system which might attract them either for reasons of principle, since they have no principles, or for reasons of advantage, since their position cannot be made more advantageous without a complete change and that change would be their end. The Red bosses maintain themselves by force, and only force can serve as an argument which could alter their attitudes and actions.

The masses under Communism still know that they are suffering hardships of every sort, moral and material, but the events of the past fifty years and more have induced a large measure of passive fatalism. But even more important is the fact that the system of espionage and repression, worked with the help of modern arms, equipment and methods, is very effective indeed in nipping all active opposition in the bud. Thus to imagine that revolution can be engineered in Russia and the others wthout any recourse to warlike actions or pressure is to rely on very problematical proposition indeed. And too much, as had been indicated elsewhere, had been done by the West to induce an utter lack of trust in it on the part of the socialist slaves.

We are left with this: parallel to the work of the dissemination of the truth in the still free world, there must be a dissemination of the same truth behind the Iron Curtain, and in practical terms very much can be done. Thus the hopes and trust in the West of the victims of Communism can be restored and a situation can be brought about in which the peoples in question will be ready to join their brother freedom-fighters when the day of the absolutely inevitable show-down comes. And come it will, as prophesied by the Communists and wiser anti-Communists for many decades. It would be foolish and irresponsible to suggest that there is any easier or less risky way of escaping the final consequences of the Capitalist-Communist process. We are now at the historic parting of the ways; it is either an heroic struggle for the restoration of Christianity and freedom, or it is the final end, the Apocalyptic era.

Meanwhile the politics of the leading Western countries are still fully in the tradition of an F.D.R., his predecessors and followers. Nothing of value can come of them. The rulers of the West must be persuaded to understand their duties or must be replaced as soon as possible. To this there is no alternative. In place of containment and co-existence there must be relentless and active opposition to all evil and an effective counter-attack. For this the moral, intellectual and material means are more than ample. In this context we hardly realise how weak is our enemy and how strong are we, if only we will understand our interest and duty.

An illustration of the way "things are planned", as indicated by Roosevelt, is provided by a quotation from the book "Far and Wide" by the well-known British writer Douglas Reed, published by Jonathan Cape, London, in the Summer of 1951, and quoting a prophecy made in 1942.

"What real purpose did Mr. Roosevelt promote through the way he used his imperial powers? He furthered the main principles of a plan for the redistribution of the earth published in 1942 (but clearly prepared much earlier) by a mysterious 'Group for a New World Order', headed by a Mr. Moritz Gomberg. What this group proposed was startling at the time but proved farsighted. The main recommendations were that the Communist Empire should be extended from the Pacific to the Rhine, with China, Korea, Indo-China, Siam and Malaya in its orbit; and that a Hebrew State should be set up on the soil of 'Palestine, Transjordan and the adjoining territories'. These two projects were largely realized. Canada and numerous 'strategic islands' were to pass to the United States (the reader should keep these 'strategic islands' in mind). The remaining countries of Western Europe were to disappear in a 'United States of Europe' (this scheme is being vigorously pursued at present). The African continent was to become a 'Union of Republics'. The British Commonwealth was to be left much reduced, the Dutch West Indies joining Australia and New Zealand in it. The scheme looks like a blue-print of the second stage in a grand operation of three stages, and substantial parts of it were achieved; what was not then accomplished is being energetically attempted now."

It is hardly necessary to stress that this report by Mr. Reed is both prophetic and highly sinister. If twenty years ago he saw much of the plan in action, today we can see it almost on the threshold of completion, especially in Europe and Africa. The quotation is taken from pp. 245-346.

The reason for which Capitalism, the Big Banks, have been the creators and financial and political backers and supporters of Communism for many decades is that the usury-cum-money-creation system involves a perpetual accumulation of permanent debt and interest burdens on the economies, and the day must come when there will be a general economic and political collapse, as the obligations have become unpayable and the currencies will be devalued to extinction.

Very great inflation could postpone the Great Crisis, but it would also destroy the key currencies.

Therefore the present global oligarchs through money have long ago made preparations to transform their power and exploitation into a stable form—Socialism or Communism, in fact universal slavery imposed by an unlimited terror with total brainwashing.

7

Making Sure of Borrowers

Now while usury Capitalism requires ever expanding fields of exploitation, it must also continually maintain the exploitability of its internal markets in each country. There must be at all times a ready and plentiful demand for the goods of the bankers—loans at interest. Woe betide the bankers if ever the day were to come when nobody needs to "touch" them, to ask for monetary accommodation. Most of us hope never to have to borrow or to lend, but the bankers thrive on the misfortunes of those in need.

Indeed in recent years the bankers' need for more and more borrowers has become so acute that they openly urge people to contract debts in many and repeated advertisements, whose dishonesty is clearly apparent to anyone who may take the trouble to think. The thesis that to borrow at interest is a means towards raising ones standard of living is quite obviously absurd, since interest payments must be added to the cost of goods and services obtained for consumption, and the borrowers often buy more than they can really afford, and thus the day of the great crash, when incomes will not suffice to pay both for essentials and interest and repayments to the usurers, is fast approaching. It must be assumed that the financiers will then be ready with the Third World War and the World State to follow, thereby "solving" the problem created by them in their own way. The World Bank already exists, and UNO. But meanwhile they still seek borrowers.

It follows, therefore, that with the help of the control which the usurers exercise over all Governments, they must bring about conditions in which no man and no firm will ever fully shake off the shackles, and especially that the State itself will be a willing borrower. Now there are several techniques by means of which the desired results can be achieved.

Before the last war, for some generations, the usual method was wars and crises. That war is an event which will contribute towards the financial exhaustion of the community, apart from a few speculators, is obvious. It is equally clear that the "classical" crisis of the past did immense damage. But it has not yet been realized that these crises were by no means catastrophes due to mysterious and uncontrollable circumstances. They were brought about quite consciously by the financiers, while everything was thickly camouflaged with the usual financial jargon, which is meant to, and does deceive.

We have noted already that the bankers control the volume of credit, of money in the land. We have noted that a change in the amount of means of exchange in circulation will alter prices, or the value of money in relation to goods and services. Now it is an obvious fact that no business is normally run for any length of time unless it brings a profit to its owners and managers. But if a business pays, then, and it is only a matter of time, it must one day become free of all debt and then be able to expand at the cost of a part of the profits, or at worst it can remain as it is and continue, to yield an income without obliging its owners to borrow anything at any time. Furthermore, if the growth of the business in general calls for more monetary capital, it can obtain this by borrowing the savings of others, but not the "money-out-of-nothing" of the bankers. In short the community would not require the most fundamental and essential services of the bankers. There would be no borrowers of their money at interest. And that would be the end of the whole system. Even the very issue of money by the banks would become impossible and monetary emission would have to return to the State, from which this function was usurped by the usurers. Clearly the bankers, like any pawnbroker, thrive on misery, and clearly they cannot allow the community ever to become debt-free and free of the need to contract further debts.

So the money-lenders have to act as soon as prosperity, encouraged by a period of expanding credit, comes too close to bringing about this potentially debt-free situation. Yet in the first instance they have to allow periods of expansion, so as to fatten the victim before the slaughter. A policy of never-ending poverty would not suit them and would also encourage too much opposition and enquiry. Capitalism must give practical proof of its benefits and efficiency. But when all this has gone too far, statements are spread through the controlled press and radio, expressed in the most obscure and deceptive jargon, which explain the need for credit contraction. A recent phrase was "We have overreached ourselves." Of course, if those responsible were to be closely questioned on the meaning of this terminology, they would explain that excessive well-being has led to inflation—the spiral of wages and prices—and this, in turn, has made competitive foreign trade difficult, and so on. It would be most convincing. But it would be only partly true.

The simple facts are these. The dangerous limit of prosperity having been reached, credit is reduced, there is less money in the land and prices fall. Now the entrepreneur, the owner of a productive business, who has made his goods to sell at a certain price which would assure him a reasonable profit, finds himself in a multiple difficulty. First of all the "credit squeeze" means that he is called upon by his bank to repay all or a part of his indebtedness, his overdraft, which he had been gradually reducing for years out of his profits. He had hoped to be able to deal with it finally in a number of years, without at the same time overstraining his resources. But the bank demands the whole sum now and, as it has full security, can enforce payment. This alone is enough to upset the whole budget of the business. But in addition the fall in prices all round will force our businessman to sell his goods at cost price or even at a loss, in order to pay the bank and keep his business going. Finally the reduction of prices is not all. The size of the market is reduced, there are fewer buyers and they buy less. So some of the goods produced cannot be sold at all, or will be disposed of only slowly, while new production has to be held up. This means that some of the workmen have to be paid off and as there are no other potential employers, all being in the same position, these men remain unemployed.

When these troubles have lasted just long enough to "bring the business community to its senses" as it were, that is, to make sure that it is again in need of loans at interest, then the bankers, with a new burst of smoke-screen jargon, announce the happy news that the crisis is passing and, consequently, a credit expansion is becoming possible. The clients of the banks meekly appear, cap in hand, to ask for loans, and the banking structure is safe. The issue of money remains in its hands, and it is burdened with interest charges—the servicing of the loan, as the jargon has it. And so it went on, every seven years or thereabouts, for many years.

In the general context of the discussions of the whole picture, in which economic considerations play their very important part, we cannot discuss every detail fully, though we would like to do so, and we indicate the essentials. However, in connexion with the question of reduced money or credit supplies after a period of prosperity in the recent past, it must be noted that such credit contraction is, in part, automatic.

Every prudent and honest businessman will, quite naturally, reduce his indebtedness when business is good, and it follows therefore that he will repay whatever obligations he may have towards his bankers. But with each repayment of his overdraft or similar accommodation from his bank the borrower inevitably reduces the amount of money in circulation, since the loan was a creation of new money, and its repayment a cancellation.

In these circumstances the banks are, of course, at liberty to lend as much, or more, money as they are given in repayment of debts, thus passing on the payments of one firm to another in the form of new loans. But in conditions of prosperity such loans to creditworthy customers may not have been possible, as the general trend was to reduce indebtedness, and not to increase it. Such conditions can only be changed by such means as inflation and excessive taxation.

Conversely, of course, inflation, following on a restoration of prosperity after a crisis, also contains elements of semi-automatic effect. Not only is more money created by new loans, but some of it is released from hoards which can take various forms, so that means additional to those emanating from the banks also come into circulation. Furthermore, in conditions of prosperity and confidence the velocity of circulation of money in all forms is considerably increased, so that the same amount of the means of exchange will bring about a much bigger turnover of goods, and this can lead to a rise in prices which is larger than the increase in the amount of money in the country. Thus, for example recent statistics shew that between 1946 and 1954 the money supply of Great Britain increased by about 15 per cent, while during the same period, the index of retail prices rose by over 50 per cent.

These phenomena would be avoided if the giving and receiving of moneys by the banks, in whatever circumstances, would not involve the creation and cancellation of the means of exchange, any more than is the case when loans are made or repaid by private individuals or firms. As we note elsewhere, the issue and cancellation of money should be the business of the State, as it had been in the past.

Here we should note, however, that it does not follow that the State, when issuing money free of interest should use it in competition with private trade and industry. It must enter the monetary bloodstream through the payment of legitimate governmental expenses and by being granted for a nominal charge to the private banks, if a surplus is available, for lending to trade and industry. This question is dealt with more fully in Chapter 10 below.

One of the further factors which help to deepen the effects of crisis, following on credit contraction, are the then inevitable strikes. Here it should be noted that often there is a hidden understanding between the operators of the financial policy and of the industrial troubles which follow. The true losers are the workers and the nation in general.

Now, however, mass unemployment is no longer politically permissible and the same results have to be attained by modified means. The methods used are a sustained inflation and taxation extended almost to the limit. The continual fall in the value of money assures that no great monetary accumulations are made possible in hands other than those of the actual money minters—the bankers. In addition the taxes achieve the same results, and again they do not affect the emission of money by the banks, which does not come under the heading of a taxable profit, being in fact a loan. So we see that whenever there is a new issue of shares on the Stock Exchange, plenty of money can be oversubscribed in a few minutes, even if millions of pounds or dollars are involved, but ordinary business remains in need of accommodation.

In these circumstances it might seem that the State, being in receipt of an enormous tax income, would not be in need of the loans of the bankers. But here, too, the stranglehold of the money-lenders was long ago assured. At no time was any Government allowed to raise taxes to so high a level as to repay whatever debts it may have had, in the days when these amounts were still very low. The very idea of taxing the business community at a rate which would have made possible the amortization of the National Debt within a relatively short time would have been opposed by all the means at the disposal of the bankers from the time when they first succeeded in becoming the issuers of money and the creditors of the State. Every newspaper and every politician would have howled at the very idea, and, indeed, most businessmen would also have kicked, believing that it was better that they should be spared an extra sixpence in the pound, or five cents in the dollar, rather than help in the total abolition of the National Debt. But once the principle was established, due to the deceit of the bankers and to the greedy shortsightedness of businessmen, that the needs of the State should be met by increases in the National Debt, the rest followed irresistibly.

The days are now long since passed when a total repayment of the National Debt was reasonably possible in any highly developed country. On the contrary, as the Debt grows and as Income Tax begins to be very largely absorbed by the "servicing" of the Debt, the need for more accommodation increases. Thus the State is never in a position to throw off the shackles of the usurer, as even its sovereign power has in practice been abandoned to the banks.

And so it is that in addition to inflation a huge Income Tax also assures that the community will be ready to borrow, while a huge Debt makes certain that the State also will remain a faithful customer of the usurers. Indeed, the immense modern income and other taxes are collected not so much to pay for the needs of the State as in order to sustain the usury structure.

Inflation also appears advantageous from the point of view of the usurers as a stable currency provides a fairly definite limit to the extent of the National Debt, "serviced" at a more or less "reasonable" rate of interest. There must come a time when an almost one hundred per cent Income Tax could not provide adequate interest on the Debt. But if the money is inflated and its value drops, then the nominal amount of the National Debt can be increased, and this gives considerable flexibility to the whole game; it gives the financiers time to make other arrangements.

An important and rapidly developing banking activity, aimed at the acquisition of new borrowers, is the encouragement of consumer loans through advertising. The false idea is encouraged that borrowing at interest can raise the standard of living. In fact this will inevitably hasten the approach of a great crisis and financial collapse, when huge numbers of wage and salary earners will find themselves unable to meet their obligations, having borrowed much from banks and bank-owned hire-purchase firms.

Today, if you want to make money, you must make it literally, by being a banker; you cannot make money by useful and constructive work. Or, alternatively, you have to become a boss in a Communist country, where you are also in control of all the economic activities and reap all the benefits.

8

Unemployment

Though we have noted that now the effects of the old crises are obtained in a more continuous form, and not in concentrated doses every seven years or so, it is still necessary to make a short analysis of the still so very recent events in this sphere. There are many who will remember the terrible and long years of mass unemployment in Europe and America. But there are not so many who realize that this unemployment was by no means a phenomenon of nature, an inevitable misfortune. It was a part of the technique by which the bankers maintain themselves in power. We have already indicated how credit contractions led to short employment. But even in periods of credit expansion unemployment did not disappear. It was a part of the system and can be eliminated only in time of war or by inflation, as at the present time. That is what is now called "a policy of full employment." This often used phrase is alone enough to shew that the managers of finance know perfectly well that employment is matter of policy, not of mysterious forces.

Now, in the absence of continuous inflation, the inevitability of unemployment under the Capitalist system can be demonstrated by two different approaches to the question: on the one hand by an analysis of prices, and on the other by a consideration of the flow of money.

Any manufactured article is sold at a price which is an accumulation of labour costs. Even the profit of the owners of the business is but a variable wage, paid to them for their work. Much nonsense has been written and spoken by Marxists and others about profit, mysterious additional costs, etc. Such matters may safely and best be considered in the light of common sense. The only difference between an employer and a worker is that the former may make a loss, while the latter is paid a fixed wage or salary and at worst may be out of work. The collection of interest on loans or from share "capital" is another question which we will consider below. But so far as true cost of a manufactured article is concerned, or even of raw materials and food, such as corn, it is a matter of paying for the work done in digging the ore, refining it, making the parts, assembling them, delivering and even selling. Even the rent charged for land and buildings is not necessarily anything but a labour cost, as these things must be kept in good repair, occasionally rebuilt etc.

But that is not all, since there is one other element which contributes towards the price, and that is the interest which the business must pay on loans to the banks and to those who advanced the original "capital". Most large-scale businesses are now public limited companies, while the smaller firms are private companies all having stock and shareholders, who must be paid a part of the profits and also, in some cases, a fixed rate of interest on the nominal value of their shares. Dividends are merely variable interest on loans.

In general terms those who earn money for work done are able to pay for all the sums which make up the total of the wages fraction of the price of all goods. It is obvious that the sum of the wages paid (including profits) is also the sum of the prices, apart from the usury element in them. Thus there could be no shortage of purchasing power, no unemployment. What is paid in wages throughout the country is expressed in the total price of all the goods, and they will, therefore, all be saleable and no man will be short of a customer for goods or services. In other words the part of the price of an article which is payment for work done can be paid by those who do the work.

But that part of the price which is set aside for the payment of interest on loans can only be paid by those who are also in receipt of such income, in addition to earnings for work done. And so we get a shortage of purchasing power, since only the few earn interest, and that shortage is concentrated on the economically weakest, who remain deprived of all purchasing power, that is who are unemployed. Indeed it could be shewn that there is a numerical relationship between the proportion of people unemployed and the ruling rate of interest.

The description of interest earning must, however, be qualified. It is economically harmful, because also unnatural, that anyone should earn interest indefinitely on a loan which is subject to no amortization. There is no parallel to such a thing in nature; and it is a proposition akin to a perpetuum mobile, known to be physically and mathematically impossible. On the other hand loans out of savings towards the true capitalization of business are helpful, providing only that there is repayment during a reasonably short period, in convenient instalments. In that case there would be no "short-circuiting" of money in payments which are useless for production or other constructive purposes, and there would be no excessive time-lag in the economic bloodstream, with money delayed at the "Capitalistic" end of the economic system.

This brings us to the other approach to the issue of unemployment, again if we eliminate any more or less artificial masking of this phenomenon. If money can earn interest at the producing end of the economic system then the flow of the means of exchange, the bloodstream of the economic body, will always tend to the "top", while at the same time leaving the "bottom", the buying end, short. There will appear a tendency towards subsidized overproduction and a corresponding shortage of purchasing power.* And this shortage, as we have noted, tends to be concentrated in the weakest members of the community, and they are then deprived of all purchasing power, that is they are unemployed. If there were proper amortization of loans, money would flow more quickly into the production of capital goods and would in general increase purchasing power, so as to bring it into balance with production.

Inflation masks these manifestations of the shortcomings of the usury system because it involves the constant "blood transfusion" which is intended to achieve, as it were, an artificially sustained purchasing power, which at the same time gives the organism more "blood"—i.e. money—than it really needs in the given circumstances, bearing in mind the level of production. It follows quite naturally that the authorities responsible for these matters tend to create a large Civil Service, are happy to have an excuse to expand armaments, and so on, all of which makes it possible to bring the excessive money into circulation. Incidentally here there is no suggestion of pacifism; this remark is purely concerned with economics, and it is taken for granted that in certain circumstances a proper measure of rearmament is essential. It is true, however, that the bankers are all too often behind wars and rumours of wars.

Finally, in connexion with the problem of unemployment and inflation it should be remembered that all the means of exchange come into being as a loan bearing interest charges. Consequently, the bankers create by book entry out of nothing, £100 for the benefit of a borrower, and demand after a given time, for example one year, say £105 in return. Now it may well be that the individual borrower had made a profit with the help of the given loan and is able to repay a sum larger than the one he originally received but the whole economic system cannot return to the banks sums in excess of the amount created and put into circulation.

It follows, of course, that the economic system as a whole must borrow the additional moneys required from the banks and engage to pay more interest on these new loans, and this interest is again paid in the same manner.

Here it will be noted that in general terms the profits made by

* This effect is accentuated by the fact that all money in circulation originates as a loan at interest.

individual units of the general system are reflected in new monetary creations, which are also partly paralleled by an overall increase in production, which reduces the inflationary effect. But such phenomena as unemployment or shortage of purchasing power are due to the time-lag between the moment the additional payment is made to the bank and the time when this money is borrowed, i.e. created and put into circulation.

The only way in which this effect can be avoided is to maintain a constant balance between increases in production and in the supply of money, both to take place simultaneously. These problems are discusssed in later chapters.

It will be observed that the greater the rate of inflation, the higher the rate of interest must be in general. If, for example, inflation is at the rate of, say, 5% p.a., then money invested at that interest would in fact yield no profit at all. Therefore, if a real 5% is desired, the actual rate would have to be 10%.

This is one of many illustrations which prove that the defects of the whole system have a cumulative and ever-worsening effect.

Note. See page 231 of Appendix.

9

The Essence of Financial Capital

If the banking system is the more important part of the whole scheme by which the materialists hold sway over the world, the method by which most businesses are financed in the modern world—the limited liability and other companies, owned by the holders of their stocks and shares and run not directly by the owners, but by hired managers—is another very important and complementary aspect of the scheme. It is banking and company financing, with its accompanying Stock Exchanges, which together make up the essential framework of Capitalism, and the root characteristic of both is usury.

If in earlier historical times it was the practice for any enterprise, be it a farm, or a shop, or a ship or a workshop, to be owned either by an individual or by a partnership, it gradually became the practice to expand partnership into Companies. But the old principle of direct ownership and responsibility was long maintained. The members of a Company were still the joint owners in a personal sense, and none could give away or sell their stakes in the business without the consent of the others.

But gradually a new practice came into operation. A share in the ownership and of the profits of the business became transferable at will and the business in question was no longer managed so much by its legal owners, the shareholders, as by managers, hired by them for the purpose. The Companies became more and more impersonal bodies and the stock and share holders became mere possessors of a claim to profits or fixed dividends, having a vote at company meetings in some cases, but otherwise in no way connected with the business. In a real sense the lawful owners became mere parasites, though their position was and is explained and justified because they are themselves (or the heirs of) those who provided the given firm with its capital and by this bought a claim to its profits.

Yet we have already noted that such capital is not an asset, but a liability. And at the present time there are few businesses which are not burdened, theoretically forever, with this liability. We have seen that the true capital of a business is land, cash in hand, machines, buildings, goodwill, etc. They are the real means of production. It is true that they were originally bought with the monetary capital which had been provided by the first or subsequent shareholders, but there are few businesses in which the face value of the share capital has any relation to the cash value of the real capital. The share capital is only the usurer's claim on the productive work of the Company—its managers and workers. But the financial capital (which gives its name to "Capitalism") is the controller of the undertaking. The moneylender is in charge of productive effort here, as he is also through money in general.

As with the banking system, so also with anonymous and collective nominal ownership of trade and industry, where management remains in the hands of experts, it is a system which grew gradually and, to a great extent, organically. We must recognize that these characteristics give the Capitalist system its not inconsiderable strength and stability and allow it to work relatively well and be generally accepted as something quite natural, as natural as the direct ownership of property and the means of production. It is the general driving force of the materialistic messianists which gave economic and social development and political change its specific direction and character and led to the particular results which, in the end, are so very harmful to the best moral and material interest of mankind.

The effective subtlety of the system lies in part in its secrecy and in part in the fact that an increasing proportion of all people, indeed now a majority, are gradually being made active accomplices in the deceptions which are at the root of the game. More and more people use banks; more and more people become, or want to become, shareholders in various companies and corporations. The deception is constantly maintained that the system is natural and beneficial and, far from being a method of finance which is dominated by a small set of financiers, is a legitimate form of economic activity which seeks to extend its benefits to all, while also, at the same time, widely spreading economic power—being thoroughly democratic and subject to popular control.

It should be understood that, just as we cannot be expert and capable doctors of medicine without long years of study and experience, we also cannot be experts in politics and economics unless we are fully informed concerning all the techniques and methods used, and have sufficient practical experience. In fact most of us have not got the requisite knowledge. Our pretended control of political and economic processes is a deception; the true and complete control remains fully in the hands of a very few people, who also derive the greatest part of the profits.

In passing it might be mentioned that this wastage of money and this massive short-circuiting of the means of exchange through channels which do not lead to productiveness, is a very real evil and leads to very real injury of the community. We might note that, for example, a very large part of the goods and services produced under "capitalistic" conditions is not only burdened with an utterly unjustified load of usury interests, but also with enormous advertising charges, which, in wide spheres of economic life, rise to as much as 80 per cent of the total cost to the public. Furthermore, there are the huge taxes, which go to pay interest, more than to cover useful expenditure.

There are businesses which own no means of production other than a typewriter and office furniture, yet they may have considerable share capital. Thus the value of this capital is not a reflection of the value of the true means of production, which may be the inventiveness or imagination of one man, but is a projection on an abstract plane of the profits of the business considered as interest and related to the ruling rate of interest. In simplified terms, if the average ruling rate of interest is 5 per cent then the value of the shares of a company will be about twenty times the profit for any given year. Thus an investment of £100 will yield £5 p.a., irrespective of the face value of the shares.

One can give at this point some examples to illustrate the estimate of value and the role of financial capital. On a basis of pre-war money values and prices it was possible to build a house in Britain for, say, £1,000. It was also possible to let one room in such a small house for £1 per week, or about £50 per annum. Therefore one room in this house would give an edequate rate of interest (5%) on £1,000, although that was the price of the whole house. Thus anyone renting and subletting two rooms in such a house, could establish a limited or incorporated company with a capital larger than the cost of the house. In fact this company could obtain control or possession of the house merely by financial manipulation. Yet its own operations would be devoid of any real financial basis, let alone constructive effort.

Furthermore another person or company, holding say 40 per cent or even less of the shares of the room company, could have effective control, as it is well known that when annual meetings of shareholders are called to vote on the affairs of the business, those who hold a bloc of some 30 per cent of the voting rights are sure to have a majority at the meeting, as few shareholders trouble to attend. Now by letting the rooms at varying rents, for example one year at £49 per annum and another year at £52 per annum, the controlling company could predetermine changes in the price of the room company's shares on the Stock Exchange. This "useful" operation would yield a profit by speculation, and this in turn would again be reflected in a share capital. Yet the true basis of the second company would be even more ephemeral than that of the first. But control of the house and of its profits would be in the hands of these moneylending parasitical abstractions.

It is with the help of such methods and techniques that financiers obtain and maintain control of economic life and get a large part of the profits without commensurate constructive effort. But if the profits of business become fixed or variable interest on the shares or indebtedness of companies, a large part of the money collected as income tax goes in payment of interest on the National Debt, which thus becomes, as it were, the "capital" of the State.

Here we have attempted to draw attention only to the basic facts of economics, to the decisive essentials. We point to the keys of economic, and therefore also largely of general, power. We sketch some of the main negative consequences of the system known as Capitalism, though we do so not in order to suggest the virtues of the alleged alternative—Socialism.

It is not the purpose of this work to describe in detail all the practical aspects of modern capitalism. We touch only some of the main characteristics, which illustrate one overall thesis. But a few words must be said about the gold standard and foreign trade. Those of us who are middle-aged or older can remember the time when in almost all countries gold coins were still in regular use. Paper money was freely exchangeable for gold. This led, quite naturally, to a fixed rate of exchange between various national currencies, whose values were determined by the gold content of their coinage. This situation was a development of conditions at the period when the goldsmiths were becoming bankers. Credit and paper money would not have been readily accepted unless "backed by gold" and also certain experiences had shewn that a lack of such a tangible link with a precious metal made violent inflations possible.

However, the decisive reason which led to the retention, in a modified form, of a gold standard to this day is that it makes possible the centralized control of credit and money by the financiers, who take good care to have the bulk of the gold under their effective control. In the absence of any form of gold standard the time might come when some private banks and States could be tempted to issue their own credit money in competition with that of the major usurers and money creators. But so long as these have the gold, they can effectively maintain the illusion that any other money would be valueless and thus few or none would accept it in payment for goods and services, or as a loan. Or loans may be raised elsewhere.

In general terms, the gold standard means that if trade between countries leads to an indebtedness of one to another which is not paid by goods or services, then it must be settled by the transfer of gold, or by a loan from the creditor or others to the debtor, naturally at interest.

Now in normal conditions, when the problem is seen in the light of basic facts and unencumbered by financial considerations, trade is a matter of exchange, of barter, of goods and services. So many tons of potatoes buy so many automobiles; so many hair pins buy so much transport or insurance; so many patents on productive industrial inventions buy so many tons of wheat; and so forth. Money, bills of exchange, and other instruments are only convenient tools of commerce, but essentially there can be no profit to any given country in terms of excess goods and services, since the value of what was sold must be equal to that which has been bought. Any exports sent out in excess of the value of imports are wasted, since nothing tangible has been received for them. That is so in the light of natural law.

But it is not so to the usurers. On the contrary, as indicated, an excess of exports is essential to them, as imports of gold are useless in most cases, gold being largely a useless metal, while the chance to lend money is welcomed by the financiers. Indeed, unless there are countries which regularly produce surplus exports and thus create the opportunity for continual loans (for example to "underdeveloped countries"), the international financial brotherhood could not create its international money, any more than it can create internal money in each country unless there are willing borrowers in trade, industry and agriculture. Without unbalanced trade, international finance would die. To maintain its opportunities and machinations, it forces governments, especially in lands such as America, to create tariffs which help export and hinder imports. By this means the materialistic messianists have been enabled to concentrate most gold, and thus the centre of global financial power, in the U.S.A. This is a major step towards Socialistic World Government. First the world is enslaved by "dollar imperialism", by the bonds of debt, and then, as described elsewhere, Socialism is made to supervene.

Of course the highly industrialized countries, America, Great Britain, Germany, France, Japan and others, receive interest on the loans made by them, in the form of the delivery of goods and services, since the money collected is useless unless converted into tangible assets. But as a result these lands are encouraged to think and act as if they must export to live, while these excess deliveries lead eventually to a growing flood of "something for nothing", "invisible exports", mostly in the form of imports of raw materials or food, produced at prices with which local mining and agriculture cannot compete, owing to higher wages. Tariffs are imposed to protect them, as also to make sure that exports exceed imports, as had been indicated, and the consequence is mounting chaos. In immediate practice the financiers are forced, in order to make the system function at all, to find ever more markets for their monetary wares. This is the basic reason for the rapid and dangerous "liberation" of huge territories in Asia and Africa from "colonialism". The bosses of high finance are not in the least interested in the freedom and well-being of the peoples of these lands, but they are in a great hurry to bring about a situation in which they will be borrowers on a large scale. It is a parallel to the efforts made inside capitalistic countries to encourage one might almost say enforce, borrowing by hire purchase schemes and much else.

But there are also, in addition, other factors. If money-lenders' markets were all, then High Finance would merely have to issue its orders to the "democratic" and "capitalistic" obedient Premiers, Ministers of Finance and Foreign Ministers, and use the present system as its tool, as in so much else. Yet the Lords of Finance and their stooges have long since declared war on colonialism, and are pushing Great Britain, France, Holland, Belgium and others out of many areas, especially in Africa and Asia but with South and Central America also in the scheme. The true reasons for this include the calculation that it is easier and less risky to rule, say, Africa directly through unintelligent and corrupt black politicians, there is no risk of being hampered by western public opinion and possible Right movements, and the path is cleared to proceed from money-lending capitalism to World Government socialism almost completely unhindered. Also the financial and political conquest of these territories yields many strategic areas and makes the rest of the world unable to resist when the show-down comes. It is a path of least resistance to objectives of maximum importance.

Yet a growing burden of debt and of interest obligations must inevitably lead to catastrophe. The day will come when the system must collapse. Already now the National Debt of the United States is greater than their total value, immense though it is, and the debt grows irresistibly by many billions every year. Similar situations exist in other lands.

The approach of the day when the whole world will be either already under Socialism, or in a state of "debt-saturation" and under full control, will be the time when the end of Capitalism will be engineered, and the era of global Socialistic slavery will be ushered in. Only timely counter-action can still save us, and for this the spread of knowledge is essential.

It must suffice to indicate these problems only in outline.

But there is one aspect of capitalism which deserves some mention, and that is the institution of limited liability. Legislation legalizing this piece of capitalistic effrontery began to be passed only one hundred years ago, and often much more recently; in general limited liability arose within the period of an ordinarily long lifetime. Yet today it is universally accepted that there are few businesses in the highly developed countries which are not run as limited liability companies.

The basic proposition of limited liability is that a company, owning a business, is not liable for the debts of that business beyond the amount of its nominal capital, that is the only money risked by those concerned in any capacity with the founding and running of a firm are the sums which were originally invested, that is lent at interest or for a share of the profits. As there is no law which prevents a company doing business on any scale, it can and often does happen that a firm with a nominal capital of, say, £100 or a similar amount in any other currency, will do business with a turnover thousands of times greater per annum than the theoretical capital, while, of course the possible liabilities are proportionately also immensely larger than the sum which is supposed to cover them. In short an individual or set of people can involve others in huge liabilities, while themselves remaining personally safe from any claims or responsibility beyond the small amount originally risked. Obviously this arrangement is almost an invitation to fraud and is often misused. The whole proposition is totally immoral. It amounts to the formula that the winnings of the given entrepreneurs are lawfully theirs, but the losses are just as legally those of their creditors, who were not even consulted about the operations which led to the losses, and still less warned about any possible weakness of the given firm.

The only "justification" for this fraudulent and immoral arrangement may be that if investors, that is holders of stocks and shares in various companies, were to be made personally responsible for losses, then the large numbers of small investors, who supply so much of the money which helps to float companies on the Stock Exchange and to sustain the game of the speculators, would be discouraged from risking their cash or would demand such detailed information about the businesses whose shares they propose to buy that commercial competition and especially speculation would become difficult or impossible. Money must be made available without too many questions being asked; the anonymity of big business must be protected. The French are logical: to them limited companies are *societées anonymes*. The name gives the show away.

In conclusion it should be noted that the financiers maintain their control over economic life and collect their profits by acting along more than one line. They not only control the emission of money and derive an interest income and other profits from it, but they also control most limited liability companies, including all the larger and more important ones. This is achieved by the fact that relatively small share holdings are enough to assure majorities at company meetings, as has already been noted, and also by the manipulation of the election and guidance of company directors. These techniques, which are based on the law which has been developed under the pressure of the financiers in all capitalist states, have put all business into the hands of the financiers.

But they have, we stress, not obtained control in the majority of cases through very massive investments of their own money. The method is not so crude as to demand that the financiers should put up all the money. On the contrary, because the money-lenders have been able to evolve means by which they have full control even though they have invested but a small part of the original "capital", they are able to finance most business at the cost of the man-in-the-street, and this almost literally, since the numbers of people who are at least small shareholders is growing all the time. And there are also large numbers of financially small people who are indirect investors by having their money in life insurance, in trade union funds, in savings funds and so much else.

The strong encouragement of savings by as many people as possible also serves the important purpose of providing means for the provision of capital goods not alone by bank creations of new money, as that would lead to excessively rapid inflation. Yet in most cases those many people who do save lose money more quickly as a consequence of the yet inevitable inflation than they earn in interest on the sums saved, unless they are invested in good equities, whose value rises with the fall in the value of money.

So it is that the two chief millstones which grind the economic producer by hand or brain are respectively the means of exchange produced by the financiers out of nothing as a loan at interest, and the limited liability companies. Both have in a very real sense acquired for the financiers the true values produced by all economic activity. And they have deprived the producers of all control, either directly or politically, through parliaments and governments. Socialism is only the logical conclusion of this process, unless we all wake up.

In addition to the control exercised by National and International High Finance through direct methods, there is the even more effective, insidious and dangerous control by means of subtle and yet irresistible pressures. Governments and firms, and even some individuals, are being effectively forced to follow the policy lines laid down in general and in particular instances by the top manipulators of Capitalism. A mere hint is often enough, passed on through many channels and so discreetly that it can never be proved, i.e. usually verbally and not in writing. And there is the overall consciousness among all experienced politicians that certain matters, especially the money problem, must not be touched if the given person is to be "successful". The dictatorship of the financial oligarchy under "democracy" is absolute.

10

The Solution of the Economic Problem

The effective solution to the shortcomings of Capitalism is not provided by Socialism or Marxism in any form or degree. On the contrary, we know that Socialism in practice can lead to the most terrible conditions.

If we reduce all that is known about the usury system to basic essentials, while leaving out a discussion of the subsidiary issues, such as gold, foreign trade, and much else, the importance of which we do not deny, we arrive at the following formula, the following solution: *The power to issue money in any form must revert to the State and money must be issued debt and interest free. The volume of emission, the amount of money in circulation, (or the amount to be withdrawn if necessary), must be determined by a price index and the value of the means of exchange, that is the level of prices, must be kept stable. New additional money put into circulation will pay for governmental expenses and reduce taxes and the authority which will control monetary issue must be a body similar to the supreme court, being composed of competent and trustworthy individuals appointed for life and independent of all private interests. And finally no debt whatsoever may be enforceable at law unless there is adequate provision for amortization within the time during which the real value created by the loan will have disappeared, with provision also for a maximum period of repayment, that is the total rate of interest charged on the loan must consist of a fraction as compensation for the service rendered by the loan (profit), a fraction as insurance against loss, and finally a fraction, making up the total, for repayment or amortization in instalments, though any debt can be paid sooner.* By these simple means the whole usury structure which controls monetary emission and the financing of the State and of business, will be eliminated. There will remain a natural and beneficient economic system.*

Yet this formula, while being a complete practical answer to the problems raised by the shortcomings of the capitalist system, is technically easily introduced and would leave the customary monetary and commercial habits of most people unaltered. Even the

* See also "Aims and Principles of a proposed Party of the Right" on p. 210.

greatest part of existing property, including monetary savings in almost all forms, would remain untouched. The solution here recommended is revolutionary and fundamental, but it is not destructive. It would come not as a shock, but as relief; not as a brake, but a release. It will assure rapid and great economic development in every country which adopts it, and it would not be necessary to bring about the required changes in all lands simultaneously, as the commercial interchanges between countries with the old and the new economic dispensations would remain largely unaltered.

When considering the formula for a solution of the problems provided by the present capitalist system, it should be borne in mind that the banking technique gives the bankers an immense rate of interest, even if we assume (and we know that this assumption is wrong) that when the bankers lend money, they really own at least ten or twenty per cent of the sum provided. If the rest, i.e. eighty to ninety-five per cent, is money made by the bankers out of nothing, by means of mere book entry, then it follows that a nominal 5 per cent on the loan is in fact 25 per cent or 50 per cent p.a., i.e. five to ten times the nominal rate. In addition the coin and bank notes (paper money) held by the banks are also not in fact their property, but are obtained from the government or central bank in return for cheque-money, i.e. book entry.

Furthermore, it should never be forgotten that there is a difference between money lent for mere consumption, and that which is lent for production. The former is unrepayable within the context of its own influence; on the contrary, it is liable to make repayment unlikely. Consequently, if we consider any lending at interest at all, it is only for production, for the creation of real capital, be it machinery, fields prepared for a harvest or any other productive investment. The hungry man needs not a loan at interest, but Christian charity; the extravagant one needs to be restrained and reformed.

The only people who would suffer somewhat are the money-lenders, usurers and bankers of every kind. Their dictatorship over most of the affairs of men, through their control of money, would end. But they would not be obliterated. They could still play an active and useful role in the new scheme of things and they could earn a decent living. If the function of monetary emission is returned to the State, and the control of its amount will be a public duty, not a private opportunity, and the bankers are deprived both of the profits of issue and the interest they can now collect on all the means of exchange in circulation in non-Communist countries, the bankers can still perform the very necessary functions of private agents of the Central Bank or Office of Issue, whichever may be the responsible institution. They can also act as agents to those who accumulate savings which they wish to invest, and reinvest as the repayments come in. Finally the bankers can still render technical services such as managing current accounts, which will be true deposits of money earned and possessed, not borrowed, handling cash transfers, cheques, bills of lading and bills of exchange etc., all for a reasonable fee. They will be able to lend such moneys as they accumulate out of profits and earn interest on them. Of course cheques would no longer originate as loans at interest, but would simply be a part of the money in circulation. They would be convenient means of exchange, as now.

But if no debts will in future remain permanently unrepaid, it would not follow that present investments should be treated other than as a debt which is subject to amortization. Only such debts as are purely speculative and financial, the by-product of the monetary operations of the bankers, and not having their origin in savings, would have to be entirely extinguished. Thus a great part of the National Debt would have to be annulled without compensation, though that part which is based on true savings of individuals or groups, would be repaid in instalments as all other debts.

As the "capital" of various firms would be repaid, the ownership of these undertakings would become concentrated in a few hands in each case, and it is certain that it would be the effective managers of each business who would eventually also be its responsible proprietors. Thus management and ownership would again be synonymous, as should be the case. Clearly the idea of limited liability would go with a new approach and, in place of speculation there would be creative responsibility alone.

On the other hand it would again be easily possible for any enterprising person or group to start their own businesses and build them up from small beginnings.

In this connexion it should be observed that any form of co-operative ownership, including co-ownership by the managers and workers, is by no means included in the general criticism of the ownership of businesses by large numbers of anonymous shareholders. Co-operation can be a very healthy and useful form of economic activity, occasionally somewhat spoiled by being made at present the tool of Left-wing politics.

But as a general rule, such is human nature, it is personal ownership, initiative and responsibility which give the best results in all forms of activity.

A stable and debt-free currency would no longer be the plaything of gamblers, a commodity to be bought or sold. But also National Debt bonds and certificates of all kinds and every sort of stocks and shares of private and public companies and corporations would cease to be the objects of permanent speculation. Trade in such paper would become impossible and the Stock Exchanges in their present form would disappear. Yet here again it should not be thought that all those who had been engaged in work connected with investments should be completely eliminated. On the contrary, their knowledge and experience could be useful in the new circumstances as they could supplement the work of the new bankers in the sphere of the reinvestments of repayments of loans and in the investments of savings. It would in all probability be much better if the determination of the suitability of various applicants for loans and accommodation would be handled by private firms, having experience and local knowledge, rather than by Civil Servants.

The new system here sketched out would place economic power where it belongs and eliminate parasitical exploitations of the community. The economic life of nations would no longer be hindered in its development and subjected to the dangers of crisis, inflation and excessive taxation. Indeed not only will taxes be reduced to a small fraction of their present level, as so much of the sums raised goes in the payment of interest on the public debt, but also monetary emission in the hands of the State will give the Exchequer a new source of income, thus further reducing the need for taxes. The new atmosphere will bring about immense changes for the better.

Not only will there no longer be the terrible choice between usury Capitalism and Communism, with tyrannical World Government as the only outcome, and between atomic annihilation and world slavery. States and nations will be free to develop and to cooperate profitably. There will be a natural balance between work and money, between prices and wages, as they will be mutual reflections of each other, and therefore there will be no need for constant strikes and troubles in order to force the parasitic system to pay a reasonable wage. In conditions of true balance the demand for workers will always be there and thus there will be an inevitable offer of proper pay. But there will also be no unnatural excessive demand for workers which enables them to ask for unjustified wages and conditions, not proportionate to their output. The present apparent opposition between management and labour will become a thing of the past, as will a social and economic consciousness of class differences, though, of course, differing capacities and efforts will lead to differing results and rewards.

With the levers of power wrenched from pernicious hands, there will no longer be any need for secrecy and deceptive jargon in economics. The processes of economic life will be seen and understood by all and they will thus be properly controlled and unable to slip back into the old ways, based essentially on a fraud of truly magnificent proportions if we bear in mind both the extent and size of its operations and the length of time during which it remained undiscovered by most people in all countries, despite its huge power; or perhaps it was precisely its power which protected it so long. But the main factor which made the biggest hoax of all the ages possible was the mixture of naïveté and cupidity which so many generations have displayed in all lands. Similarly, too, most of us will swallow the most amazing political deceptions, the utter effrontery of which remains apparent only to a small minority. But of that more below.

Under a natural economic dispensation the class of political-economic parasites and exploiters would disappear and this applies equally to Capitalism and to Communism. It is the former which supported the latter, its spiritual and in some cases even blood cousins, to set up another and more logical form of economic exploitation with its corresponding political approach and method. In both cases the underlying materialism and ultimate greed were the same driving force.

We do not suggest that a class of rulers can be created which would be entirely devoid of ambition and material wants and still be effective or efficient, but we do say that it is quite impossible to visualize the continued existence and maintenance in the exercise of its power of a class of pure parasites, holding power ultimately only for the sake of its material benefits to that ruling class. Every person (and group) must in the end justify himself in the eyes of his fellow men if he is to be tolerated at all, and especially if he has power and its fruits, whether in the form of prestige, or money, or both. Sooner or later the body of the nation, the social organism, will expel or kill the superfluous and parasitic factor.

At the same time the long continued existence of a class of unjustified parasites is also made impossible by the fact that such a situation will lead to the decay of that class. It has been the relative strength and source of stability of Capitalists that they have in many respects justified their wealth and power by the positive contributions they have made to economic and social life. They were by no means unmitigated parasites and they became almost completely such only in the final stages of Capitalism's decay.

On the other hand the class of Communist bosses, despite torrents of words to the contrary, has never been anything but an unnatural, harmful and purely parasitic clique, at the root expressing the most extreme forms of parasitism towards which the Capitalists are driven inexorably by the logic of their own system. This they know, and it is for that reason that their true leaders have created Socialism.

However, it by no means follows that all those who have been caught up in the stream of either Capitalism or Communism, in practical and not verbal terms, must be considered as enemies of society who can in no circumstances render it any useful services. On the contrary, apart from those individuals who have committed serious crimes—and this would apply almost entirely to certain sections of Communist leadership, it is desirable that not only many of those who are at present bankers or stockbrokers etc., but also very many who are now, in the various lands behind the "iron curtain", active as managers, administrators, scientists and so on, should be ready to find their way into the inevitable new dispensation of tomorrow.

The new way should be one in many respects very close to the liberal conceptions of nineteenth-century England or present-day America. It is the creatively active man who should be economically the most valued, and the personnel of the ruling machinery, whose functions should be very limited in scope and power, should be drawn from those circles which have achieved socially and nationally useful success. It may be objected that in the past such an approach led to failure and to unhealthy consequences. That is true, but the reasons must be sought in the shortcomings of the usury-capitalism which accompanied the efforts to work a truly liberal society. It was the possibility of making excessive profits, of accumulating too quickly a large fortune, of making too much money by usury and especially by the manipulation of the machinery of monetary emission, which made it impossible to give the system balance and stability.

Rich men became artificially too rich; their wealth was increased by the system far beyond the value of the services which they had rendered to society or the nation. At the same time the working masses remained artificially too poor and their reward for hard and loyal work was far less than the true values which they produced. But even worse was the fact that real power passed not so much into the hands of, say, industrialists, but into those of the bankers and financiers and their political nominees.

Under Communism, that product of nineteenth-century Capitalism (a fact which is even illustrated by the tastes of the Soviet rulers, which are in everything mid-Victorian), the shortcomings of Capitalism have been accentuated and speeded up. In both cases power passed into the hands of useless and even harmful, and therefore also inevitably criminal, parasites. The materialism of the type could not save it from perversions.

It is now absolutely necessary to make the choice in each individual case. If the world is not to be abandoned to final slavery and moral and material collapse, then there must be a positive, constructive and beneficial counter-revolution in the best sense. There can be no question of a return to the past anywhere, but there must be a return to organic and basic Christianity, to natural law in the Divine sense.

We do not suggest that the place of Communism can or should be taken by restored Capitalism, and still less by an allegedly democratic Socialism—a deliberate deception. Both expressions of modern materialism—Capitalism and Communism—must and will give way to a new form, yet one essentially very old. It will not be a classless dispensation, since such a thing is neither possible, nor desirable, but it will certainly be a way of life in which the success of persons or groups will not imply a loss to others. If a man or a group does well, all will have gained since new values will have been created, and yet they will not have been used through monetary techniques as a means of acquiring something more than the actual value produced, thus inevitably both creating and stealing. And if something has been acquired without a corresponding creation of true value, then that something has been taken from those who are economically, socially and politically weaker and unable to resist the theft, all the more so as they do not even understand the processes which have led to it and the fact that they have been the victims of such events. All that such people were given in the past was the lies of Socialism, which did not solve their problem, but made it worse. What could be done partially and, as it were, surrepticiously by usury, could now be done openly and in extreme forms by political power, backed by terror. It is a poor compensation to be told that it is done "in the name of the people".

The theory of "Social-Democracy" and the like is a superficially attractive abstraction, based in part on a misconception, fostered by Marxism, of the class factor. There will always be differences between people, functionally and qualitatively, and thus there will always be classes. That is not an evil in itself, but even a useful phenomenon. Another confusion results from the inability to distinguish correctly between the personal ownership of property and its control under Socialism as being two forms of the same thing, with an outward and formal legalistic and great moral difference. Far from being an evil, classes can in certain circumstances be both inevitable and useful. Only cynical demagogues can play on jealousies which sometimes arise or can be fostered. Yet what deserves to be attacked is any form of a parasitical and tyrannical class. Useful ones must be welcomed and encouraged, be they artists, scientists, industrialists, traders, farmers, or administrators.

The reforms here proposed would assure not only that production and consumption are balanced, but that any increase in production or productive capacity would be supported without delay by the requisite finance, and without imposing an unjust and destructive burden. Therefore total production and consumption would be able to expand rapidly and beneficially, assuring a state of material well-being which is unimaginable at present. This is especially important in this age of atomic power and automation in industrial production —both factors about to assume immense importance. It would mean that an ever-increasing number of people would have to work only very short hours in order to make an adequate livelihood, and thus the benefits of leisure for cultural pursuits would become the heritage of all. Only moral and intellectual training would still be needed to make sure that these opportunities are not wasted or misused, as they are so often today by the various hippies, drug takers, drop-outs etc. A real culture is essential if any income in excess of subsistence requirements is to be wisely spent.

In addition to factors already mentioned, there is yet another which must and will be cured by the proposed reforms. Under the existing debt-money system it is inevitable that there is an artificial pressure on all business and the State to borrow money at interest. In part this means that there is a financial interest and even compulsion to persuade or force the economy to borrow more than is always necessary for the capitalization and expansion of production. If this were not so then the amounts of money as a debt at interest which could be created by the banks would be insufficient to maintain that rate of expansion and inflation which the operators of the game require both economically and politically.

This situation leads also to the compulsive selling which is so obvious a characteristic of Capitalism. If business is "capitalized" to provide a "proper" pretext for the creation of new money, then also that money, that "investment", must yield sufficient interest or profit. It would be not only unprofitable, but would be an admission of the artificiality and wrongness of the system if moneys were to be issued too often in fact, if not in principle, interest free, or even at a "loss" (of course there is no real loss, since the money, the "capital" was created out of nothing at all).

Now this leads to the enervating and demoralizing "salesmanship" and advertising which pervades and almost dominates the lives of the victims of usury-capitalism-cum-democracy. Because not only are goods and services marketed actively, overcoming "sales resistance", but also wrong ideas, peddled by the controlled political parties, newspapers, radio etc. And so we have arrived at the "consumer society", meaning that it is not the provision of adequate necessities which comes into question, but the using-up at all costs of the products of a financially forcibly "fed" system of parasitical exploitation. It will be readily understood to what an extent all this is in step with the godless materialism of the "establishments" of High Finance and Marxism.

In conditions of a balanced economy and of sound ideas and principles there would be sufficient finance available for the necessary expansion and improvement of the economy, but without creating an unnecessary and unhealthy urge to, ultimately, feed the usury-parasite. Also, and this is morally and psychologically important, individual men and women should not be under the constant influence of materialism in all that it means. It should not be a "status symbol" to have much money and what money can buy. People should be able to earn enough with reasonable ease, and stop at that point which best accords with their true wishes. And let nobody say that everyone wants to be a millionaire. Most people do not, and prefer other and greater values. And we see all around us in the Western world the evil consequences of too much money almost forced into the hands of demoralized and immature people, and this process is welcome only to the proponents of The Revolution; like all disease and putrefaction they thrive on decay and weakness. The suggested reforms will end this state of affairs.

II

The Role of the Banks under a New Dispensation

In the previous chapter we have discussed the basic overall stipulations for a new social and economic order, involving also new political methods. These outline proposals are in themselves probably sufficient as a framework, within which a number of specific solutions can be developed, in accordance with the needs and traditions of various countries. Therefore we would not attempt to overstress anything more. If we set out below some further details regarding banking and associated functions, it is by way of discussion, by way of the submission of the picture of a possible scheme in some greater detail.

Basically we would have three stages of economic activity: the central bank or office of emission, which we will call The State Bank; the private banks, acting largely as the agents of the State Bank; and the clients of the banks.

Standing independently of the State Bank would be the committee whose function would be to determine the volume of new money to be created and put into circulation, or the amount of money to be withdrawn by not renewing loans and by taxation. As indicated above, these decisions would be taken in accordance with a price index, and certain other subsidiary considerations. When new money has to be issued, this would be done simply by authorizing the State Bank to enter the given sum in its credit books. Thereafter it would be put into circulation in the form of coin, banknotes and bank credits, circulating mostly with the help of cheques. The proportion of each would be determined only by practical convenience, the demand of the public.

The State Bank would have three main sources of income: the profits of emission, taxes and profits (interest) from loans to private banks and clients. It would have to cover two main outlays: its own expenses and the needs of the State—administration, defence, diplomacy and so on.

The Private Banks would have money coming to their coffers from the following sources: loans (subject to amortizations etc.) from the State Bank, money deposited with them by clients, charges made for handling private accounts, and interest plus amortization on loans made to clients. The banks could also handle credit insurance and earn profits from it. Thus the money coming to the banks would be under two main headings of loans or deposits and of profits.

Clearly if the State Bank lends the Private Banks money and this is repayable in instalments, while at the same time more money will be lent, then in fact new loans and repayments will largely balance and cancel out, leaving a profit in favour of the State Bank. On the other hand the same situation would apply as between the private banks and their clients but with the difference that in general there will be a turnover of borrowers, whereas the private banks would be in permanent relationship with the State Bank.

The private banks' clients would look to them for three main types of services; deposit accounts from which money can be drawn in cash or transferred by cheque, loans to customers, especially for the creation of capital goods, and the acceptance of loans from clients who have savings, and in this case amortization repayments can be re-lent to the banks, as long as they are willing to take loans at interest, as well as the discounting of commercial Bills.

If the State Bank charges the Private Banks interest on loans, it does so as it is lending the credit of the Nation, and thus the Nation must gain when accommodating individual borrowers, thus reducing or eliminating taxation. If the State Bank lends to private banks, it will need to charge only a low, or no credit insurance premium. It follows that the total rate charged by private banks in dealings with their customers will be higher, and in addition these banks would be entitled to add further low interest as their own profit. Its rate would be controlled by free competition, as private banking would not be a monopoly. Also if the State Bank were to have a few private, as well as official, clients, it could influence interest rates, though it should not truly compete with private banks, over whom it would have an unfair advantage.

In this situation there would be a need for a new form of bank rate. The basic rate of interest charged by the State Bank, to which the private banks would add their own profits, would have to be such as to attract a sufficient volume of savings, bearing in mind that lenders to the banks would obtain approximately the same interest rates. If the rate is too high, the creation of capital goods would be hindered and thus economic progress would be slowed down; if the rate is too low, people with spare money may prefer to spend it, rather than invest through the agency of the banks. Consequently this new bank rate would have to be an act of policy, and no fully automatic circumstances could determine it. But its determination should present no great difficulties.

Here it could be noted, however, that the State would, if it wished, be able to bring about forcible savings through taxation, while ignoring those who may wish to save, and lending money to the private banks at a very low, nominal, rate of interest, or even free and only subject to insurance and amortization. Again, such matters would be a question of political and social policy. But clearly it would smack of Socialism if the State were to take money from the general public in order to lend it, directly or through private banks, at a low rate of interest to those who wish to capitalize their businesses in the true, not usury-financial sense.

The possibility of lending money at interest through the agency of the banks raises the question of the admissibility or even need for a leisured class. Other means by which it could sustain itself would be through the ownership of land, houses and so on, and such acts as the purchase of sleeping partnerships, more or less sinecures, in active businesses of every kind, and it would be open to people to spread the risk by having a stake in many firms. Most such forms of property, yielding an income, could be inherited by heirs. It had been said in ancient times already that there can be no culture and civilization without slavery, i.e. that their highest forms can not be developed and sustained unless there is a class which is financially independent during several generations. Income from investments and property now takes the place of slavery. It would be difficult to deny that even in modern conditions the development of a cultured and civilized class, exerting a good influence and providing a good example, is desirable. Also such a class can best provide impartial and incorruptible public servants of all kinds.

However, it would not be in the interests of the State and nation as a whole if such a class were to become too large and too wealthy, and there might be a real danger, in the conditions of great and growing prosperity which would ensue on the establishment of the new dispensation here discussed, of the appearance of a mass of rentiers who would soon become not an asset, but a burden. But to this tendency there would be natural and effective counter-balancing factors, as well as the possibility of the necessary governmental policies. In the first place investments through the banks, being subject to amortization, like all loans, would not be continuous if there are no new borrowers. In that case repayments would remain on the hands of their owners and would either lie "idle" on deposit, or be spent on consumer goods. Secondly few active entrepreneurs would tolerate indefinitely the burden of a sleeping partner; they would prefer to treat his investment as a loan, to be repaid at once or in instalments. Finally the weapon of taxation would remain as a means of pruning the tree of financial independence if and when necessary.

But in any event it is important to bear in mind that in the conditions described in these lines a financially independent, or semi-independent class would not benefit from the present theoretically everlasting debts of the State and private business, from speculation and especially from the right to issue money created out of nothing and its lending at interest to governments and individuals. It would not be possible to describe a leisured class under the new conditions as an unmitigated and economically and socially evil parasite. On the other hand there is much to be said, for example, for provision for old age and illness through thrift, rather than by relying on effortless provision by a Welfare State, dependent on the votes of the most unproductive and irresponsible mass. Then the feckless in trouble can be helped by charity, both private and official, but not in a way which implies that such assistance is a right. That approach destroys independence and a sense of responsibility and makes people more likely to accept in the end the status of mere slaves.

As had been stated already in the preceding chapter, investments through the banks would be to firms owned by individuals or partnerships, or to co-operatives, directly and not through the medium of stocks and shares, and these loans would be repayable in instalments. Thereby the need for a stock exchange would disappear and what remains of its former functions would be absorbed by the banking system in its new form. Debts for the creation of capital goods would not become a permanent burden on economic life, but would be repaid as the real values created by them disappear through wear and tear or have created sufficient profits to have covered repayment. It would, therefore, be important to understand that what is proposed, though seeming to be approximately the same as the capitalist system we know at present, would in fact be basically different in several very important respects. Yet commercial life would continue as now, but freed from the ever-present threat of crisis, inflation, war and excessive debt burden. True progress would be limited only by the amount of work people are willing to do, and it will not, as now, involve consequences which must bring about "financial stringencies", a fall in the value of money, and the rest. It is well known that even apart from atomic power and automation, which are already in operation and will dominate the immediate future, the possibilities of economic expansion and the betterment of conditions everywhere are so immense, that few of us can even adequately imagine them. We have only to throw off the chains of usury and its attendant phenomena, to enter the era of extraordinary prosperity.

Yet there is the apparent, though not real, paradox: we seem to be preaching the heaven-on-earth of the materialists, while in fact we stress again that only by abandoning the tenets and techniques of materialism will be achieved true liberation and true progress, material and spiritual.

Two points should be made clear. Firstly, while it may be best that investment from savings, as a repayable loan, should be placed through the private banks, to assure a proper selection of creditworthy borrowers, sufficient credit insurance and other requisite conditions, it should also be permissible to lend money directly from person to person and firm to firm, always providing there is amortizaion within a reasonably short time.

Secondly it should be pointed out that in the circumstances here proposed the rate and extent at which savings would become available and would be absorbed in the creation of capital goods, would be naturally controlled to provide the ideal volume, giving the maximum healthy rate of economic expansion and growth. And also this development of the whole system would take place in a manner which would not produce a permanent and parasitic debt and interest burden.

Such lending as there would be would in no way abolish the maxim that money must be spent but not lent into circulation.

An economic system purified and cleansed of all the manifestations of fraud, usury and parasitic power, no longer subject to crises and not retarded by the brake imposed by all the various manifestations of "Capitalism" described in this work, will without any doubt whatever provide conditions for an absolutely unimaginable development of useful production, accompanied by a reduction in the time spent by so many people in purely economic activities. In political, social, moral and psychological terms the problem will no longer be that of constant want and danger, but that of great and lasting affluence. To make well-being a fetish, to forget the virtues of work and sacrifice, to think only of more profits and less effort, that would indeed be dangerous.

Only a truly and deeply religious approach to life could provide the proper answer to the problems which boundless affluence would raise. It is true, of course, that many lands and races would lag far behind for a long time, being incapable of organized, efficient and sustained effort, of proper political and social organization and of the civilized use of leisure. However, there can be no doubt that the nations of the Northern parts of the globe would enjoy great benefits as soon as the natural system is installed, as would the extensions of Europe in South America, South Africa, Australia and New Zealand. A full formula for the controls and restraints of a moral nature which would become necessary cannot be propounded here, and we must content ourselves with merely stating the need for it.

When we mention the National Debt we have, of course, in mind also the various regional and city debts which are a part of the financial burden carried by the people. Therefore, since the producers must include in their prices not only their directly paid tribute to the money-lenders-cum-issuers, but also their indirect payments through taxes and rates etc., we see how great and widespread is the load.

And since it grows continually, the problem of a "sufficient" inflation to prevent unemployment on too large a scale becomes ever more insoluble, as the additional moneys issued in connexion with inflation are a further interest-bearing set of debts.

A discussion of the functions of banks would not be complete without mention of foreign trade. For centuries this has been carried out mainly with the help of bills of exchange, and it is a major function of the banks to discount them, i.e. to lend the money to the creditor at interest even before the bill is due to be paid. Ultimately the bills between the various countries are set against each other and should cancel out. Very often they do not do so, and then the countries remaining in debt must either pay the difference in gold or borrow it from the bankers. And as in internal trade, so also in the foreign one, the banks welcome trade imbalances, since without them there would be no banking opportunities on the "money-markets" of the world.

Yet in the light of common sense a debt between countries which remains outstanding for more than a reasonable time is quite simply money's worth wasted, values uselessly lost. Just as individuals should normally not spend more than they have so also countries should limit their purchases to their recources. Except in special circumstances, purchases made with the help of loans at interest can only harm the economy and benefit the usurers. Capitalization loans made to other lands should be subject to amortization like internal debts in a natural dispensation.

In the sphere of attempted solutions of the problem in practice there have been quite a number of initiatives. We shall limit ourselves to mentioning only two or three of the most recent ones.

Usually they bear in mind both the fact that capitalistic moneys are issued as a debt by private banks and also that the US Constitution demands issue solely by the State, debt free. In its modern form this method of monetary emission began with the founding of the Bank of England in 1694 by William Paterson, who said openly that "The Bank hath benefit of interest on all moneys which it creates out of nothing". They then printed banknotes; now it is mostly book-entry money, passed on by cheque.

The Act of Parliament which authorized the setting up of this private bank was entitled "An Act for granting to their Majesties several Rates and Duties upon Tunnage of Ships and Vessels, and upon Beer, Ale and other Liquors: for securing certain Recompenses and Advantages, in the said Act mentioned, to Such persons as shall voluntarily advance the Sum of Fifteen hundred thousand Pounds towards carrying on the war against France". Not only the thing being done, but even the very name was a deliberate fraud and deception, to conceal the essence of the deed. To create money out of nothing is to make a valid and effective claim on all goods and services for no return, which is fraud and theft, made worse by the circumstance that this money is lent out at interest.

In the USA, in the State of Minnesota, a patriotic lawyer named Daly mortgaged some land with a bank and then refused payment on the grounds that he had received no value for the land, the money being created unconstitutionally out of nothing. The case was brought before a patriotic Justice of the Peace, Judge Mahoney, who gave a fully lawful decision in favour of Mr. Daly. The consequence was not that the bank appealed, but that Mr. Daly was debarred on the grounds that he had been told not to institute proceedings bearing on money matters! And not long after that Judge Mahoney died....

The same Mr. Daly was lawyer for a group of other American patriots, also in Minnesota, who went to a bank with Canadian Dollars and asked for US ones. Having received them they then sued the bank on the grounds that it had given them unconstitutional money, a statement which is incontrovertible. The court gave a wrong verdict against them, but the matter received much useful publicity and may be appealed again and again.

Now there is a most intelligent and conscientious US Congressman, Mr. Rarick, who has brought a Resolution before the House to repurchase the stock of the Federal Reserve, thus bringing the issue of money under the control of Congress as demanded by the Constitution.

And there are other Americans also carrying on the fight with energy and great ability.

In Great Britain there is a long tradition of most knowledgeable work for Monetary Reform, and there have been several writers on the subject of the greatest importance.

In the British Parliament a very close friend of over thirty years of the writer of this work, the late Captain Henry Kerby, M.P., who understood the matter better than anyone else in the House, put down two Motions:

On the 14th January, 1964, Captain Henry Kerby, M.P., put down the following Motion in the House of Commons:

"THE EMISSION OF ALL MEANS OF EXCHANGE:
That this House notes with approval the patriotic actions of Mr. Wickliffe B. Vennard, Senior, Lieutenant-General P. A. del Valle, Mr. Jerome Daly and other Americans in presenting a legal complaint to the United States Courts whose purpose is to enforce the issue of money only by Congress in accordance with the Constitution, thus preventing the further emission of the means of exchange by private financiers as a debt at interest and for their sole benefit at the cost of the State and people, the money to be issued constitutionally and as a public service, and to be spent and not lent into circulation, thereby removing an immense and illegal burden on the nation and an unjustified private control over public and private life through the control of all money and its value and distribution; and calls upon Her Majesty's Government to do likewise and to return the sovereign power and duty of coinage, the emission of all means of exchange, in accordance with ancient tradition, to Her Majesty the Queen."

On the 22nd December, 1964, Captain Henry Kerby, M.P., put down the following Motion in the House of Commons, to replace his first one on the question in the previous Parliament:

THE EMISSION OF ALL THE MEANS OF EXCHANGE
That this House considers that the continued issue of all the means of exchange—be they coin, bank-notes or credit, largely passed on by cheques—by private firms as an interest-bearing debt against the public should cease forthwith; that the Sovereign power and duty of issuing money in all forms should be returned to the Crown, then to be put into circulation free of all debt and interest obligations, as a public service, not a private opportunity of profit and control for no tangible returns to the British people; and that the volume of money be controlled so as to maintain stable prices:

That the nationalization of the Bank of England did nothing to solve this problem as the bank only serves a subsidiary purpose and almost all money is still created out of nothing by mere book entry by private banks:

That the aims of those who want to assure private property and free enterprise, as well as those who want to protect the British people from unfair exploitation, would both be best served by restoring the power of issuing money to Her Majesty the Queen, in accordance with ancient tradition and law, as is also demanded by the American Constitution, which gives the right of issue solely to Congress, so as to assure the State and Nation the benefits of that emission and relieve them of the immense and growing burdens of a parasitical National and private debt; and to make certain that control passes to *the taxed and is taken out of the hands of the present hidden and unlawful beneficiaries of taxation, much of the proceeds of which they collect as interest on all money and immense debts:*

And therefore this House calls upon Her Majesty's Government to introduce the required legislation, to assert the proper sovereignty of The Queen in Council in this most important of all sovereign functions, to assure unprecedented prosperity with true sovereignty and liberty.

It is not generally understood that for many centuries, in Britain and in almost all other civilized countries, the power and duty of coinage, i.e. of the issue of money in all forms—coin, notes and book-entry credit passed on by cheque, etc.—was vested solely in the Crown or State. For this reason the tradition still persists of putting the Sovereign's portrait on the coinage, though in fact since the end of the seventeenth century, the reign of William and Mary, by far the greatest part of all the effective means of exchange are issued by private bankers *out of nothing by mere book entry*, to be lent at interest to the State and to private borrowers. Thus real power passed from the State to the private bankers.

There is ample evidence from many independent sources to prove that most of the means of exchange in modern conditions originate with bankers. In America it is aptly called "fractional reserve banking," meaning that if you have a pound in cash in the till you can issue ten or twenty times more in the form of "credit" on the books, which is mostly circulated by cheques.

Not a few Heads of Central Banks of Issue have stated the facts at public enquiries or in the press, including the chief of the Canadian Bank of Issue, also Mr. Marriner Eccles—at one time in parallel position in the U.S. Federal Reserve—and the late Mr. Reginald McKenna, former Chancellor of the Exchequer and Chairman of the Midland Bank. They and many others confirmed that it is the function of banks to create money out of nothing and lend it out.

In the United States of America, the Constitution clearly provides in Art. 1, Sec. 8, Clause 5, that only Congress shall have the power to coin (issue) money, regulate the value thereof and of foreign coin (rate of exchange). Yet obviously this constitutional provision has been completely ignored in practice almost since American independence. In the United Kingdom, too, the spirit of the old laws and traditions has been circumvented.

Yet this is no mere academic matter, but a question of supreme importance, affecting the Sovereignty and very existence of the State and country. It has been said that there should be no taxation without representation, yet private financiers can issue "imaginary" money out of nothing by mere book entry and lend it at interest, they acquire the profit of issue and of interest gratis, at the cost of the whole community. This is taxation in the fullest sense, accompanied *not* by the representation of the taxed, but by the complete power of the true tax collector, who is the ruler. The basic truth of no taxation without representation is turned upside down and inside out.

It follows that the power of Parliament in general, and especially with regard to Money is non-existent, and all true sovereignty is in the hands of those *private* individuals who issue all money and determine its value and distribution. If even the State borrows from them, having abandoned its own powers of coinage (emission) to private financiers, how can that State claim to be truly sovereign? The *real* basis of the power of the money-creators and money-lenders lies in the fact that few know the truth about this financial "hidden hand."

Conservatives with knowledge and long historical memories will recall that the original Tories were Jacobites. Today this question does not apply to the Crown as Her Majesty enjoys the loyalty of all Her subjects. But the spirit of the old Jacobites expressed a sounder understanding of the functions of the Crown as fount of Sovereignty, to be exercised with Counsellors. In the context of that conception it was natural that the power of monetary emission should belong to the Sovereign, and long experience has shewn that that proposition was sound.

On the other hand the old Whigs were the proponents of "Dutch Finance," of the issue of the means of exchange as an interest-bearing debt by private bankers, and of the domination of the State by High Finance, not the Sovereign in Council, the King and people. With the decline of Liberalism in Great Britain it might be thought that Socialist Labour is the heir of that tradition.

It is the claim of Socialist leaders that theirs is *not* the Party of the Big Money Men. The test is this: will Labour understand that the "nationalization" of the power of coinage (emission) is the supreme necessity? And not the confiscation of the fruits of many peoples' labour and invention. If the Socialist Party does not pass this test and continues to protect parasitical finance, if only by its silence, then it will lay itself open to an attack which it could never repulse, however long it may postpone the show-down.

Here, then, are some basic propositions which should be known to all, and which are behind the intentions of the Motion:

1. All the means of exchange, with the exception of a very small fraction (coin) are created in the books of private banks when they lend to the State and private borrowers. Conversely, when a loan or overdraft is repaid there is less money in circulation.

2. Even notes and coin come into circulation only in exchange for book entry purchases of Treasury Bills by banks, and thus are virtually issued by the bankers.

3. It follows that those who have the power to "create" *out of nothing* all the money in each country and the whole world and lend it as stated, have total power over all States, parties, firms, radio, press, individuals and so on. Therefore the powers of Parliament are largely ephemeral.

4. It is essential that the issue of money be as needed by the whole nation and hence free from private or political influence. Consequently it is essential that the Queen in Council should resume the power and duty of monetary emission. If new money is *spent* (not lent) into circulation, taxes could be reduced to a small fraction of their present and growing burden and the National Debt will gradually disappear.

5. Banks should only be able to lend moneys they have earned or borrowed. Their other functions would remain.

6. With the release from the debt and tax burden and with the issue of money in accordance with the needs of exchange the country would experience unexampled and lasting prosperity, with no slumps and unemployment. Financial principles and policies would be open and broadly understood; instead of being Master, Money would become a public servant.

And the fight goes on. More and more people in all countries are becoming aware of the question. This book has been published in Spain as "La Lucha por el Poder Mundial", thus making the problem understood in the Spanish-speaking lands. Great work is being done in almost every country. But this is the beginning.

12

The Political Attack of the Usurers

As soon as the possibilities of large scale usury and all its attendant phenomena and developments became apparent, it also became clear to those who worked the game that certain principles, habits, traditions and beliefs, certain ways of government and of life, stood as a barrier to "progress", to the developments of the parasitical system, whose logical end had to be the subjection of the world to the rule of its leaders.

It would be foolish to claim that all the things known to the world before the rise of Capitalism were perfect. Being tainted with original sin, humanity cannot hope to achieve the perfect state in this world, but when we apply ourselves diligently to the study and practice of true Christianity and the other great and positive cultural influences, we do attain real progress and an approach to betterment. However, with these qualifications in mind, it would be possible to claim that in olden times the majority did live altogether happier lives, and that they achieved this in Europe when Christianity was a living force. Since then we have seen immense technical and material developments, but true betterment, which is an outcome of both spiritual and material factors and influences, has escaped us. On the contrary, the world is in a very unhappy and dangerous condition, and is getting worse.

Christianity and some of the other great Faiths teach the immorality and consequent impropriety of usury. Yet we have allowed it to become, as we have seen, the dominant factor in our collective and personal lives; more so than most of us realize. And inevitably parallel with the conquest of usury there came the spiritual domination of materialism. If the founders of the money-lending scheme were certainly guided by the materialistic messianism which is at the root of their thought and actions, it must be admitted that the rest of us have allowed ourselves to be subverted by bribery for generations. In addition to bribery there was false flattery.

A whole complex of wrong ideas, known by their proponents to be falsehoods, was proposed and fostered for many generations. Deceptive ideas of freedom and equality were preached, first to the Middle Classes who had as yet little power, but not a little ability and even more ambition, and this line led to the revolutionary movement in England of the seventeenth century and in France of the eighteenth. The Crown was either removed or reduced to a weaker status, and the old rulers were swamped by an influx of new people. At the same time, too, the influence of Christianity was greatly undermined. In fact the dangers which arose from these situations were not the result of the appearance of new rulers, most of whom were, as individuals, competent and conscientious, but they were the result of the fact that the active ambitions of the new rulers were fostered and led by subverters, who grafted wrong principles on to the social and political changes which, in some respects, were inevitable.

Then, in the nineteenth century, the line of attack was taken a step further. The aristocracy having been replaced by a Middle Class and the Crown by a puppet Republic, while the most superficial and deceptive teaching took the place of the old Faith, the time came to remove also the Middle Classes and put in their place the alleged representatives of the people. And so, in the twentieth century, there came the Russian revolution.

The teaching of Liberalism and Socialism, the ideas fostered in certain Masonic Lodges, and the theses propounded by some of the various sects which appeared like mushrooms in so many lands, all pretended to serve some lofty and exalted cause. But all, in fact, served only the cause of the usurers, of the materialistic messianists, whose march towards world domination was furthered by these falsehoods. Not that each of them did not contain very much more than a grain of truth. They could not have achieved the success which did accompany them at times, if they had not propounded some ideas which were true, or if they had not tried or even succeeded in curing some ills which were real and some injustices which called for reform. All this we take entirely for granted. But it is the fundamental and overall conception, the real purpose of the game, usually, but not always, unknown even to most of its direct leaders, which really matters.

All the vain and ambitious men, greedy and disloyal, who weakened their Church and their King, enriched themselves in the name of popular control of wealth. They seized power as an alleged expression of its passing into the hands of the people, the Nation. These men preached liberty for all, while in fact claiming it only for themselves, and propounded equality, meaning only that they themselves were at least the equals of the rulers they overthrew. And they topped all with the slogan of fraternity, by which they meant a docile and unopposing loyalty of the masses to themselves. All these men cleared the ground for the money-lenders who held all the strings in their hands, since none of the clowns, bursting and blinded by their ambitions and follies, could do anything effective unless the financiers provided the means.

And so we have come to the time when all power is in fact centralized, and not only in each State, but throughout the world, in the hands of a few men, who hold the purse strings.

It would be a long story to analyse all the many deceptions which are a part of the process of our spiritual and political degradation, fitting us to be no more than the slaves of the bankers. The teaching of equality, whose purpose is to reduce all to the level of the lowest, is one of the main lies which lead to so much of the way of life today. Yet the untruth of the proposition is so obvious that it seems almost a waste of time to discuss it further. We are not born equal and we never will be born equal. It is entirely untrue to suggest that all that matters is the conditions in which we are born and bred. They play a role, it is true, but to begin with we are not equal in appearance, intelligence, temperament, character or physique. It is an obvious fact that some are fit to be rulers, and others to be ruled. It is clear that a few do possess the capacity for original thought and practical initiative and others are almost devoid of it. It is true also that the quality of our capacities, their tendency towards good or evil, construction or destruction, is to some extent inborn. Even talk of equal opportunities is usually loose and shallow, a mere matter of clap-trap. Of course there should be no barriers to the advancement of anyone anywhere, but that is all that can be attained. Opportunities will vary inevitably from the first day in each person's life, for innumerable and obvious reasons.

The acceptance of the simple fact that men are not equal, and that not all men are fit to rule, just as not all men are fitted for many other occupations, does not imply the proposition that all men are not entitled to liberty. On the contrary, in the first place every man and woman, whatever his or her intellectual capacities, is God's creation, possessed of an immortal spirit and soul, and as such entitled to the fullest respect; we have been made in God's image and to offend against man is to offend against his Maker. Each human being is entitled to love, as that is the basic rule of Christianity. Furthermore, Christians are taught that humans have been given a free will. Thus to try to bind that will and impede the dictates of conscience is a grave offence against God and man. If liberty is considered in the light of moral law, it is not only something to be permitted, but something which must be defended. It is, however, not the same thing as unfettered "democratic" rule by chance majorities, swayed by unscrupulous deceivers. From these, men must be protected, just as they require protection from robbers and perverters.

We have been taught also that men and women are equal in everything. It is another falsehood, calculated to mislead us and to make us unable to oppose our enslavers. The suggestion is as preposterous as that all men or all women are equal among themselves. God has made us men and women, to perform entirely different functions. To claim that these functions are the same is manifestly absurd. This leads inevitably to the conclusion that if you try to force men and women to live their lives not as such, in all that that implies, but in some standardized hermaphrodite way, then both sexes will be unhappy, inefficient and on the way to doing not good, but evil.

God made humanity not only of two sexes, but made an equal number of each. Indeed in Russian and other Slavonic languages the words for half and for sex are the same, or similar. The misunderstanding arises because it is assumed that the different functions of the sexes are not equal in value. This is absurd: men and women are of equal value and one man and one woman together form a complete unit. It is, however, natural and right that one must be the head, and it is the man; the family is the embryo of the State, the basic social unit. This fact is symbolically stressed by the Orthodox Church in making a marriage ceremony in fact a coronation, with the use of crowns for the bridegroom and bride.

The basis of "democratic" propaganda is the proposition that full freedom can be achieved by all members of a nation and of all humanity only if and when everybody has an equal vote, when the mass of the people are the legal Sovereign, the only source of authority. This whole proposition is even more absurd than the suggestion regarding the equality of the sexes. In the latter case, after all, we only have to clarify terminology and establish the difference between the equality of function and that of value. But when we come to consider the equality of every person in every land as a formula which is put at the foundation of the modern State, then we are truly in the presence of a lie whose effrontery is breathtaking. The sly implications of the formula are that it is impossible or at least rash to attack it, for by doing so, you court too much opposition; you have to tell, in effect, all those who care to listen to you, or to read what you have written, that in your own view most of them are not your equals. But we cannot shirk this issue, nor would we serve our fellow-men best by descending to the level of cheap and vulgar clap-trap.

We do not know the qualities of those who may read these lines and we readily and gladly assume that, if our readers have got as far as this, they are of a quality at least as exalted as our own. But while we take so immodest a view of ourselves, we also know that were our wife to be in need of a serious operation, we would not rush into the street and ask Tom, Dick and Harry for their collective views on what ought to be done, imagining that in this sense the voice of the people is the voice of God. We would go to see a competent surgeon and leave the matter to him and to his colleagues, and we would not even take a vote among the nurses and porters at the hospital. Each sane man would in such conditions accept the rule of the aristocracy, of the best.

Yet we are told, with the full backing of the law of most States, and of their press, that on matters which affect the well-being and even the very existence of Nations and all mankind, and not only of one person in need of help, Tom, Dick and Harry, and their wives, are competent to vote. The falsity of this elaborate and solemn buffoonery is quite obvious. In so highly intelligent and cultured an ancient country as Great Britain it was said on good authority that the average intellectual age of the recruits to the armed forces in the Second World War was some fourteen years. And these people, capable of reading little more than strip cartoons or football reports, if they read at all, are the technical Lords of Creation! It is well, of course, that this nonsense is not really put into practice, but it is not so well that the limitations and guidance are provided not by the natural leaders of a nation, but by the agents of the usurers. There is much confusion of power and freedom.

In Britain and in other countries the right to vote was granted only in quite recent times and the franchise was usually extended only gradually from the top downwards. At the same time much of the older structure of the machine of government remained. Especially in countries which still retained monarchical institutions in some cases even after the Monarchy itself had fallen, there was retained a certain practical assurance of continuity and stability, of effective and useful rule. But the political theories and the parties which were formed to carry them out are proposed by the agents of the financiers and managed by them. The voters are given only a strictly limited choice, and even then their ultimate decision is obtained by means of various effective measures, usually pressures of a kind not noticed by the superficial observer. That even supposedly elective Chiefs of State are the nominees of banks is a fact which is often openly mentioned even in serious memoirs and letters. Who else can afford elections?

It has been a notable feature of British history that the struggle of Parliament, i.e. of the men and forces it represented, and nominally the struggle of the people for an assertion of their power at the cost of the limitation of the power of the Crown, was centred mostly on the question of the control of money. This theme is, and has been for many generations, a fundamental and, indeed, the most important aspect of the unwritten, but traditional and practiced British constitution. Parliament, and since recent decades specifically the House of Commons, controls money and is thus assumed to hold the true levers of effective power. As we have noted in another place, the American Constitution specifically provides for the control of money and its value by Congress, and in this the law of United States, as in so much else, is a variation of the British theme.

Yet the irony of the true situation, so very widely unknown in Britain, America and everywhere else, is that just when Parliament wrested ultimate sovereignty in general and monetary control of emission, taxation and expenditure, in particular from the King, it failed entirely, as also the U.S. Congress, to become the effective master of finance. The powers which were taken from the Crown immediately fell into the hands of the financiers, and still remain there to this day. It has been openly admitted by more than one Chancellor of the Exchequer or Secretary of the Treasury that the mysteries of finance are unknown to them and that the technical details of a budget speech are prepared by Treasury officials. In fact of course control does not lie even with the officials, but with the banks which are the true source for the emission of the means of exchange and which control their value and distribution.

As in so much else, the power taken from the traditional and natural Sovereigns in the name of the people, in fact, passed into the hands of the Materialists.

This brings us to the consideration of one of the reasons which made the Russian revolution so essential from the point of view of the financiers. They can afford to overlook the existence of states like Ethiopia, where absolute Monarchs rule a primitive society, and the coinage is still largely composed of silver, minted on behalf of the State. But Russia, huge in size and population, developing rapidly, in all respects one of the two or three true great powers in the world, could not be allowed to remain a country in which, though many aspects of modern capitalism were in being, the true control of money and credit remained ultimately in the hands of the Crown, itself not only disinterested and incorruptible, but entirely devoted to the welfare of the Nation. Thus it is not surprising that taxes were the lowest among the great nations, as was also the national debt, and external trade gave an annual surplus, so that the gold cover of the paper money issue was greater than the face value of that issue, and it was growing. Every paper Rouble could have been exchanged for gold on the same day, and there would still have been more gold in the treasury vaults. It was the biggest gold reserve of all. Indeed it would have been correct to say that in essentials capitalism was not in charge in Russia, and only some of its techniques were being used. So, sooner or later, this "bad example" would have destroyed all the true capitalistic systems. This was the unknown basic reason for which the financiers backed the revolutions of 1917. The substitution of Communism for national liberty under the Czar solved the problem of the materialists in more than one way.

Not only has a most dangerous competitor been removed, but the country has been made a base for further attacks, and with the help of atomic weapons, subversion and disinformation on a global scale, and an all-embracing terror, including the techniques, of brainwashing, slave-labour and moral perversion. Fortunately for all, Russia will survive its enemies.

The crimes that have been committed for generations past in the name of "progress", while every attempt to stem the evil tide was termed "reaction" or "obscurantism", are already well beyond recapitulation. Indeed their sustained increases is such, that it has long since numbed the senses. Supposedly nice and sensible people quite readily assume that regicide is a virtue, excessive attachment to religion is a sign of backwardness and blindness, it is fashionable and proper to applaud every Left-wing revolution and to be horrified at any movement to the Right. In short everything which makes for demoralization and subversion of established and traditional Faith, authority and morality, is accepted, and all that may hinder such "progress" is rejected. Yet these trends are by no means natural and, still less, really beneficial. They are required and encouraged by the financiers, the materialistic messianists, who cannot maintain and increase their hold on humanity unless they can also break down its moral fibre and common sense.

The trend towards a mental and moral degeneracy, an utter spiritual decay, which any still healthy person can easily observe in the modern world, is not an inevitable process due to mysterious and uncontrollable forces. It is a process just as consciously initiated and directed as the political, social and economic life of nations and the world. Indeed this negative and evil trend, which in the first place finds its expression in the destruction of religious faith, is an integral and organic part of the whole scheme of increasing world control.

When the Bolsheviks came to power in Russia in 1917, Lenin and his closest collaborators, working in tune with the overall plans of which their revolution was a part, at once declared that the arts— the theatre, cinema, ballet, literary books, painting and sculpture, and even sport—would be encouraged and supported by all the means at the disposal of the Communist State. The Soviets were quite right from their own point of view. They well understood the importance of the influence of these factors on the spiritual and mental life of the people and, therefore, they well understood also the political implications of these things. It is hardly necessary to prove that they could not act otherwise and we will assume that this is self-evident. To control only the activities of political agitators and propagandists, while either attempting to eradicate all manifestations of higher culture, or trying to reduce them only to the crudest forms of the political advertising of Communism, would have been to court disaster, and it was not possible at one stroke of the pen to deny Russia's cultural heritage and past.

So it was that the Communists have tried for more than fifty years to mould all manifestations of the arts to their purposes, while gradually attempting to put a "Socialist Realism" in place of true art and the manifestations of a free spirit and mind. Their success has been very limited indeed, and that is due to the fact that Soviet rule and all its works has at no time become acceptable to the mass of the Russian people, or to the other nations more recently enslaved by Communism.

The same cannot be said of the West, or indeed, of the whole still free world. Because on the one hand true materialism is far more widespread in the West than it is in Russia under the Soviet surface, and because on the other hand it is a fact that the way of life generally known as "democratic" and "capitalistic" is far more acceptable in everyday life than the rule of the Soviet Communists, the parallel manifestations of a godless materialism in art have become far more widely and deeply rooted and to a much greater extent a part of life. Yet all this is just as consciously invented, directed and financed in the West as in the USSR and the satellites.

Literature and the press are being invaded by pornography for its own sake and with an increasing Left-wing bias, while the intellectual level of the printed word for the masses is now so low as to be almost unbelievable. Painting and sculpture are being debased by the introduction of the so-called "abstract", "Futuristic", "Cubist", etc., and in general "progressive" forms. Utter rubbish, easy to produce and entirely devoid of meaning or beauty, is peddled successfully. All depends here on a gift of the gab, an easy and impressive patter, which appeals to the shallow and stupid snobbery of pseudo-intellectuals. It is true that some healthy minds still resist and even counter-attack, and we have not all been conquered yet.

In the sphere of music, however, which affects a much wider circle of people, indeed the great majority, the demoralizers have achieved very considerable successes. There are few in the more developed countries who do not hear music in one form or another every day, be it by radio, television, the cinema, dance hall or concert. It is true, of course, that good music is still heard and even still written, but the evil influence of musical perversions cannot be overstated. We have in mind especially jazz and its various developments. To those who have given these questions some thought, it is known that rhythm can have a very considerable influence on people's mood and even state of mind and intellectual development. It is obvious that certain rhythms can provoke certain excitements and passions. Not all are bad, and the music of a military band is completely harmless to adults and children. Good music, especially in its highest forms, has been known since ancient times to be a valuable tonic, a positive spiritual and cultural influence.

Sir Charles Cochrane, a universally recognized authority on all that is connected with the stage, mentioned in his memoirs that jazz originated in the Negro bordells of New Orleans. Now we are by no means inclined to consider the Negro beneath us; we are all the creation of the Almighty and all must play the role assigned to them. But we would not be unfair to the black Africans if we suggest that those of them who, some generations ago, had the misfortune of being forcibly transplanted from their native land and their habitual ways of life to the strange and largely unnatural conditions of a big white American city, are bound to be open to demoralizing and debasing influences, and probably to a much greater extent than white men. And, furthermore, the "artistic" products of the brothels of these in any case already rootless and debased ex-slaves, must be something which could hardly, at a first glance, claim acceptance as a positive contribution to art.

During the past fifty years we have seen this musical abomination systematically fostered throughout the world. And we have seen its inevitable accompaniments, the disorderly, sensuous and quite uncivilized dances which are now becoming a part of the life of a large section of the younger generation, being advertized in the most attractive light, while no appreciable resistance is evident anywhere. We are far from any sort of puritanical prudery and hypocrisy and we readily recognize that love and sex have their proper and attractive parts in our lives, unless we dedicate ourselves to the monastic life on a far higher spiritual level. But whatever we do should be both decent and also in tune with our respective national traditions and cultures. If we abandon them, we expose ourselves to the evil influences of the anti-culture of the materialists.

At the present time, however, we see the world being gradually brought under the spell of a pseudo-civilization in which all forms of art and entertainment, indeed all manifestations of life in general, are being standardized. The cheap, the easy, the nasty, the perverted is being pushed forward, while all that was deeply rooted, of value, is being eliminated. We seem to forget that all that which is worthwhile must be maintained and protected by efforts, themselves encouraged by a positive love of the values in question. A culture and civilization which are not loved and protected will die, and the nations which abandon them will become the slaves of their perverters, being unable to act purposefully or to judge correctly the various influences to which they are subjected.

The bad influence exerted by modern pseudo-art is all the more pernicious for being actively supported by those who both seek to dominate us after having weakened us, and who contrive, within the framework of their general system, to make this "art" in all its forms pay. The answer to this is not just a rejection of bad art alone, but an attack on the whole scheme of world subjection and its roots. The answer is a part of the struggle for liberty, the true freedom which leads to betterment, but not the licence which debases.

When proper reforms have been instituted, the press will no longer be subject to the financial pressures, through advertisers, themselves not financially free, and it will be able to serve the community well and at the same time survive.

The struggle for the souls and bodies of men, for their complete enslavement and utter exploitation, has been going on for centuries. There have been occasional local successes of the forces which stand for true liberty, protected by Faith and by the natural rulers of the people, but in general, and especially in more recent generations, it must be admitted that the materialists have been winning. They are now almost within reach of the final prize, of world rule. By subversion, infiltration and revolution the enemy has gradually extended and deepened his rule. Within living memory there remained one bastion of Christianity, of true freedom and progress—the Russian Empire. It is typical of the long preparatory work which has been done to condition mankind for its own destruction, that such a statement, we know it well, will come as a shock or an absurdity to most people who may have cared to read thus far. Yet we would urge them to look at the matter in the spirit of complete detachment and to consider some of the facts we shall mention, before deciding finally whether the claptrap and propaganda of recent generations has been fair and true, or not. It is an undeniable fact that the fall of the Russian Monarchy has opened the floodgates of Communism and that now this criminal conspiracy is spreading its hold over the whole world. More than that—since the Russian Revolution the brakes have been off everywhere and the world is sliding headlong down the slippery slope towards catastrophe.

We have already noted that a series of revolutions since the seventeenth century have gradually given power to the materialists, though they often worked through dupes who certainly did not imagine themselves to be opposed to Christianity. And there were well-planned stages. The sights were gradually lowered: first the Kings were attacked, then the aristocracy, then the middle classes, and when all these had been eliminated, the proletariat, the working masses, were, in the deceptive name of their own dictatorship, finally and fully enslaved. In the realms of belief, too, there were stages which ran parallel to the political attacks: the great traditional Churches of ancient times were replaced in leading countries by sects which had whittled down the Christian truth and teaching and introduced some dangerous falsehoods. Then a laical and unreligious line of thought and public education could become dominant. After this the unqualified attack on all religion became possible. The toiling masses were to be automatons without a soul, without a heart and without a head. Such an assault on God's creatures proved to be largely ineffective, but it has done immense damage and is still being pursued with energy.

If a profitable consideration of the overall strategy of a counter-attack is to be considered, it may suffice to base it on an appreciation of the global events of the past one hundred years. It is approximately this period which has seen the final preparation for and the achievement of the Russian revolution and the final crystallization of the Capitalist system, both of which are the means for the attainment of world power by the materialistic messianists. Not only did the revolution of 1917 give them the use of the Russian and later also the satellite bases, but it brought about the completion of the philosophical and political structure—Marxism—which is the final stage of the conspiracy before its last battle.

These events are, of course, a part of a long process. For generations, and even centuries, wars and other events have been both fostered and used in order to bring about great social and political changes and even revolutions. An excessive inheritance and income tax has also served the purpose of eliminating certain classes and the influence which they were able to exert. Yet these taxes serve no useful purposes, as they are not collected primarily in order to defray the expenses of government. It is the structure of immense national debts and similar factors which is the predominant excuse for the collection of these taxes.

It is true that in still very recent times there were people whose possessions and income were much larger than their usefulness to society could justify. Such huge accumulations of wealth were possible as the result of certain characteristics of the Capitalist system. The matter was made even worse by the fact that the system also allowed employers to pay workers wages which were scandalously low. The income differences between the very rich and the poor were too great.

Yet it does not follow that it is desirable to destroy the possessing classes entirely, that it is not socially desirable to have a stable set of people, materially able to develop and preserve culture, and enabled also to give the state and society the services of impartial and incorruptible men. The alternative of assuring that only the slick and dishonest speculator, here today and gone tomorrow, shall have the chance to acquire "Capital" and income, is anti-social. It cannot be denied that in all countries the old landowning class provided much of immense and lasting value, which will be very difficult to replace.

Even if we leave out of account the largely false arguments in favour of internationalism of the financiers and their Marxists stooges, it is undeniable that the so-called "Atomic Age" with its almost unlimited potential power for global destruction or global enrichment, with its immensely increased speed of communications and with the consequent increasing interdependence of nations and continents, does provide strong arguments in favour of a closer integration of the world. But all depends on the purpose of integration and on who will be responsible for whatever manifestations of international co-operation may be found possible or even essential. That a hungry man must eat is a truism, but it does not follow that he must swallow anything which comes to hand, as he may then poison himself. Also if he is hungry, it does not follow that he must swallow an excessive amount of food. The quality and the quantity must be just right.

Similarly with the question of international collaboration, which is now being fostered by those circles which are least of all interested in the true well-being of mankind. We must not let ourselves be stampeded by empty or false slogans. If once a centralized world power is established, with atomic weapons and complete political and economic control in its hands, it will be too late to repent. World Government is not a universal cure for all ills, any more than the League of Nations or the United Nations Organization are cures for wars, famines or the spread of evil.

At the present time we are being conditioned for World Government through the "educational" process of the work of the League of Nations, followed by that of the United Nations and its UNESCO etc. But in 1955, as had been prearranged ten years previously, the revision of the Charter of UNO had been proposed. This is a step towards the conversion of UNO into the World Government, and it is not surprising that all the many organizations throughout the world which work towards universal federation are very busy in trying to make sure that the revision of the charter will lead to the desired end—the abolition of national sovereignties and the imposition of a central world authority.

Now at a first glance the proposition that the very existence of humanity is threatened by the A and H bombs seems incontrovertible. It is true that it may well be argued that these bombs, as well as other methods of mass destruction, will never be used, just as gases and bacteria were not used in the Second World War, because both sides had them, but we must agree that such arguments can never be a complete substitute for more concrete assurances of safety.

But as soon as we have disarmament, accompanied by effective inspection, to make certain that nuclear bombs and even worse weapons are not being made, we have in fact a supranational authority. We must agree that that idea in itself is not one which we can reasonably or safely reject. All that we do reject is a world power which is founded in fact for the purpose of giving authority and its fruits to the Materialists, while only pretending, but in no way really protecting, the true interests of humanity and each nation. We know, too, that such a power would quite naturally try to acquire as many means of coercion as possible; it would not destroy and forbid certain armaments, but merely try to acquire and control them.

That the present partisans of World Government are not concerned with the freedom and well-being of humanity can be clearly seen from the fact that they do not make the disappearance of Communist slavery a condition for the establishment of a World Parliament in place of UNO, yet even now, if voting were proportionate to population, the Communists and their friends would have a majority. That alone apart from all else, would be a sufficient argument against all the present schemes of the world federalists. That such circles are concerned not with virtue or well-being, but only with power, emerges clearly from the fact that they missed every chance to destroy Bolshevism, were at all times happy to work with it in the League, UNO and so on, and are now concerned not with the betterment of a sick and suffering world, but merely with coexistence with a bloody and criminal conspiracy.

Only when that criminal conspiracy, as well as the other evils we mention in this work, has been eliminated and the rule of moral law has been established in most leading States can one think seriously of setting up a world authority.

But it would be essential that such a body should never be such as to be capable of becoming the tool of global tyranny, another short cut to the aims of Marxism. That authority should derive its powers from the collective agreement of all or most of the world's countries and should perform the limited functions of an international police, not government, and it should be controlled by, say, the International Court of Justice at the Hague.

Fundamentally, however, real peace and safety, but without tyranny, can be assured only on the basis of a true understanding between the leading nations of the world—America, Britain, Russia, China, Japan, France and others. But there can be no agreement while there is an Iron Curtain and Communism.

The steps being taken since the end of the last World War to create a European State are a part of the preparations for the destruction of national states and the establishment of a World Government.

13

The Foreign Policy of the Financiers

As in internal policy of each State, so also in its foreign policy and relations, there is an interplay between a number of influences, some of them being entirely proper and rooted in the given country and consciously pursued in that country's interest. But there are also factors, influencing home and foreign policy, which are by no means rooted in any given land and are in no way attuned to the true interests of that land, but which originate with the materialistic messianists and which are operated through the medium of the financial machinery which now covers the whole globe, except where its products and counterparts takes Socialistic political forms.

It may be taken for granted that every country has usually tried to pursue a foreign policy which was intended to assure safety from attack and often also possibilities of territorial expansion, or the acquisition of new lands. But any expansion of territorial holdings, however great they were in certain cases, was always an exceptional event, while a static condition was more usual, even if it was sometimes disturbed by smaller wars. The latter often ended without any notable outward consequences. It would be fair to say that self-defence and the maintenance of the *status quo* both territorially and politically was the most usual policy in all countries throughout the world, based on a natural and sound instinct and on long experience.

It could also be said that, until relatively recent times, there was no factor of international and worldwide importance, which affected the policies of various countries. Each pursued its own line in its own interests, and if blocs or alliances were formed, they were not intended to be something to be spread over the whole globe, but merely a localized event, a policy undertaken by two or more countries whose interests seemed to coincide.

Clearly in such circumstances national sovereignty, the full independence of each State, was a reality, though it might be said that some were more independent than others; obviously weak states could not always assert themselves in all against stronger ones, and had to depend for survival on the protection of others, whose interests were served by this line. But there was no worldwide, supra-national authority which in any way pretended to limit the sovereignty of states.

This situation came into being, very gradually and insidiously, when the old-time goldsmiths had discovered the economic keys to global power and when the financiers and bankers began to establish their network over the whole world, paralleled not by accident, by certain subversive and sometimes secret societies and sects. After generations of the development of these forces, there came the time when the idea of global union and world government could be openly proclaimed and the first steps towards this could be officially initiated. So it was that there appeared first the League of Nations and then UNO. And now it is, theoretically, only a matter of time before UNO is converted into a World Government.

If that were all, it would still be possible to argue that there is nothing to fear, providing only that Communism has disappeared or has been eliminated by the time when this world assembly and government are set up. It would hardly be safe, in the view of most normal people, to establish a central government, with atomic weapons and all the other technical wonders at its disposal, if that government were dominated by the Communists, as it would today, since they fully or indirectly control so large a proportion of the world's population.

However, the position is quite different. As we have noted, there is not only no anti-Communism inherent in the policies of the materialistic false messianists but, on the contrary, Socialism in suitable form is the ultimate régime which they wish to impose on the world. Consequently, as we have seen, there is no effective anti-Communist or even anti-Socialist policy, but only a pretence of such policies, intended to lull the unsuspecting mass of the peoples of the world. Indeed, it is the class of the so-called "intellectuals" who are being groomed for the lesser leading roles in the new dispensation, and also as the spearhead of the attack on the world's still remaining liberties and faiths. It is now quite easy to define these intellectuals even by the picture which their sponsors give of them in the press etc. In their earlier youth, at their university, they were always Communists; it is implied that they are now past that sensible, but raw, stage and are now very sophisticated men of the world. It is not suggested that they have really changed and least of all that they are Christians. They are always the friends of great financiers, great liberals, great progressives.

If such an "intellectual" is caught, then there is an immense outcry in the press and radio of the world, but the villains are by no means those who were found out having very close relations with the Soviets, while also holding key posts in the West, but the men who gave them away. It must be admitted that men such as the late Senator McCarthy, of the USA, inadvertently helped these misleaders by themselves sometimes putting vague and generalized sweeping statements, often sensational, in the place of proven facts, and yet Mr. McCarthy was, in principle, on the right track, and the healthy instinct of the American masses told them that that was so.

Of course, if an "intellectual", besides being a deep pink, is also homosexual or at least thrice divorced, then he qualifies all the more. It is his function to make all issues muddled and muddy and deliberately to mislead, and at the same time to substitute coexistence and then collaboration for a natural and healthy resistance to Communism or, better still, an effective counter-attack.

In broad outline the global foreign policy of the financiers, which increasingly affects the foreign policies of each separate state, and which is imposed by the pressures which can be applied through the levers of finance, subverting individuals, often unnoticed to themselves, forming public opinion and directing the flow of trade and money in desired ways internally and externally, amounts to the attainment of a Socialist World Government, though the name of Socialism will not eventually be used at all. Therefore there are two simultaneous lines, two coinciding aims. On the one hand everything is done to further internationalism in every form, in the realm of ideas and in practice while ostensibly retaining the democratic system of rule and the capitalist form of economy. On the other hand nothing is done to weaken Socialism and Communism and all is done to encourage their spread. As this is not so officially and, indeed, the very opposite is supposed to be the accepted policy of the West, some will find it hard to accept this statement of fact at a first glance.

Yet it is a fact, and this can be seen from a consideration of the trend of world events in the past fifty years, and indeed during a much longer time behind the obvious scenes. The larger strategy of the financiers clearly had to give them full control in a number of suitable countries, which could then be used as a base for further operations along the capitalist and Socialist lines, whichever was found to be most suitable. The countries selected as first bases of operations suggested themselves as the result of chance, experience and calculation. In the main the first centre of operations developed, as Capitalism itself grew, in Western Europe and especially in those lands which were becoming great maritime trading and colonial powers. The economic social and political conditions which grew up there, not a little guided by the financiers, were best suited for the firm establishment and wide dissemination of the correct ideas and practices. The United States of America, when they became independent, were also included into the basic sphere of influence of the capitalistic money-creators and money-lenders. Through America the influence of the system spread over the Northern and Southern New World and later over many other territories.

In these lines we will not be able to enter into all the details of the picture, but in broad terms and for the purposes of the problem we have here in mind, we can divide the world approximately into two main parts: one part is the world of western Europe and its extensions, such as the United States, South Africa and so on, which had developed in relatively sheltered conditions, in which the problem of national self-defence from immediate and immense dangers was almost completely unknown. Wars were almost always small-scale affairs, or were fought far away or at sea. Frequent and massive invasion, great destruction and the need for immense efforts and special political organization of the effective and rapid defence of the fatherland were more or less unknown in the areas we have in mind. As a result, as we have also noted in another context, the appearance and survival for long periods of lilliputian states, and the preoccupation of individual citizens with their own business for generations, be it in trade, industry or agriculture, were possible. In this atmosphere it was not alone possible to lay the foundations of modern capitalism, but to assert its power over a relatively very weak state. The money-lenders succeeded the landowners as the effective rulers of the West.

In the East, in the great land mass of Eurasia, including Russia and China, there developed the conditions typical of the other part of the somewhat divided world we are considering. Here wars were more often than not great catastrophes, involving huge armies and whole nations and costing very much in blood and treasure. Furthermore the enemy was often on the very doorsteps for generations and centuries. And it was not only national independence, but often also the Christian faith which had to be defended. Weak states could not survive for long, nor unruly nobles and insubmissive commercial classes. The central authority of the Crown and with it often also the spiritual power of the faith were maintained with conscious and traditional perseverence, as the only alternative was complete catastrophe and utter elimination. No class of money-lenders could here hope to become the rulers by the means which were so easily open to them in the West.

But there was an Achilles' heel also in this world. If an open attack by warlike means would be effectively repelled, an insidious penetration by moral and political poison could destroy the social and governmental structure of the Eastern States, Socialism provided here a formula which fully achieved the aims of the materialists, and yet did not alert the protective instincts of the people, since the State was to remain as strong as before, and even perhaps stronger. There was at the same time a long preparatory campaign of spiritual demoralization by the substitution of the false faith of materialism for the old beliefs and the anti-Church of Communism for Christianity or the other established faiths. The old spiritual and political structures of the East have temporarily succumbed to an attack to which they could find no immediate defence, but it must be noted that the roots are intact.

Having first established a major bridgehead in the East by the political capture of Russia, the materialists were enabled to spread their power through Socialism, while at the same time preparing to convert Capitalism in the Western world to another form of Socialism, thus bringing both halves of the world under a common denominator, their own stable and undisputed power. Of this we say something in Chapter 6.

Far too little attention has been paid to the immense consequences of the Second World War. This war was ostensibly declared in order to prevent the continuation and spread of the power of Nazi Germany and to a lesser extent Fascist Italy and militarist Japan; it was intended to prevent the establishment of a military dictatorship over a large part of the globe. We must assume that Hitler's anti-Semitism, whatever we may think of it, was a secondary point. But the result of the war has been the exact reverse: another and a far worse militarily strong dictatorship has spread it rule far and wide. The war was lost. The winner was a third party.

But was that an accident or was it foreordained? It is superficially easy to explain the apparent mistakes of Western Allied policy by such arguments as that it was necessary to yield much to Stalin because he was able to exert great pressure by the threat of a separate peace. Alternatively it was claimed that Roosevelt was so naïve as to believe that he could trust dear old Uncle Joe, and this after he had been in power in a first class state for so many years and with so much information and advice at his disposal. No, Roosevelt was not naïve, nor was General Marshall naïve in China, when he wanted to compel Marshal Chiang Kai-Shek to enter into a coalition with the Reds, as King Peter's Premier, Subasitch, had been forced to join with Tito or Mikolajczyk with the "Lublin Committee" Reds. All that was necessary was to legalize the Communists.

In 1939 Poland had been given an Anglo-French guarantee against not only Hitler (openly), but also the Soviets (in a secret protocal added to the Treaty). Yet Poland was brutally handed to the Communists without even the pretence of a protest. In the Far East Stalin and his murderous colleagues were given the major fruits of victory literally for a few days fighting; they gained not only the Japanese military stores and industrial installations in Manchuria, but soon afterwards the whole of China, despite the fact that its Nationalist Government had fought loyally at the side of the Allies, as had Poland and the others. Was this again naïvete? No wonder there are so many good Americans who speak of treason.

The Allied attitude to Japan was all the more shocking in the last phases of the war, since it has been known for not a few years that the Japanese government had offered to surrender before the atom bombs were dropped on Japan, and the only condition was that the person and position of the Emperor were to remain inviolate, a condition which was granted in any event after the final surrender and was thus not worth any further bloodshed. But not only was Japan subjected to an unnecessary atomic bombardment, but the Soviets were quite unjustifiably enabled nominally to participate in the Far Eastern war, and were thus inexcusably given the enormous fruits of victory for almost nothing at all. And all this comes after we have been told by eminent and well-informed Americans that in any event Japan had been consciously provoked by Roosevelt to attack at Pearl Harbour, so as to enable that president to involve his country in the war. We are not here in the least concerned with a defence of Japan and its actions and motives, but we are concerned with the establishment of the truth. It is arguable that Japan could have been persuaded to remain neutral and it is a fact that that country was willing to surrender in time to make is absolutely unnecessary to Bolshevize the Far East and to give the Communists all the fruits of a hard-won victory, as had also been done in the West.

And when the war against Hitler was over and the West held almost all the military and economic and especially the political and psychological cards, and when the Soviets could have been overthrown in a short time and without great effort or cost, with the atom bomb only in western hands, not only was nothing done against Communism and its bastion, but far more than was necessary by any stretch of the imagination was handed to them for less than the asking. At the same time anti-Communism was compromised and weakened in countless ways, as we have pointed out in other parts of this work.

It is quite impossible to escape the conclusion, especially bearing in mind that obviously the Western camp is managed from a central HQ, largely in the USA, that all this is an expression of an overall global foreign policy. Even the forms and functioning of UNO are fully attuned to this plan. No national interests are served by this policy, it does nothing to defend freedom or to protect Christian civilization. The only force which gains consistently is Socialism.

But while a Socialistic dispensation is the ultimate aim, policy in the West is meanwhile concerned with the maintenance of the capitalistic *status quo* and every attempt at its overthrow or basic modification leads to the most intense attack. Any State which has tried to throw off the shackles of the usurers has become the target of an aggressive coalition of other countries, a coalition and eventual attack which was, of course, thickly camouflaged. The ostensible reason for enmity was defined in a way which did not disclose the true causes.

An effective counter-measure to such tactics in the future would be the immediate and complete disclosure of the policy being pursued and the reactions to be expected, thus making it impossible for the financiers to mobilize public opinion anywhere against the "offending" country. And since true credit is based on the physical wealth and productive work of any land, and not on gold or the prestige of the money lenders, the threat that no more loans would be granted to any country prepared to throw off the yoke would be an empty bluff.

The reply to this attempt to dragoon the world in the interests of materialism should not be the proposal to substitute the discords of conflicting national interests. The dangers and problems which face all nations simultaneously will, if they are openly declared and explained make it possible for the first time to establish the harmonious collaboration of all, especially if the Great Powers, freed from evil oppressors, are determined to achieve this aim. And then the dangers of atomic annihilation will be enough to persuade all to settle their differences at the International Court at the Hague, rather than by war. But first we must assure the liberty of states and individuals.

Yet this freedom is being rapidly reduced, while pretended policies seem to extend it. An important example is the African policy of the major powers which followed Mr. Harold MacMillan's speech on "The Wind of Change" in the South African Parliament. Obviously the ground had been well prepared in advance, and then there began the setting up of absolutely artificial "independent states" nominally governed by totally incompetent native politicians. In fact, of course, all power passed fully into the half-hidden hands of the chiefs of international high finance.

Only some ten years ago the whole African continent was a "desert" to the backers of world government, via capitalism and communism. There was, archaic States such as Ethiopia or nonentities like Liberia apart, not a single sovereign borrower in Africa. All the lands were controlled from London, Paris, Brussels, Lisbon or Madrid, so that there was borrowing only, if at all, in those capitals. Yet at the same time the financial pages of the world's press were full of "inspired" complaints about the "shortage of international liquidity", translated into plain English—a shortage of bank-created international debt-money, needed for profits and control.

After "freedom" came to Africa and splendid statesmen such as Mister Kenyatta, chief of the excellent Mau-Mau, and others of a related type, all on the make, were installed as Presidents and Ministers, and after things were then well organized by means of bloody revolutions, murders and the establishment of dictatorships, all most democratic, there were not none, but three dozen "sovereign" borrowers on the continent. One might suggest that they are all most unlikely ever to pay interest on the loans, let alone repay the sums lent, but then these accommodations, like "aid to underdevelopable countries" and so on, are deliberate gifts anyway. They serve the purpose of creating sufficient sums of money in the approved manner, as a bankers' loan, and they give control.

Through a "United Europe" dictatorship on to a United World once the path is smoothed. The great Empires are no more, the world is fully controlled by finance or communism, or even both, and all might have been well were it not for some peoples who have the guts and foresight to resist the take-over, be it fully consciously or by instinct.

So in Africa we see the Portuguese provinces refusing to submit, as well as heroic and capable Rhodesia. And there are many people all over the world and, of course, in Rhodesia itself, who fully understand the global role of that country. This is not in fact (whatever the intentions of some may be) a refusal of local village pump significance; it is resistance to world-enslavement which has already upset the time table and the successful deception of opinion everywhere by the proponents of World Government.

Whites and Negroes have the same basic rights and opportunities in Rhodesia and there is no apartheid on the South African model. The Europeans and Natives are happy and support the Government. The writer has been to Rhodesia, as to many countries all over the world, and the first of five visits was immediately after UDI. He knows all the leaders personally. Mr. Ian Smith, the Premier, and Mr. John Wrathall, Vice-Premier and Minister of Finance, are able and honest men. And there are others who are even better informed about the wider global significance of their fight, about finance, money and politics, such as Lord Graham, Duke of Montrose, former Minister of Agriculture and then of Defence and External Affairs, Ralph Nilson, chairman of the Rhodesia Front Party, Donald Goschen, member of a distinguished British banking family, Harvey Ward, Head of the News Service of Rhodesian Radio and Television, and many others. Rhodesia has survived since the end of 1965, and it is in the interests of us all that it should survive the world-wide attacks of the common enemies until the whole struggle has been successful. Out of that context even such as Rhodesia will, in the end, succumb. But there is no sign of any weakening.

And while a struggle, artificially made to appear as one between races, goes on in Africa, it is extended also to many other countries. It is obvious that the fostering of friction between races, the giving of unjustified influence to people by no means capable of making good use of it, and the encouragement of race mixing, all serve the purposes of the Revolution, the take-over.

In the United States there is propaganda in favour of "Black Power" and immense sums are spent on effective subversion along these lines. Again if "power" is given to obvious incompetents and worse it passes in fact out of the hands of reliable and experienced rulers and administrators into those of the agents of Revolution.

No Christian should ever treat anyone, be he Negro or of any other race, badly in any respect whatsoever. This is indisputable. But from that it does not follow at all that everyone is equally capable and that we are all equal. We are not. At the same time laws which enforce "integration", in fact race-mixing, and forbid any choice between persons are an unmitigated evil, apart from being a denial of freedom. They are meant to and do help global and national subversion.

In the general realms of the centralization of control we have also seen a new phenomenon: the creation of "paper gold", "special drawing rights". As we know, gold is still maintained more or less fictionally as a means of "backing" moneys, and this helps to maintain centralized control of finance throughout the world. But there is too little metallic gold, and to raise its value by many times would strengthen a South Africa which is insufficiently submissive and would create other problems, such as speculation in gold which might allow much of it to get into "wrong" hands.

So the top financiers have created documents out of nothing, like all their moneys, which are to supplement the gold supply and perform the same function. It may postpone, so the usurers hope, the inevitable day when the debt and interest burden on the economies will be such as to bring about the collapse of the major currencies and the break-up of the present order. The operators of the Revolution hope to complete the Socialization of the world before the Great Crisis, for which our camp must prepare the alternative.

Meanwhile we see the cheque system developing ever further in the direction of monetary credits being passed on by such instruments as Credit Cards. This would obviously provide immense further interest profits for the bankers, but more especially all-embracing total control over every person everywhere. Mere numbers in computers will be able to tell the central controllers everything they want to know about every man, woman and child everywhere. And so we can see the day approaching when, to quote the King James Bible, The Revelation of St. John, Chapter 13, Verses 15 to 18 : And he had power to give life unto the image of the beast, that the image of the beast should both speak, and cause that as many as would not worship the image of the beast should be killed. And he causeth all, both small and great, rich and poor, free and bond, to receive a mark in their right hand, or in their foreheads : And that no man might buy or sell, save that he had the mark, or the name of the beast, or the number of his name. Here is wisdom. Let him that hath understanding count the number of the beast: for it is the number of a man; and his number is Six hundred threescore and six (666).

Before leaving the subject of the enemy's foreign policy, we should note that the significance of Israel and of Jerusalem, the intended capital of the world, is very great. Now it may seem that the Soviets are opposed to Zionist conquests and are backing the Arabs. In fact the communists play their usual role of agent-provocateur, and they give the Arabs enough arms and encouragement to fight without real hope of victory, thereby justifying further Israeli conquests until they have what they have always wanted,—the whole area from the Nile to the Euphrates. This view has been, independently of us, formulated by the great expert of Arab affairs, the former Jordan Arab Legion Commander, General Sir John Glubb—Glubb Pasha and by H.M. King Faisal of Saudi Arabia. But should Israel ever be in real danger then both the USA and the USSR would come to its rescue being always in collusion. The sooner the Arabs understand the facts the better for them. Their only chance of survival is to work on the lines we propose, while abandoning policies which, for over fifty years, have brought nothing but defeats.

14

Some Historical Illustrations

Long prepared, Marxism finally triumphed in Russia over fifty years ago. It is of little more than academic interest to distinguish between the two phases of the revolution, that of February, when the old régime fell and was replaced by a government in which the Left and Socialism played a decisive role, and of October, when the Communists took over. The revolution was applauded throughout the western and still supposedly Christian world. It still is. And if anything about the Soviets is attacked, it is not their Socialism, or internationalism, but any Russian elements which may be detected in them, and, indeed, Russia itself, which are attacked. And when liberation is mentioned, it is always the freedom of all countries other than Russia which comes into question, though including such lands which are a part of Russia. It is Russia which is bad, not Communism. This is "logical": Russia was the main bulwark of Christendom, in the decades before the First World War, against the advance of the materialists; it is the enemy. Communism was the tool with which Russia was laid low, and which now serves as a bulldozer, to clear the ground for a central world government; Communism is not a true enemy, though in its Soviet form it may be imperfect.

We find, thus, that the two "opponents" in Moscow and New York-Washington, with the latter's branch in London, in reality drive the game towards each other, while supposedly engaged in "mortal combat". But this combat is kept strictly "cold" or if it does get a little hot here and there, it is at once localized, and never is it allowed to become a danger to the Communists. If there are shortcomings or weaknesses in the West, the Marxists gather a harvest of lost or enslaved souls; if the Soviets exert great pressure, the plutocrats step in and lend money to stem the red tide. The formula of the dialectical materialism of the Marxists serves both camps equally well: the Soviets maintain that materialism is justified by the thesis that conditions determine outlook, and the financiers echo the same thought by stating that, in order to prevent the spread of Communism, one must raise the standard of living. In one case one brand of internationalists obtain political control, and in the other case the parallel internationalists, the creators of the first-named, obtain economic control. You can turn to the alleged Right or to the Left, and you fall into the same trap. It is as simple and as neat as that. But the true path, which accords both with high principles and with our best interests, remains completely concealed. We shall try to reveal it.

It should be noted, when considering questions of the political "Right" or "Left", that Conservatism in democratic conditions is merely a part of the technique of government an effective trick. Under the present materialistic dispensation Conservatism is not meant to be an opposition to false "progress" but only a stabilizer and a temporary fixative of "progress" already achieved by pressure from the Left. It is also a trap for those who seek, often instinctively and unconsciously, a means of practicing some real opposition to subversion. Thus all the means for countering the game of the subverters are put under control, or at least made ineffective. This method of neutralizing possible enemies is well-tried. On the other hand any real opposition is immediately labelled "fascism", or by some other name equally meant to be disparaging, and all the guns of the enemy are turned on it. (In this context we are by no means implying that recent fascisms were unjustly attacked.) The situation calls for an entirely new course, based on old and true principles.

If, however, the attacks on Russia, which have been so prominent a feature of Western political propaganda for several generations, are claimed to be unfounded, we cannot escape the need for at least some details regarding Imperial Russia. We will not shirk this need for an apologia, the more so as elementary justice requires that the truth be stated. We will demonstrate that the attacks on Russia were deliberate falsehoods and were pursued only because Russia could not be made one of the chief tools of the policy of global enslavement unless the traditional Christian Monarchy and the influence of the Orthodox Church were completely overthrown and eliminated. Fortunately for the whole world the enemy of us all has not succeeded in full measure and will be defeated in Russia.

Unbelief and an attachment to various subversive ideas had affected only a small part of the educated Russians. The mass of the people were at all times completely attached to the ancient Monarchy and the Church. As the power of the Throne remained considerable even after 1905, it was impossible to give the life and work of the State and of the Nation a direction which suited the would-be subverters. Though it was possible to remove individual Emperors by assassination, it was not possible to arrange for the occupation of the Throne by a nominee of the financiers, as is the inevitable rule when supreme power is nominally elective.

It is true that in some Republics attempts were made to overcome this difficulty. In France, after 1871, the Parliament of the Third Republic had a Royalist majority, and the Constitution, including the clauses which dealt with the election of the President of the Republic, was designed to serve a parliamentary Monarchy; it was intended to hold only one election at Versailles by the two Chambers combined, and the person to be chosen was to have been the Comte de Chambord, Duc de Bordeaux, the lawful Pretender to the Throne of the Kings of France. However, the plan came to nothing as Prince Henry insisted on being King of France by the Grace of God, though he announced his willingness to institute a Parliament, while the political leaders were mostly in favour of a King of the French by the Will of the People, and limited by Parliament; symbolically it was the white standard with the Fleur de Lys against the Tricolour. The full Monarchy was lost by only one vote; and, as an alternative did not arise, the Republic remained in France; later there was a Masonic majority and a trend even towards anti-clericalism. France, once without any doubt the leading country in Europe and the world, has not yet recovered.

In the United States of America the intention of the founders of the State had been that the President should be in fact elected by an élite and should not be dependent on true popular election. But that which may have been possible in a country of small size and few people, where all those who mattered in any way all knew each other, became quite impossible in a country occupying the greater part of a large continent and having a population of scores of millions. The checks and balances have been largely upset or eliminated, and there is no truly impartial power which is able to defend the people from those who have led them astray.

While it must be emphasised here that there is and should be no intention of presuming to interfere in the internal affairs of any country, other than our own, we are tempted to make the following general observations about the possible and, perhaps, desirable future position in countries having a Constitution such as the United States of America.

In the first place it should be noted that as soon as the power of the usurers is broken, it will not again be possible for private financiers to dispose of such enormous funds as to be able not alone to influence, but predetermine, the outcome of presidential and other elections. Incidentally, it does not follow that under a natural economic dispensation there will be no very large fortunes. On the contrary, it is undesirable, for practical and psychological reasons, to set an artificial ceiling to achievement, even as expressed in money, and it is not a Henry Ford (the big one) who does damage (and in any event his influence was limited), but the bankers who control all the money of any country and of the whole world. Thus, negatively, the overwhelming corruption which is the dominant feature of western political life today would be removed almost completely. In so far as there would be competing candidates, their backing would be such as to give each a relatively fair chance; the total costs of election campaigns would be greatly reduced, since none could afford the present huge sums for advertising, bribery and so on.

But there is yet another consideration which may be of value. As we have noted, the people as such are not able to defend their own interests consciously, as their knowledge and abilities are very limited in 99 cases out of 100. Therefore a Constitution, however well-intentioned its formulation, cannot be worked in the true interests of the people unless there is an absolutely impartial arbiter. The laws are the rules of a game played by the political leaders. There must be a fair umpire, if that game is to be well played and the rules are to remain respected.

Now, for example, the American Constitution makes the excellent provision for presidential elections that they are to be based on electors, on indirect selection. Surely it would be possible to get as close as humanly practicable to real impartiality, ability and prestige by making sure that the electors are not mere nominees of political parties but are chosen by the people as the candidates of such bodies as the Churches, the trade unions, Veterans, charitable trusts, universities, the Senate and Congress, the States or provinces. It may well be that such arrangements would not even call for a revision of existing Constitutions and there could certainly be no break with their spirit.

Thus the people's real freedom, as distinct from a deceptive and even dishonest formula, would be assured, and the honour and efficiency of the State would be enhanced. The President would be above parties and above suspicion. He would be able to protect the people from usurers, deceivers, the servants of subversive forces and other enemies. He would be able to encourage virtue and raise the standard of public and private life.

In this connexion, too, it should be observed that, to take two very different examples, the situation of Russia was not to be compared with that of America. Russia had, for many centuries, to maintain a never-ceasing struggle for its survival. No natural boundaries, no oceans or high mountain ranges, separated it from its actively aggressive and expansionist neighbours. Tartars, Poles, Germans, Swedes and others tried to conquer it. Napoleon came with his twenty-two allies—the Grande Armée. There were periods when, for hundreds of years, Russia was almost continually at war, defending itself against one or more would-be invaders. In the circumstances there was an absolute need for a State able to mobilize the country at short notice and rule it effectively in conditions of great strain. It was the strong Monarchy which provided the answer to the problem of survival, and Russia did survive. It should not be thought that it began its history as the huge State it is now. It began as a small Grand Duchy, with its capital in Kiev, now the chief city of Little Russia, or the Ukraine. Later the capital moved towards the North, and it was finally Moscow which became the focal point of the Empire. But even in the early eighteenth century, when Charles XII of Sweden attacked Russia, his country had a population larger than that which was subject to Peter the Great. The Swedes were defeated by a country with a smaller population.

How different the position of the United States! Two oceans on two sides of the country gave complete protection, the more so as the seas were dominated and pacified by Great Britain. The two land frontiers were those of Canada and Mexico; one a land of empty spaces and few people, the other a land which was a military zero. America, after having attained its independence, was threatened by little more than Red Indians. In such a happy state one could safely leave one's affairs to a Tammany Hall. The true business of the country was in the hands of competent private individuals. They could devote most of their energies to the pursuit of happiness, for the survival of the country was, in those sheltered conditions, not a problem, or so it seemed.

But it was just these deep differences between the United States and Russia which led to present conditions. In America penetration of the machine of political and economic leadership was possible, and it has taken place. In Russia no penetration of the Government was possible, and it was overthrown. Some of the reasons which made this possible will be noted below. For the moment we must note that the two leading Great Powers of the world are both, in different ways, in the hands of the materialistic messianists.

There is, however, a difference between the two camps, and this problem will require more detailed discussion. It may prove to be one of the keys to the fate of the world in the very near future. But before we can consider this more fully, we must obtain a truer and clearer picture of Russia, the real and not the mythical Russia of the revolutionary propagandists and their conscious and unconscious dupes.

Before concluding this chapter we should note that while the present leaders of the United States have repeatedly stated, especially when catching votes, which it is customary in democratic states to buy by this or that form of bribery, that it is their policy to oppose Communism and even to liberate the oppressed nations, they have also just as readily contradicted themselves at other times and stated the exact opposite. But words, especially at election time, are not to be taken seriously. Deeds, however, do count. And it is a fact that America and the West in general have never done anything effective against Communism and for the establishment of freedom, but have helped to sustain the Soviets, the governments of the satellites, and such as Tito. We have indicated some of the chief reasons for these evil policies.

It should be added that, in addition, there is also a semi-automatic compulsion, rooted in the character of Capitalism, which has inclined the American Governments for a long time towards pro-Soviet policies. The existence of Communism and the fact of its rule over half of Europe and Asia and now Cuba and Chile, has enabled American finance, which controls the State, to sustain an economy based on subsidized overproduction. Massive armaments, subsidies to many countries and other related forms of expenditure keep up the high level of production and financial expansion; all this provides a money-lender's paradise. If the Soviet were to collapse, then with them will go this whole artificial economic structure. There would be a great crisis, or war.

But this state of affairs cannot go on forever, as the phantastically expanding debt and credit structure, the huge and unjustified monetary emission, the relentless inflation, must lead inevitably to a catastrophe. This fact is well known to those who operate the game. They reckon that they will be able to foist a World Government on us all, led by themselves, before the collapse comes. It is a terrible gamble. The nations of the world are the losers in any event. It is a case of heads I win, tails you lose. Either we shall be involved in a crisis which would make 1929-30 look like a picnic, or we shall become the slaves of the global Socialist state, perhaps after a Third World War.

There is only one way out: the still free world, or at least powerful and responsible elements in that world, must help to bring about the liberation of the nations now under the Red yoke. In this connexion we must consider Russia. Only fundamental reforms in the West and parallel changes behind the Iron Curtain, with the immense markets of the East opened to America and all others can restore a virile and expanding balance to the whole world and give us prosperity without life-and-death gambles and global conspiracies for the seizure of power.

In the summer of 1959, the American President, Senate and Congress passed an unanimous resolution (law) favouring the liberation of a long list of enumerated parts of Russia. Though outwardly this resolution was thinly camouflaged as anti-Communism, it was in fact a declaration in favour of the complete destruction of Russia as a state, and its division into a large number of separate units. This action could be paralleled by the proposition that all the 50 States of the USA should become independent, or all parts of the United Kingdom, such as Scotland, Wales, Northumbria, Wessex, and the rest, or all the parts of historical Spain or France, but with the difference that such parts of Russia as the Ukraine have never been independent states. This highly mischievous act of the American government is not merely political nonsense, but is calculated to play fully and immediately into Soviet hands, while completely alienating all true Russians, few of whom are even nominal Communists. When a common front against the common enemy should be the basic rule, such glaring irresponsibility can only confirm ones worst suspicions regarding American policy and its makers, suspicion shared by very large numbers of sound and patriotic Americans. The hand of friendship and anti-Communist collaboration should, instead, be stretched out to the Russian people, as to all the other victims of Communism behind the Iron and Bamboo Curtains.

15

The True Russia

If ill-disposed people want to destroy someone morally, they do not employ elaborate and subtle arguments. The most effective mud-slinging is the simple repetition of a few nasty statements, quite regardless of their truth. It is a long time since an experienced man said: "Spread calumny repeatedly; something will stick." A too specific accusation invites investigation and provokes suspicion; a vague and sustained torrent of dirt will do damage.

The campaign against Russia was, therefore, not only concerned with problems of an alleged imperialism or of a supposed cruelty and lack of freedom. The simple statements that Russians do not wash, were held down by masses of police and by frequent flogging, that their rulers were uncivilized fools, and so on, were found to be adequate. They created a whole "school of thought", well established for generations. Cultured and grown-up men in the West repeat as truisms statements which are quite preposterous in the light of the facts.

Now let us glance at a story which is the standard jack-in-the-box whenever Russia is mentioned, the Russia in which life may now be bad, but in which it was far worse under the Czars, and before the "interesting experiment" of Communism was begun. This is the clap-trap story of Siberia. The place where untold thousands of innocent people spent their lives in chains. And associated with this is the story of the Russian knout, the Russian gallows, the Russian secret police.

Even in early mediaeval times Russia knew no death sentence for ordinary crimes and not even for murder. Death was the punishment only for the most serious crimes against the State, as in all other countries. The punishment for murder was some twelve to fifteen years of forced labour in a Siberian settlement. In addition there were small numbers of political prisoners in Siberia. Lenin, whose brother had been involved in a plot to assassinate the Emperor and who had himself worked actively for the overthrow of the Czar and all established law and order, and who would have been in serious trouble with the authorities in any country whatsoever, spent some time in Siberian exile for his efforts. (In passing we should note that this fighter for the "rights of the proletariat" was a member of a landowning family of the small nobility and gentry, an illustration of the social insincerity so typical of all revolutionary Socialists from Marx onwards.) Lenin has himself fully described this horror. He took with him his wife and his hunting guns and dog. He wrote openly for opposition papers both in Russia and outside and supplemented the adequate sum he was paid by the Imperial Government to support him, and his wife wrote letters to her mother complaining of the difficulty of getting really competent maidservants. The horror, the misery of it all! Of course, as soon as Lenin himself was in power, he introduced the reforms he had been taught during the years spent plotting in the West. Now millions of innocent people are scientifically exploited until they fall dead in the camps of Siberia, while the West, apart from an occasional grunt, shrugs its shoulders. After all, they are only Russians. They are used to it.

But are they? Let us consider the knout. All corporal punishment was abolished in Russia in the later part of the last century, and it was forbidden in all schools. In England the viciously cruel cat-o'-nine-tails was abolished outside the prisons only a few years ago. It is true that in Britain small children are no longer publically hanged for stealing things of the value of a shilling, but that did happen in quite recent times, and in the 1870s a proposal in Parliament to limit the flogging of British soldiers to one hundred lashes, instead of the then permissible maximum of six hundred, was quite strongly opposed by those who thought that the army might get out of hand if treated too softly.

And then the dreadful Okhrana—the secret police of the Czar—which maintained his cruel tyranny. Of course no moujik would presume to compare it with the Sureté, the Special Branch of Scotland Yard, the Federal Bureau of Investigation. After all, the Okhrana failed to sustain the régime. Was it not the well-known Russian publicist, the late Mr. P. B. Struve, the founder of Russian Marxism and one of the companions of Lenin, but later an opponent of Communism, who said in exile in Belgrade: "The Imperial régime made one big mistake in not hanging us all in time." The number of policemen per hundred of the population was lower in Russia than in any other European country. That was a mistake.

An apologia for pre-revolutionary Russia would not in itself be justified here. We shall have to undertake it in outline because so much malicious nonsense has been systematically spread about Russia for generations that its true character is almost universally unknown. Yet we cannot consider humanity's overall policy for survival if we do not consider dispassionately and scientifically whether Russia is a positive or a negative factor, whether Russia can be trusted or not, whether the Russians are an influence for good or bad. There is today no problem of any kind whatsoever which can be seriously considered entirely without taking Russia into account. Therefore a proper understanding of Russia is essential. Here we shall do no more than give a few outlines.

We would stress, however, that when we say "Russia", we mean a historical State and nation, and not the present passing régime, based on a criminal conspiracy, hatched in the West and not in Russia. There is danger in the present fashion, deliberately encouraged in certain quarters, of confusing Russia and Communism and of saying "the Russians" when one speaks in fact not about them, but about the Soviet Communist members of the aforesaid conspiracy, aimed as much against Russia as against the whole world.

Let us not emphasise Russian views on this matter. To put the problem into proper perspective it may be best to quote the views of Sir (then Mr.) Winston S. Churchill on the role of Russia in the First World War, as set out in "The Great War", published in instalments by George Newnes Ltd. after the war. The actual quotations will be from parts 15 and 16, pp. 949 and 950, and 1006 and 1008.

"Surely to no nation has Fate been more malignant than to Russia. Her ship went down in sight of port. She had actually weathered the storm when all was cast away. Every sacrifice had been made; the toil was achieved. Despair and Treachery usurped command at the very moment when the task was done.

"The long retreats were ended; the munition famine was broken; arms were pouring in; stronger, larger, better equipped armies guarded the immense front; the depots overflowed with sturdy men. Alexeieff directed the Army and Koltchak the Fleet. Morever, no difficult action was now required: to remain in presence; to lean with heavy weight upon the farstretched Teutonic line; to hold without exceptional activity the weakened hostile forces on her front: in a word, to endure—that was all that stood between Russia and the fruits of general victory. Says Ludendorff, surveying the scene at the close of 1916.

" 'Russia, in particular, produced very strong new formations, divisions were reduced to twelve battalions, the batteries to six guns; new divisions were formed out of the surplus fourth battalions and the seventh and eighth guns of each battery ...'

"It meant in fact that the Russian Empire marshalled for the campaign of 1917 a far larger and better equipped army than that with which she had started the war. In March the Czar was on his throne; the Russian Empire and people stood, the front was safe, and victory certain.

"It is the shallow fashion of these times to dismiss the Czarist régime as a purblind, corrupt, incompetent tyranny. But a survey of its thirty months' war with Germany and Austria should correct these loose impressions and expose the dominant facts. We may measure the strength of the Russian Empire by the battering it had endured, by the disasters it had survived, and by the recovery it had made. In the Governments of States, when great events are afoot, the leader of the nation, whoever he be, is held accountable for failure and vindicated by success. No matter who wrought the toil, who planned the struggle, to the supreme responsible authority belongs the blame or credit for the result.

"Why should this stern test be denied to Nicholas II? He had made many mistakes, what ruler had not? He was neither a great Captain, nor a great prince. He was only a true, simple man of average ability, of merciful disposition, upheld in all his daily life by his faith in God. But the brunt of supreme decisions centred upon him. At the summit where all problems are reduced to Yea or Nay, where events transcend the faculties of men and where all is inscrutable, he had to give the answers. His was the function of the compass-needle. War or no war? Advance or retreat? Right or left? Democratize or hold firm? Quit or persevere? These were the battlefields of Nicholas II. Why should he reap no honour from them? The devoted onset of the Russian armies which saved Paris in 1914; the mastered agony of the munitionless retreat; the slowly regathered forces; the victories of Brusilov; the Russian entry upon the campaigns of 1917, unconquered, stronger than ever; had he no share in these? In spite of errors vast and terrible, the régime he personified, over which he presided, to which his personal character gave the vital spark, had at this moment won the war for Russia.

"He is about to be struck down. A dark hand, gloved at first in folly, now intervenes. Exit Czar. Deliver him and all he loved to wounds and death. Belittle his efforts, asperse his conduct, insult his memory; but pause then to tell us who else was found capable. Who or what could guide the Russian State? Men gifted and daring; men ambitious and fierce; spirits audacious and commanding—of these there was no lack. But none could answer the few plain questions on which the life and fame of Russia turned. With victory in her grasp she fell upon the earth, devoured alive, like Herod of old, by worms...

"In vain the Imperial Family, deeply concerned for their own existence—apart from other issues—approached their Head. In vain the leaders of the Duma and every independent figure in Russia made their protests. In vain the Ambassadors of the Allied Powers dropped their elaborate hints, or even uttered solemn and formal warnings under the direction of their Governments.

"Nicholas II, distressed, remained immovable. He saw as clearly as they did the increasing peril. He knew of no means by which it could be averted. In his view nothing but autocracy established through centuries had enabled the Russians to proceed thus far in the teeth of calamity. No people had suffered and sacrificed like the Russians. No State, no nation, had even gone through trials on such a scale and retained its coherent structure. The vast machine creaked and groaned. But it still worked. One more effort and victory would come. To change the system, to open the gate to intruders, to part with any portion of the despotic power, was in the eyes of the Czar to bring about a total collapse. Therefore, though plunged daily deeper in anxiety and perplexity, he was held alike by all his instincts and his reasoning faculties in a fixed position. He stood like a baited animal tied to a stake and feebly at bay.

"It is easy for critics never subjected to such ordeals to recount lost opportunities. They speak lightly of changing the fundamental principles of the Russian State in the stress of the war from absolute Monarchy to some British or French parliamentary system. It would be a thankless task to assail convictions so confidently asserted. Nevertheless, the martial and national achievements of Russia in the three terrible campaigns already described constitute a prodigy no less astounding than the magnitude of her collapse thereafter. The very rigidity of the system gave it its strength and, once broken, forbade all recovery.

"The absolute Czar in spite of all his lamentable deficiencies commanded Russia. It can never be proved that a three-quarters-Czar or half-Czar and the rest a Parliament, could in such a period have commanded anything at all. In fact, once the Czar was gone, no Russian ever commanded again. It was not until a fearsome set of internationalists and logicians built a sub-human structure upon the ruins of Christian civilization, that any form of order or design again emerged. Thus it is by no means certain that the generally accepted view upon the practical steps is right, or that the Czar for all his errors and shortcomings was wrong. After all, he was within an ace of safety and success. Another month and the accession of the United States to the cause of the Allies would have brought a flood of new energy, encouragement, and moral stimulus to Russian society. The certainty of victory, never again lost, was to dawn like a new sun beyond the wastes of Asia and the Pacific Ocean.

"Only another month till daybreak! Only another month and the world might have been spared the tribulations of the two most grievous years of the war. That month was lacking. A brief but hideous hiatus marred the scene. Meanwhile Nicholas II, casting his eyes now towards the Providence he sought to serve, now towards the family group he loved so well, clung chained to his post.

"All sorts of Russians made the revolution. No sort of Russians reaped its profits."

To these observations we are tempted to add Sir Winston S. Churchill's summing-up of Communism. He wrote the following in the London "Daily Telegraph" on the 4th December, 1930:

"Those who, like myself, are inveterate opponents of all that Bolshevism stands for whether in subversive corruption or despotic rule, are prone to dwell upon its root characteristic. It is unnatural.

"A monster has been born into our modern world . . . It possesses the science of civilization without its mercy, the fanaticism of religion without God, the exploitation of human passions and appetites without any ideal beyond their gratification—and that not achieved.

"I have repeatedly warned my Liberal and Socialist friends . . . that they will never get any satisfaction out of the Russian Communists. We are in the presence of a sub-human degeneration which, if not luckily inherently morbid, would reduce great nations, nay, all mankind to the conditions . . . of the White Ant. Or again, it is a cancer bacillus feeding and spreading itself upon the starving body, thriving by the very process which tortures and destroys its victim.

"Undeterred by this advice, many have tried the experiment. All have been disillusioned . . . All in turn have sought to clasp that clammy hand. All in turn have recoiled, injured, infected, or at least defiled by its chill, poisonous sweat . . .

". . . Will the Soviet Government 'get away with the goods' in Russia? Will they succeed in diverting the wrath of the Russian people at the horrible and utterly needless privations which they are now enduring, into a harmless and imaginary canal?

"I am by no means sure that they will not. The combination of the powers of Terrorism without limit or compunction, and of caucus machinery, newspapers, the broadcast, and the cinema, applied to a primitive people, isolated from all external news and bowed in grinding toil, is not to be measured.

"It is by no means certain that, if these forces of soulless barbarism and modern inventions once got us down, we could ever recover or escape.

". . . My only regret is that Europe and the United States did not make a more resolute effort to rescue the Russian people from the awful fate by which they are now gripped."

As true today, as it was written some forty years ago, and certainly prophetic.

Now let us set the views of a leading Russian opponent of Czardom, one of the chief gravediggers of Russia, against those of Winston Churchill.

The following is an unabridged and exact translation of a letter written in 1917, after the February revolution, by the late Mr P. N. Miliukoff, leader of the "Kadet" (Constitutional-Democratic) party and (when he wrote, some two months after the February-March 1917 Revolution) Foreign Minister in Kerensky's Provisional Government of Russia, to Prince Paul Dolgoroukoff, the Chairman of the Central Committee of the Kadet Party. This letter is now in the possession of a former leader of this party, personally known to us, and we are acquainted with the circumstances in which the letter had reached him. It is in Mr. Miliukoff's own hand and was published in the Russian paper "Russkoye Vosskressenie" (The Russian Resurrection), Paris, 17th April, 1955.

"In reply to your question as to how I look upon the coup d'état which we have brought about and what I expect of the future and how I evaluate the role and influence of the existing parties and organizations, I write you this letter, I confess, with heavy feelings. That which happened we had, naturally, not wanted. You know that our aim was limited to the achievement of a republic or a constitutional monarchy with an Emperor having nominal powers, with the dominating influence in the hands of the intelligentzia of the country, and equal rights for the Jews. We did not want complete ruin, although we knew that the coup d'état would at any rate have a bad effect on the course of the war. We assumed that power would be concentrated and would remain in the hands of the first Cabinet, that we would soon stop the temporary disorganization of the army and, if not by our own hands, then with the help of the Allies, we would attain victory over Germany, having paid for the overthrow of the Czar only with the temporary postponement of this victory. One must admit that some even in our party had pointed out the possibility of that which later happened, and we ourselves watched the organization of the working masses and propaganda in the army not without some worry. There is no escaping it, we were wrong in 1905 in one direction, now we are wrong again in the other. Then we made a wrong estimate of the strength of the men of the extreme Right, now we did not foresee the dexterity and consciencelessness of the Socialists. The results you can see for yourself.

It is quite obvious that the leaders of the Council of Workers' Deputies are leading us quite consciously towards financial defeat and economic collapse. The shocking formulation of the question of peace without annexations and compensations, apart from its complete senselessness, has already now fundamentally spoiled our relations with the Allies and undermined our credit. Of course this was no surprise for the inventors. I shall not explain to you why all this was necessary. In short I shall say that here there was played, in part, a role by conscious treason, in part by the wish to fish in troubled waters, in part by a craving for popularity.

Of course we must confess that the moral responsibility for that which happened lies on us—i.e. the Bloc of the State Duma. You know that the firm decision to take advantage of the war in order to bring about a coup d'état had been taken by us soon after the beginning of the war. You also know that our army was to have gone over to the offensive the results of which would at once have stopped at the root any hints at dissatisfaction and would have called forth in the country an explosion of patriotism and jubilation. You will now understand why I hesitated at the last moment to give my assent in the carrying out of the overthrow; you will also understand what must be my inner feelings at the present time.

History will curse the leaders of the so-called proletarians, but it will also curse us, who called forth the storm. You may ask what one must do now—I do not know, i.e. inwardly we both know that the salvation of Russia lies in a return to the Monarchy, we know that all the events of the past two months clearly prove that the people were incapable of receiving freedom, that the mass of the population, which does not participate in meetings and congresses, is in a monarchist mood, that very many indeed who vote for a republic, do so out of fear. All this is clear, but we cannot admit it, an admission is the collapse of all our work, of the whole of our life, the collapse of our entire idealogy (Weltanschauung—G.K.), of which we are the representatives. We cannot admit, we cannot counteract, we cannot join up with those of the Right and obey them, having struggled against them for so long and with such success—that we cannot do. That is all that I can tell you."

In general no comment is needed on this remarkable letter, which is of considerable historical importance and even now politically most valuable, when there are still so many in the West who are prepared to make great efforts and expend much money in backing the very things which Miliukoff (who knew better than anyone) renounced over fifty years ago. But it may be well to point out one or two details well known to Russians, but, perhaps, not always obvious to our non-Russian friends.

The author admits, both openly and by general implication, that the whole conspiracy against the Imperial régime was treason and ended in failure.

He states that the mass of the people of Russia were in favour of the Monarchy and that those who wanted to overthrow it were seeking power for themselves. It is in this light that we must consider the phrase that the nation was not ripe for liberty; this is mere demagogy, and the real aim was not freedom for the people, who had it, but "freedom", i.e. power, for the intelligenzia—for Miliukoff and his type, and their hidden backers.

The Bloc of the Imperial Duma mentioned in the letter was the block of the opposition parties; there were also supporters of the régime in the Duma.

Those who understand the causes of events will be able to read much between the lines and in this respect, as in all that is openly stated, the letter is very valuable.

Naturally, the implied comparison between the Monarchy and the rule of the opposition as being a choice between authoritarian government and liberty, is also demagogic casuistry, and quite consciously so, since democratically the will of the nation was in favour of the Czar and the political and administrative structure of the Empire, which was democratic and in no way totalitarian or dictatorial. Indeed events proved conclusively that it was the Imperial Throne which had stood between Russia and godless tyranny. It was Leo Trotsky himself who had written after his fall and exile that if the White Armies had fought the Russian Civil War under the banner of a people's Czar, they would have won in a fortnight.

Before we leave the subject of the First World War, it may be well to mention that, during the first three years of that struggle the Germans, according to the memoirs of General Ludendorff, the Chief of Staff, kept more than half their troops on the Russian front. In addition Russia had to deal with almost the entire military machines of Austria-Hungary and Turkey, both at that time Great Powers. Therefore Russia alone had to bear the burden of almost the whole might of the Central Powers, during a long period of the war. That could not have been done unless the régime was both popular and efficient.

Naturally this statement invites comparison with the successes of the Soviets in the Second World War. But whereas the Empire did not yield considerable parts of the country to the enemy, in some areas fought on enemy territory and began the war at the same time as its allies, and was the first to make a great effort, so as to save France, and in addition also supplied the bulk of its own ammunition and other necessities, the Soviets could not even defeat Finland, when not occupied on any other front, yielded an area containing more than half Russia's population to the Germans at one time, were heavily supplied with all necessities by the West, and incurred losses out of all proportion to the results attained. Both in peace and in war the Soviets maintain themselves by terror.

Furthermore, it is a most noteworthy fact that the Communist government of Russia mobilized just prior to the war, and especially during it, precisely those spiritual and intellectual forces which were the basis of the old régime. All the glories of the Czars were remembered, and the nation was not invited to defend Marxism, but Holy Russia. Also, and this is immensely important, victory would have been impossible but for the tremendous mistakes of Hitler, who made it clear that he was attacking not Communism, but Russia. It was he who forced the Russians unwillingly to defend the régime in defending their country. Let others be warned.

16

Some Details about Russia

But, of course, military achievement is by no means a decisive measure of a nation's worth, unless other factors also demonstrate positive capacities and virtues. We again remind our readers of the fact that we are not concerned with an apologia of Russia; we are concerned with an estimate of a possible Russian role in the events of the future. And we are unable to make that estimate unless we know something of Russia other than the malicious untruths which have been spread for so long for reasons which have little in common with the true interests of humanity.

In the first place it is necessary to point out that Russia is not a country built by imperialistic expansion and containing a small ruling minority which is a more or less oppressive parasite on a subject majority. It is true that, politically, the Communist party is, temporarily, a very small ruling minority, but there has never been a ruling race. By far, the greatest part of the territory of both European and Asiatic Russia is inhabited by the Great Russians (approximately the RSFSR, the Russian Republic, in the USSR), who make up some 54 per cent of the total population of the whole of Russia from the Baltic Sea to the Pacific Ocean, almost half way round the northern globe. A large area in southern European Russia is inhabited by the Little Russians or Ukrainians (the word "Ukraina" means borderland, but originally it was the cradle of mediaeval Russia with the central, all-Russian, capital in Kiev), who constitute about 21.5 per cent of the total population. In the west, on the border of Poland, there is the much smaller territory of the White Russians (Bielorussians, as distinct from the politically "White" Russians), who make up about 3.5 per cent of the whole population of Russia. Thus the three branches of the Russians are together approximately 79 per cent of the whole number of inhabitants of Russia on both sides of the Ural. All the other ethnical groups, many of whom also belong to the white race, total only some 21 per cent, little more than one fifth, and they are largely intermixed with the Russians geographically. Among these the Turkomans are the biggest group, but in all there are well over one hundred different races living in Russia, with their own languages and religions, though again the huge majority belong to the Orthodox Church, while there are also not a few Muslims, Buddists, Jews and so on.

Russia is not only the largest single territorially uninterrupted political unit the world has ever seen, but also, among the very big states, the most uniform racially, linguistically and in the sphere of religion. At the same time all races had the same rights before the revolution, and the same lack of rights since. The only exceptions were the Jews before 1917 (they made up about 4 per cent of the population), as they were slightly disqualified in certain respects, and also such very primitive tribes as the Eskimos, who were subject to special laws for their own protection.

A general picture of the historical basis of Russia can be obtained from the late professor Charles Sarolea, of Edinburgh University, a great and profound expert of Russia, who wrote in the English Review in June 1925 that it was certainly wrong to affirm that the Russian Government (of the Czar) was by nature anti-democratic. On the contrary, the Russian monarchy was essentially democratic, just as that of Saint Louis. It was, wrote the professor, of popular origin and the Romanov dynasty owed its accession of power to the will of the people. Furthermore, professor Sarolea wrote that the Russian monarchy was probably the European Government most favourable to progress. It corresponded to the most modern type . . . It led public opinion rather than followed it . . . Often the Czarist régime was able to accomplish in a few years tasks which had taken several generations in other countries. These reforms had been far more radical than those which followed the French revolution. Serfdom was abolished by a stroke of the pen. The administration of the law was completely reformed. The country was covered with a network of railways. At the same time the development of industry was enormous and reached a prodigious scale.

To these observations of professor Sarolea one might add that, indeed, serfdom, which then affected about 30 per cent of the population of Russia, was abolished by a simple decree of the Emperor Alexander II in 1861. A few years later the abolition of slavery in the United States required a very costly Civil War. Furthermore, in Russia the liberated peasants were given land at the cost of the larger landowners, while in America the slaves were left as poor as they had been and still as much at the mercy of employers. By the beginning of the First World War very little land remained in the possession of the old Russian estate owners, most of it having passed to the peasantry.

A detailed discussion of the administrative and legal system of Imperial Russia is not necessary here. It may suffice to say that independent experts, including British lawyers, who had made a study of the Russian Code of Laws and Judiciary, state that they were the most advanced and impartial in the world. This has always been freely admitted even by opponents of the régime. As for the way the country was governed, we can judge it best by considering the practical progress which was possible and which can best be seen in the light of the figures. And this was progress attained not in conditions of slavery and the complete deprivation of the working masses of even elementary necessities and sufficient food, but while the standard of life of all Russians was rising rapidly.

In the sphere of education the Imperial Government had set the target of obligatory elementary education for all to be achieved in 1922. In the years between 1908 and 1914 10,000 schools were opened annually, that is almost one thousand new schools every month. It can well be imagined what great practical problems this involved: the provisions of finance, of building materials, of books, of teachers and so on. An investigation made by the Soviets in 1920 shewed that 86 per cent of all children aged 12 years could read and write; and they were, of course, the products of education before the revolution. It may be well to consider that in other similarly large territories, under the administration of others, such a high standard of education has not been reached even today, except in the United States.

The Russian Imperial universities were of the highest academic standards, and education in them was so cheap as to be accessible to all who wanted it. Since the revolution the number of places available to those who seek higher education has risen only by about 8 per cent, a rate of progress far lower than that which was usual under the Czars in the decades before 1917.

Today the Russian masses are kept in semi-starvation by the Soviet tyranny for two reasons: Socialism is inefficient, and, an even more important reason, it is a part of the system of terror to keep the population short of food and other necessities, to discourage thoughts of reform and revolt, while all spare energies after excessively hard work are engaged in trying to get enough to survive. Long waiting in queues at the shops, systematic overcrowding and so on are also part of the same technique; if there is no peace and no privacy, there is less likelihood of "counter-revolution", while only those who have sold their souls to the devil and are reliable are given a higher standard of life.

But before the revolution Russia was one of the chief exporters of foods, even after enough had been retained by the producers. Let us compare, for example, the Russian production of cereals with that of the world in 1913 (in millions of poods, one pood being forty Russian pounds):

Cereal	World production	Russian production	Percentage
Rye	2 378.0	1 593.3	67.0
Wheat	4 971.4	1 554.8	31.2
Oats	3 324.6	1 087.0	30.3
Barley	1 771.4	750.4	42.3

It will be seen that Russia alone produced a very substantial part of the world's cereals. In the last years before the First World War the Russian production was greater than that of Argentina, Canada and the United States combined, by about 25 per cent, and Russian exports were greater than those of the United States by some 366 per cent. Similarly advantageous figures could be quoted regarding all other agricultural products.

Intensive Soviet Communist propaganda, willingly echoed in many interested quarters in the West, had led to the firm establishment of the impression that Russia before the revolution had almost no industry, which had been created since by the Bolsheviks. Yet in fact industrial progress in Russia took place on such a scale and at such speed as to leave even American tempoes in the shade. On the other hand, after the Communists came to power, Socialistic inefficiency has made progress not only slow, but also far more costly.

In 1963 the United States Information Service published a material entitled "Modernization in the U.S.A. The Roosevelt Years", by David Cushman Coyle. Mr. Coyle is an eminent writer and had great experience of affairs under President Roosevelt.

The second paragraph of the material is as follows:

"During the nineteenth century the United States had seen a considerable development of heavy industry, stimulated by railroad building and expanding production of steel. Most of the country, however, was still agricultural. There was a notable resemblance between the nineteenth-century economic growth of the United States and of Czarist Russia, especially after about 1870. Both countries started comparatively late and their growth rates were rapid toward the end of the century. Industrial output per capita grew at an average rate of $3\frac{1}{2}$ per cent per year in Russia, and $2\frac{3}{4}$ per cent in America, during this period, compared with only 1 per cent in Great Britain."

So we see, on the authority of an American Governmental publication, and the facts are true, that industrial growth in Russia during the decades before the revolution was faster than in legendary America. What would have been achieved by now, had there been no Communism? Clearly Russia would have been now the greatest industrial as well as agricultural power in the world, and by a huge margin. Instead it lags behind in production, cannot feed itself adequately and has a population little more than half that which would have been likely but for the revolution.

But not only was industry before the revolution more efficient. It was also more humane. Already in the first half of the eighteenth century, more than one hundred years before such problems were tackled at all in any other country, a law was promulgated in Russia limiting the hours of work in factories and mines. In the later part of the last century the measures taken to protect the health, safety and well-being of the Russian workers were such that in 1912 the American President Taft was able to say that the Emperor of Russia has passed workers' legislation which was nearer to perfection than that of any democratic country.

The production of coal in Russia rose as follows: in 1885 a total of 259·6 million poods, in 1905 1 179·8 million poods and in 1913 it was 2 159·8 million poods. The production of petroleum rose from a total of 491·2 million poods in 1906 to 602·1 million poods in 1916. At one time Russia was the greatest oil-producing country in the world. The production of iron ore in the Russian Empire was 46 628 thousands of poods in 1870, 105 360 thousands of poods in 1890, and 562 800 thousands of poods in 1913. Finally the production of gold rose as follows: in 1864—1399 poods, in 1894—2622 poods and in 1914—4047 poods. Similar progress was made in all other metals.

The progress made in production of every kind of industrial produce was immense. This was reflected in the trade figures. The total weight of goods carried in Russia in 1900 was 5 200 million poods, and in 1912 it was 15 764 million poods; in 12 years the turnover had been trebled.

Russian foreign trade appears thus:
In millions of Roubles.

Average	Exports	Imports	Favourable balance
1899/1903	793·3	630·2	163·1
1904/1908	1 046·0	769·5	276·5
1909/1913	1 505·4	1 139·6	365·8

(Then the approx. gold rate of exchange was 10 R. to £1; $1=2·50 R.)

The first railway was built in Russia in 1837, thereafter progress in railway building was as follows, in versts:

1844–1846 — 260 v.; 1877–1879 — 20 782 v.; 1913–1915 — 73 852 v. In 1916 the total length of the Russian main lines was 100 817 versts. (1 verst = approx. 1 km.)

(See also Appendix)

At the end of the last century, in 1900, the Russian commercial river and canal tonnage was 11 130 000, while the total British merchant tonnage on the high seas at that time was 10 750 000; Russian internal tonnage alone was greater than that of the then leading maritime power, and in addition Russia also had a merchant fleet trading on the high seas.

For better or for worse, in the period before the First World War it was the gold holding of a country which was a guide to its financial health. In this connexion we can give a comparative table, in millions of Roubles, for the year 1913: (Ten Roubles were then approx. $4).

Central Bank	Gold	Banknotes
Russian State Bank	1 550	1 494
Bank of France	1 193	2 196
Bank of Germany	411	930
Bank of England	331	263

As will be seen, Russia had the world's biggest gold reserve and the issue of paper money was more than covered by the holdings of gold. In 1912 32 clearing houses in Russia had dealt with 31 000 million Roubles, yet in 1906 the amount, in but 5 clearing houses, had been 12 000 million Roubles; in six years the turnover was almost trebled. And there was no inflation.

It would be fair to claim that a sign of the efficiency of a Government is the smallness of the taxes it has to impose, as well as the limited size of its National Debt, given the "classical" methods of Capitalism. At the same time it is obvious that Russia, one of the major Great Powers, had to deal with very considerable governmental expenses of every kind. In this light the Russian Imperial Government will be seen to have been the most efficient.

Direct taxes in Roubles per inhabitant, in 1912

Country	State Taxes	Local Taxes	Total
Russia	1·28	1·38	3·11
Germany	5·45	7·52	12·97
Austria	5·12	5·07	10·19
France	6·44	5·91	12·35
Great Britain	10·01	16·74	26·75

Indirect taxes in Roubles per inhabitant, in 1912:

Country	State Taxes	Local Taxes	Total
Russia	5.95	0.03	5.98
Germany	9.31	0.33	9.64
Austria	9.90	1.38	11.28
France	13.11	2.89	16.00
Great Britain	13.86	—	13.86

In the year 1908 the National Debts were, in Roubles per inhabitant.

France	288
Italy	189
Netherlands	178
Belgium	172
Great Britain	169.8
Germany	135.6
Russia	58.7

This was soon after Russia had been involved in the Japanese war, while the others had been for long at peace. By 1914 83 per cent of the interest and amortisation of the Russian National Debt was paid by the profits of the Russian State Railways.

Now these few figures, which can be checked and extended by anyone who may be interested, show clearly that the Russian Empire in the period just before its collapse was in a most flourishing condition. That this prosperity and progress, when life was free, extremely cheap and not under the threat of unemployment, was in no way due to the merits of the Imperial régime would be an absurd assumption. All men of all races had equality of status and opportunity to an extent greater than in any other country and paralleled only in America. No land was then as truly democratic as Russia. But no land was as cruelly maligned.

We have already mentioned that the Jews were not granted full equality. The reason for this was by no means a mean or mistaken anti-Semitism. The policy may not have been entirely wise or right, but it would never have attracted any attention at all, were it not that the Jews were involved. No other race would have been able to make and maintain so great a volume of plaintive and even aggressive propaganda throughout the world.

The Russian policy towards the Jews was not anti-Semitic, since it did not consider race, but only religion. This policy was largely pursued in the interests of the Jews themselves. The Russian peasants were very unbusinesslike and some Jews were continually tempted to settle in the village and indulge in extortionate moneylending. Then there came the moment when the simple villagers had had enough, and the poor Jews became the victims of a pogrom. Such events, despite propaganda to the contrary, were never encouraged by the Government. And so it was that the Jews were not permitted to settle in any but Jewish villages while in the towns and universities of Russia outside the region in which they had lived for centuries the Jews were limited theoretically to a maximum of four per cent, this being their proportion of the total population. This rule was, however, broken very often indeed with the full knowledge of the authorities. On the other hand Jews had equal rights in the courts of law, and Jewish rabbis, just like the priests of the Orthodox Church, were paid a Government salary, in addition to the sums provided by their flock. There was no civil marriage or registration of births in Russia, and all ministers of recognized religions had to perform the functions of registrars.

The fable that the persecuted Jews of Russia fled from Czarist oppression and came to the freedom of England and America is most flattering to the English and Americans. Unfortunately the story is not true. The sad fact is that, before the First World War, the two countries we have mentioned were the only ones in the world in which there was no obligatory military service for young men. We have very often had the experience, when going to a very efficient Jewish tailor or watchmaker, of being greeted with a friendly smile and the remark: "Oh, so you are also a Russian!" Never did we hear a bad observation about Russia, but always a story somewhat as follows: "I have been here for forty years; I am now sixty and have grandchildren." They all left at twenty—the age for military service. We do not blame them, and we are grateful to them for their unfailingly kind reminiscences of Russia. But there is a small, but influential minority which made anti-Russian capital out of such as these things for many years. They have misled the West.

In addition to the many Russian Jews who remember their old homes with nostalgia, there are still very many people of all nations —British, Swiss, German, French—who spent most of their lives before the revolution in Russia. Many of them came back to their old countries completely Russianized and only dreaming of the day when they could return to the country whose way of life, language and often also Faith, they had adopted.

The famous and powerful Russian Prime Minister Stolypin, had had the firm intention of recommending the abolition of all laws which in any way discriminated against the Jews. He was assassinated in 1911 as the result of a conspiracy by one of the Socialist organizations and, unfortunately, his murderer was a Jew. Nevertheless such legislation would have been passed soon and this, and so much else, was prevented by war and revolution.

* * *

Further details can be found in the Appendix.

17

The Background of the Revolution

It may now well be asked, ironically, if the Russian revolution has taken place at all. Perhaps such a paradise still exists and all that one has heard to the contrary may be a great misconception. In short what did and what did not bring about the dreadful catastrophe of 1917?

The misrepresentations which are persistently spread about these events and about the country in general are a conscious part of a plan for the subjugation of the world. These deliberate lies can be ignored by those who wish to understand the true facts, and we would repeat that on a proper understanding of these facts depends the fate of the globe.

A living organization may succumb to disease if two factors are present: there must be a virus, capable of provoking the disease, and the organism must have become weakened and its anti-toxins become at least in part ineffective, so that the virus cannot be resisted and destroyed. In addition, the infected organism faces two possibilities: the disease will overcome and kill it, or, alternatively, the organism will not succumb, but will ultimately eliminate the virus and disease. Such is the situation which applies to Russia.

The Russia which emerged from a long struggle for survival at the end of the seventeenth century, had for hundreds of years to devote the greater part of its energies to uninterrupted wars of self-defence. Across the open plains of the West and East there came many would-be conquerors—the Tatars, the Swedes, the Germans, the Poles and others. The first-named succeeded in imposing their largely indirect rule on Russia for almost three centuries.

In the Middle Ages, in the early period of Russian history, a thousand and more years ago, the then capital, Kiev, had been one of Europe's largest and most flourishing cities. The Grand Dukes of Kiev and All Russia were related by blood and by marriage to the Kings of England, France, Hungary, Norway and others. Russia was an integral and leading part of the continent, a Christian country with a great present and an immense and seemingly assured future. But fate had put Russia in a most exposed position, where only a very tough and very energetic nation could have survived. Western Europe, sheltered for a thousand years from the storms which shook

Russia, but which Russia held up, was able to create a highly complex and developed culture, which made up in outward brilliance what it might sometimes have lacked in depth. Politically Western Europe could indulge in feudalism, chivalry, lilliputian States and parliamentarianism. It was a way of life which would not have survived for as much as a single day the strains which Russians bore for almost the whole of their eleven centuries as a united State.

But much of real value emerged in Western Europe. The technical achievements of the past centuries, especially since the Renaissance, had become a factor without which no State could effectively live and survive in competition with others. In the realm of ideas, too, there was an energy and productiveness which was both dangerous and advantageous.

At the same time Russia had been largely separated from Western Europe and forced to devote too great a part of its spiritual energies and material efforts to defence. Only towards the time of John the Terrible, the contemporary of Queen Elizabeth I, did contacts with the West begin to be re-established. But the English merchant adventurers who went to trade in Russia, often expected the inhabitants of Northern Muscovy to be monsters with one eye in the middle of their brows. It was a mysterious place of which little was known. And it knew too little of the West.

Inevitably, as the one-time invaders had been reduced to manageable proportions, and Russia itself had become strong enough to devote more attention to progress, rather than to mere existence, as the result of the colonization of the largely empty spaces of Siberia (a land as good to live in as the region on both sides of the US-Canadian border)—leading Russians began to study the West and its many positive achievements. Towards the middle of the seventeenth century they had decided to pursue a policy of the gradual absorption of Western methods and ideas and their adaptation to Russian culture and practical requirements. In part this again was a policy of survival, but on a higher plane than the mere repelling of invaders.

However, the Russia of that time was a land of the most extreme conservatism and tradition. It was inevitable that there were many who were violently opposed to any reforms whatsoever and who felt that any admittance of the influence of the Catholic and more especially Protestant heretical West would lead Russia towards the abyss, towards the rule of Anti-Christ. If these people were to revisit the earth today, they might be able to claim that they were then entirely right!

But then the problem was not so much one of general philosophical conceptions and of far-sighted policies; it was a matter of immediate effective competition, of becoming a Great Power, or being crushed after all, despite a millennium of effort and sacrifice. The situation called for radical action and the man appeared who was to prove capable of so acting.

Peter the Great, Czar of Moscow and Emperor of All the Russias, the last of the Romanovs in the direct male line, succeeded to the Throne when still a minor. His elder half-brother John was intellectually weak and the two Princes were proclaimed Joint Czars, with their older sister Sophia as Regent. It was the later part of the seventeenth century. Not long afterwards Peter, though only sixteen years old, annulled the Regency of his sister, while ignoring his brother, and actively assumed full powers. A man of immense physical size and strength, of huge will-power and great intellectual ability, Peter was a crowned revolutionary. He did in a few years that which others would have attempted during decades or even generations. It is in such cases impossible to say what would have happened if Peter had not done that which he did, but it is certainly arguable that Russia might not have survived, and it would obviously never have become what it was after him, and remains to this day: a Great Power of the first rank and a cultural and political force which has shaken and still will shake the world.

It was Jean Jacques Rousseau who wrote in the same eighteenth century in which Peter died that his too rapid reforms would bring about a great revolution in Russia, as they had split the nation. The masses had remained as they were, rooted in the old Russia with all its faults and its great virtues, while the leading classes were westernized and separated from the bulk of the nation. It was largely a true estimate, and the prophesy proved to be correct. This view is also held by very many Russians.

Those who have read "War and Peace" by Count Leo Tolstoy will remember his description of the Russian upper classes of the time of the Napoleonic invasion, a little less than a hundred years after the death of Peter I. Many spoke little Russian and habitually used French in conversation. The Russian armies which liberated Europe from the French yoke of the time came back to Russia infected with the revolutionary ideas of the country they had just defeated. In little more than a decade the Decembrist conspiracy proved to be the first manifestation of a revolutionary movement in Russia which established a tradition. The ferment among the intelligentzia was not to cease until the final cataclysm.

But it was not a fight for the liberty of the masses, or for their well-being, which came into question. All the leaders of the Decembrist plot of 1825, whose aim was the total elimination of the entire

Dynasty by murder, and the freeing of the serfs, accompanied by the establishment of a parliamentary régime, were themselves owners of serfs, and not one had thought of liberating his own peasants, before fighting for the liberation of the rest. These motives were quite incidental, largely make-believe and a façade. The true motives were the struggle of the irreligious rationalists against the forces which represented a Christian conception of life and the State. These guiding influences remained the underlying force of the revolutionary movement to our day, and it is not surprising that not liberty, but only a terrible tyranny, has been the ultimate outcome of all the subversive efforts of almost a full hundred years.

In these circumstances it is also not surprising that the revolution was entirely the work of the westernized upper middle class intelligentzia and a part of the aristocracy. It is not surprising that so many revolutionaries, especially at the time when the Bolsheviks achieved power, were westernized Jews, followers of Karl Marx, himself one of them. The revolution of 1917 would not have been possible but for the reforms of Peter the Great two hundred years before. A dose of western blood transfusion was necessary, but an overdose, taken too quickly, has almost killed Russia. But Russia has survived, and there are some who ask whether it is not now the West which is also ill with the same spiritual poison. The West and Russia will have to solve these problems together.

If we have seen that there were great weaknesses in the Russian State and social system, if the Russian religious and cultural structure was vulnerable, there were also weighty factors making for strength and stability. We have shewn that the Imperial régime was capable of immense efforts, we have shewn that it gave Russia great prosperity without loss of personal freedom or the excessive subjugation of the Government and the business community to the usurers. The Church was basically intact, weakened only by the institution of the Holy Synod and the Procurator-General, established by Peter the Great in the place of the Patriarchate, as one of the means by which he tried to overcome conservative forces. The Imperial Throne was unchallenged by the mass of the people and it was sincerely devoted to the cause of their well-being. But between them there was that rootless and demoralized stratum of the westernized upper middle class and intelligentzia which made infection by the virus of revolutionary disease possible. If most of the leaders of the Bolsheviks had been imported from the East Side of New York, all the members of the Provisional Government of Prince Lvov and later Kerensky, had been members of a St. Petersburg Masonic Lodge. They, too, were spiritually a western import into Russia. We should bear in mind that freemasonry must here be considered not in the light in which the average Anglo-Saxon brother sees it, but in the light in which it was a factor in Russia.

The virus of revolution was an emanation of the conspiracy of the materialistic false messianists, who want to establish the one world state, ruled by themselves. All the subversive movements of the past three hundred years can be traced directly to this origin. As we have seen, the apparently anti-capitalistic line of the conspirators was in fact but one aspect of their policy, while they were at the same time the originators of usury capitalism. They have always employed apparently quite different methods, so different that most people were utterly deceived and did not notice their common origins and the shared ultimate objectives. But the aim is one and the same. Thus it is not surprising, for example, that western "public opinion", the greater part of which is manufactured to order by the conspirators—who control most of the press, radio, cinema and even governments, while officially attached to democracy and capitalism—applauded and even aided the revolutionaries in Russia, believing them to be the liberators of an oppressed people, only waiting to be freed. And when it became obvious even to the blind that Marxism had brought not increased liberty to the Russians, but complete slavery and a ruthless terror, "democratic" public opinion remained for long years more or less silent, and if hard pressed to pronounce unfavourably on the godless tyranny, it remarked that Bolshevism was bad, but, after all, Czarism had been worse. Bolshevism was an interesting experiment and, anyway, the Russians were so barbarous that one could expect nothing else.

The writer had been told by a British Labour Member of Parliament, well known as an intellectual Left-winger, that Marxism was a very sophisticated system which had been completely ruined by the barbarous Russians. Now this is a key to much which we have seen in more recent years. We all know that there are numbers of formerly leading western Communists and fellow-travellers in America, Britain and elsewhere, who are now the leading proponents of the idea that Communism is an evil despotism, that the Russians are its oppressed victims, and that the world must do all in its power to rescue the Russians and the others now under the Soviet yoke.

The one-time backers of the Soviet dictatorship over the proletariat have suddenly turned against it, and quite sincerely so. At first sight it would seem that these people, having for many years observed Marxism in practice, and being kind-hearted souls, have come to the conclusions that they were wrong and that, in all conscience, they must now reverse their views. But such a generous assumption would not always be correct.

As a rule, it is not a reversal of the fundamental line which we observe, but a tactical change, while the ultimate objective remains the same. As we have seen, Capitalism, Socialism and Communism, Liberalism and Democracy, and much else, can be used and are used as a means of furthering the cause of world domination by the materialistic messianists. Now they find Communism in Russia has got out of hand in some respects. It is no longer the completely acceptable tool it was intended to be when so much treasure, effort and goodwill were showered on it. While Communism must not be simply removed to make way for whatever the Russian people may really want, it must be replaced by an "improved" alternative régime. The prisoner must be transfered from one jail to another, but he must not be allowed to escape on the way.

Another way of saying a similar thing is the recent statement by a British Premier, that Soviet Communism is but an expression of the old Russian imperialism. This is the Conservative version of the thesis that it is the Russian nation which is to blame and, by implication, not Communism.

What is the real trouble? Why is Russia always the alleged enemy and Communism in its present Soviet form, though not in general and in principle, also unacceptable? These phenomena, if observed at all, and few people do observe them, seem full of contradictions and inconsistencies. But if the root causes of events, and the true makers of policy, are once clearly discovered and understood, then all becomes obvious.

18

The "Case" against Russia

The Russian Christian Empire was a powerful bulwark, preventing the spread of the subversive doctrines and practices which opened up the paths towards the domination of the world by the materialists. That this Empire must be attacked and overthrown was, therefore, a foregone conclusion. But an acceptable excuse had to be found in order to mobilize sufficient support for a consistent and sustained policy which would require great efforts and even sacrifices. It would not have been enough in, say, the late eighteenth and early nineteenth centuries to claim that Russia must be considered an enemy because it was not ruled by a Parliament based on universal suffrage. Before the Reform Bill in the first half of the last century England was ruled entirely and openly by the aristocracy and gentry and it was only within the lifetime of old people that the working masses of Britain received the vote, while women were finally enfranchised only in very recent years. Even the unadulterated accusation of expansionist imperialism would have sounded very strange if it had come from the British and others. After all, there are still many men alive today who fought in purely imperialistic wars. Indeed it was impossible to discover a convincing case against Russia on any really true basis. But the case had to be made.

It was made; a great historical misunderstanding was carefully and "scientifically" planned and fostered for not a few generations, adorned with various clap-trap trimmings, of which we have already mentioned a few. The basic case against Russia was made convincing and effective by being presented in the form of a dangerous threat to the very existence of Great Britain and others and of their possessions. In fact, also, Russia was presented as the enemy of all that was decent and right.

The artificially created historical misunderstanding about Russia amounted in outline to this: For hundreds of years England, Spain, Portugal, France and Holland had competed and defended themselves on the high seas, while building up their overseas empires. They all had this in common: the metropolitan territory was relatively small, and the colonial and colonized possessions were enormous. In each of these empires the ruling race was far less numerous than the ruled races. In the end, during the 18th century, these struggles ceased, as a sort of modus vivendi and division of spoils was achieved. And just as this had came about, there appeared the new, post-Petrine, Russia, with a large fleet, active in the Mediterranean, while some units more than once circumnavigated the globe.

In these circumstances it was not difficult to foster the impression that Russia was an expansionist and aggressive power, threatening the liberties of Europe. A campaign of slander began, which, of course, made no mention of the fact that Russia was not a maritime and colonial power, that its population was homogenous, being predominantly Russian, and that its interest in the sea was only limited to obtaining openings to ice-free ports and to controlling the Straits which were the entrance to the predominantly Russian Black Sea.

Yet what was in fact the real effect of Russian foreign policy after the time of Peter I? Where, except in Poland, did Russia obtain new territories to which it was not entitled by some reason other than conquest? Russia grew from small beginnings in the South and centre of the area which is now European Russia, and gradually grew by the colonization of the surrounding space, largely uninhabited, or inhabited only by marauding nomads. The bulk of Russian territory lies in the great plain which stretches across Central Europe and beyond the Urals to the Pacific. Russia naturally tried to reach the sea and especially the ice-free ports, but in the process no great nations with a long history of civilization and independence were weakened or destroyed. In Central Asia certain areas had to be occupied and pacified because their few inhabitants were restless marauders, who continually raided peaceful Russian lands. But the main stream of Russian colonization was through Siberia and across the Behring Straits into Alaska, in lands which were before the coming of the Russians completely wild and unused.

But while in North America the Red Indians were almost exterminated and deprived of almost all their lands, the natives of the territories which became part of the Russian Empire were given full protection and equality and all the advantages of a well-organized administration and a truly Christian civilization. No one was deprived of his possessions. In the Caucasus, for example, the leading oil magnates were local Caucasians, and not the nominees of bankers from the capital.

Before coming back to the Caucasus, it may be well to say a few words about Poland. This unhappy country has often been the cause of anti-Russian agitation. In the first place it must be said that all Russians are the friends of Poland and desire good relations with their Slavonic neighbour. In the second place it should be remembered that it is a regrettable fact that there has been a see-saw, a swing of power and influence, between Warsaw and Moscow for centuries, and it was the Poles who were the first to attempt an expansionist policy towards the east; at one time Polish armed units even reached the Urals. Then Russia became stronger, and Poland weaker, and the pendulum swung the other way. It is now time to stop it and to find a permanent and mutually satisfactory modus vivendi. But both sides must abandon exaggerated claims and desires to hold territories inhabited by the members of the other nation. When Russia took part in the partitions of Poland, that ancient and gallant Kingdom was in so weak a condition that the Prussian and Austrian initiative would have undoubtedly succeeded. Russia, for strategic reasons, had to take a share of the lands of Poland, so as to prevent a deep German penetration towards the centre of Russia, the more so as the east of Poland was inhabited by Russians of the Orthodox faith, who had been conquered by Poland many generations earlier. But, it should be said that all Russians regret the partitions and want to see Poland free and prosperous, and a friend of Russia.

And how was it that the Russians came to the Caucasus? For generations Georgia and Armenia, ancient Christian kingdoms, were hard pressed by their powerful Muslim neighbours—Turkey and Persia, and by lesser Muslim states in the Caucasus itself. It was an entirely unequal battle. Repeatedly the Georgians asked for Russian protection, beginning in the seventeenth century. But Russia was not yet strong enough to challenge the Turks especially beyond the great Caucasian range. But at last, at the very end of the eighteenth century, the Georgian plea for protection by incorporation in the Russian Empire could be granted and the last King of Georgia and his nobles became incorporated into the Russian nobility. Within a few years a member of the ancient Royal House of Georgia (another branch also being the rulers of Armenia), Prince Bagration-Mukhransky, was one of the chief commanders of the Russian army in the war against Napoleon. He fell at the head of his troops at the great battle of Borodino and was buried on the battlefield. The Prince was a national hero of Russia and a monument was erected over his grave.

After the incorporation of Georgia it was necessary to pacify the other Caucasian territories, inhabited by Muslims under Turkish protection or leadership. But here, too, the natives were given all the rights of Russian subjects and they retained all their properties.

Soon after the pacification of the Caucasus during the first half of the nineteenth century, there followed the need to deal with the dreadful conditions under which the Balkan nations lived within the Turkish Empire. Indeed the liberation of Greece had already taken place in collaboration with Great Britain and France, in the middle of the first half of the century. But there remained under Ottoman and Muslim misrule several nations which were mostly Slavs—blood relations of the Russians—and mostly members of the Orthodox Church, to which also the huge majority of the peoples of Russia belonged. It was natural that Russia should not ignore the position and the repeated pleas of the oppressed nations. In the 1870s a victorious campaign brought the Russian army to the gates of Constantinople. Turkey signed a treaty of peace and the Christian Balkans were free.

But on no account could this be accepted; this act was clearly an expression of Russian acquisitive imperialism. Already the Straits were endangered and Russia might take them. And then, it had to be assumed, half the world would be lost. So the terms of the treaty were whittled down and Britain took Cyprus from the Turks as a reward, presumably just to shew that it was only the theoretical threat of Russian seizures which was to be feared, and not the reality of a British one. Yet if, and who will dispute its truth, it is proper for Great Britain to acquire and hold Gibraltar, Malta, Cyprus, Aden, Singapore, Hong-Kong and so much else, why was it so dreadful a threat to the peace of the world if Russia did consider that it should control the Straits? But that was not the true issue. It was not Russia in an aggressive posture which was the enemy, but Russia in a defensive one; this made "progress" impossible.

Yet defence has been the continuous tradition of Russian history, imposed on the country by circumstances. A notable example was the Napoleonic invasion of 1812, the culmination of the whole period of the French revolutionary wars. The French Emperor was driven, like Hitler, to this fatal step by the British naval blockade. When, after his political end, Napoleon looked back on his campaigns, he said: "I was defeated by the storm-tossed ships of England, on which my Grand Army never set eyes." Of the then inevitable battle of Borodino he said: "This battle proved that the French soldiers deserved victory, and that the Russian ones were invincible." On the rock of Russia he broke his back. It is a fact of history that all who have ever challenged Russia seriously have ceased forever to be great powers.

After the total annihilation of the French armies and those of its allies and after they had been driven out of Russia, there were many among the chief military and political advisers of the Emperor Alexander I of Russia who considered that the Russian armies should stop at the boundaries of the Empire and leave France and all Europe to their own devices. It was assumed that the power of the invader was broken forever, and, consequently, no Russian interests were served by a further pursuit of the beaten enemy. As for acquisitive conquests or the extension of Russian influence, none thought of that, although Europe was entirely at the mercy of Russia. There are few countries, if any, which would have missed the chance.

The Emperor Alexander was more generous than his advisers and he decided to follow up the liberation of Russia by completing the liberation of Europe. The French armies, rapidly re-formed by Napoleon, were pursued. A series of victorious battles brought the Russians, with their Allies, the Austrians and the Prussians, who only recently had been grovelling in the dust and either imploring Russian help or fighting at the side of the French, to Paris, and Alexander I personally led the entry of the armies into the capital of France.

What was the peace which the complete master of Europe dictated to a broken and helpless opponent? Was it a demand for astronomical material compensation, for the cession of territories, for the break-up of metropolitan France? Did Russia demand the disarmament of France, the imposition of Russian occupation troops or a puppet régime? No. All that the Emperor Alexander I demanded of a France which was to retain all the lands it had held before the wars began, was that the legitimate King, Louis XVIII, the brother of the pseudo-judicially murdered Louis XVI, should establish a régime in which he would rule together with an elected assembly. As soon as the dust had settled, the Russians withdrew and went home. The Czar went to the Congress of Vienna not to dictate, but to decide in amity. Even the representative of France was admitted as an equal. Russian policy assured fifty years of peace. How unlike the aftermath of 1918 and 1945, when the true Russia was absent.

Let us compare this with the terms imposed by the "democrats" of recent times. Let us consider the consequences of Versailles. Was there peace or stability? Was there any betterment? Or would it be true to say that the world went relentlessly from bad to worse?

We held no brief for Hitler and his Nazis at any time. We knew that they would sow an evil seed and also that they would attack Russia, while, whether intentionally or not, furthering the cause of Communism. We foresaw the defeat of Germany and we welcomed it. But the things which were done in and to Germany after 1945 can only be the cause of a further worsening of the spirit, mind and condition of the world. To divide Germany and half Europe and Asia and give a large part to the Soviets and their agents was to lose the war completely and open the door to the unrestrained spread of the red pestilence. To arrange the Nüremberg trials and put on the bench of judges and among the prosecutors (even quite apart from the impropriety of ex post facto laws) the representatives of the most immoral and criminal organization the world has ever seen, is to make western justice a mockery and reduce relations between peoples to the level of the jungle.

Compared with all this, the noble actions of the Emperor Alexander I of Russia are as far from the criminal and dirty actions of today as a nunnery would be from a brothel. And we do not seem to have reached the end of the slippery slope. Our senses are so dulled that we hardly understand how vile are the times and how dangerous the prospects.

The pacific role of Russia is also illustrated in recent times by the twice repeated initiative of Nicholas II, who unsuccessfully appealed to the leading countries to agree to a sweeping programme of disarmament. Not disheartened by these refusals, the Emperor founded the Court of International Justice at the Hague, meeting all expenses out of his personal funds.

Americans who are acquainted with their history will know well that, from the very beginning of American independence, Russia had been a steadfast and active friend of the United States. Suffice it to remind them of the fact that when a Civil War was being fought in the United States, which threatened the unity of the country, and when Great Britain and France were prepared to recognize the belligerent status of the Southern States, so as to give international legalization to the splitting of the State, Russia actively intervened to help to preserve American unity. Two Russian naval squadrons were despatched to San Francisco and New York respectively, to prevent any other naval intervention in the internal affairs of America. After the war the American Government sent a special mission to Russia, headed by an Admiral, to thank Russia for these actions, which had preserved America. Very soon after that Russia sold Alaska to the United States for the nominal amount of some seven million dollars, which even then was a small amount in the given circumstances. Was that an example of expansionist imperialism?

While it would be impossible to discuss the whole matter in detail in these lines, it is well to remind ourselves of the fact that the true motives which actuated some of the chief actors behind the scenes of the drama of the American Civil War had little to do with slavery or its abolition. The true aims of the wire-pullers were financial. It was a complex picture, in which the ambitions of Napoleon III were used in order to foster the adventure of the Mexican Empire. The division of the United States into two weaker units, both subservient to the international financiers, then still based on London, was one of the major intentions. There is reason to believe that President Abraham Lincoln was assassinated not by an angry friend of Southern gentlemen, but on the instigation of financial circles, who knew that he intended to continue to issue US Government money free of interest, in accordance with the Constitution. The intervention of the Russian Empire must be seen in the light of the same circumstances.

This is one of a number of major reasons why that Christian Empire which had been the friend of America had to be overthrown; it also follows that it is, conversely, in the true interests of America that that Empire should rise again. And let us note that the financiers who have made Communism possible are now just as much concerned with dividing up Russia as they had been anxious to divide the United States. The reason for this is that smaller and poorer countries are more easily managed, until the day arrives when universal Socialism will have all the means of compulsion at its disposal, but then it will be too late to come to ones senses. Do it now.

The theory that Russia, as such, is dangerous, is based upon a deliberate falsehood and is a part of the plan by which the materialistic messianists wish to conquer the world. It is a thesis which is all the more pernicious at the present time because it plays straight into the hands of the Soviets, since it amounts, as we have already pointed out, to the proposition that the enemy is not Communism, but Russia: Thus Communism will be spared and Russia, the greatest potential ally of genuine anti-Communism, will be attacked. The patriotic Russians, as at the time of Hitler, will be forced to defend their country and thus also, though unwillingly, the hated red régime.

19

Policies which Mislead

The consequences of such a confusion of issues will be, in this atomic age, a most terrible cataclysm. But there is nothing vague or haphazard about this deliberate policy. The plan is to reduce the whole to a manageable condition, geographically, politically, socially and economically. No Great Power, or potential Great Power, must remain intact. It is, therefore, not surprising to see everything done which can contribute to the break-up of the large units—the British Empire and Commonwealth, Russia, China, America. For many decades much money and efforts have been spent in founding and fostering various anti-Russian separatist groups and movements, best known among which are the "Ukrainian" Organizations. These paid Quislings represent nothing but their foreign employers, who want to use this means, and others, in order to assure that Russia will become pliant and unable ever to rise again. We are told that self-determination of every little unit is desired by all, yet in fact the true trends are towards the formation of larger political and economic units.

And ultimately, when all has been achieved and the splintered, beheaded and stupefied world is in the grip of the materialists, the atomic threat will be the final and irresistible sanction. Even the present Soviet methods of total terror and deliberate underfeeding will no longer be necessary in their most extreme forms.

It will be small comfort to the patriotic Americans if we can tell them that their country, being a major base of the conspirators, may be the last to succumb openly. The fate of the possessions of Holland and France and others is clear. That Great Britain is under attack has been obvious to sound, patriotic Britons for a long time. Of the various plans which are being operated to deal with Russia, we will say more below. But none of us should imagine that his country is immune. The double attack from both sides of the Iron Curtain is aimed at us all equally, though some are being reduced earlier, and some later. In this connexion it is terrifying to observe the complacency which exists in certain Conservative circles in Britain and elsewhere.

We must all hang together if we are not to hang separately. There must be an international plan of counter-attack. But before we can discuss it, we must consider the outline of the attack on ourselves.

Lenin had stated, and he repeated in outline a proposition which had been propounded much earlier, that the attack of the Social-Democratic Marxists would, after Russia, be directed via China at the western countries. Just as the now classical German manœuvre against France was the sweep through the Low Countries, or at least Belgium alone, and then towards Paris, so the classical Communist and especially Bolshevik line of global attack is the circle from the West to Russia, and then through the Far East back to the West. And, as prophesied, this line had been followed.

Lenin also told us repeatedly, as did Stalin, that the Communist must and will pursue a flexible policy which will permit temporary tactical retreats. Those who are deceived by talk of co-existence, should look up the authorities; they are available in most reputable libraries, at least in Europe.

But Russia was not merely the corridor through which the Communists were to pass towards world dictatorship. It was also the chief base of operations, once it had been seized. And more than that: as we have already mentioned, Russia had been the chief bulwark against the red flood. It is not surprising that Karl Marx hated Russia. Furthermore, we should bear in mind that if the conspirators, as we have noted already, are hoping to transfer Russia safely from one prison to another, the same also applies in general to the whole world. There is no intention of letting usury-Capitalism disintegrate and be replaced by a dispensation which would be based on truth and worked in the interests of the peoples. It is permissible only to give way to Socialism in one form or another; the form of world control can be changed, "improved", but it must not be relaxed. It is for that reason that the observant will have noticed that attacks on Communism and discussions of its true nature are always incomplete and guarded and that consideration of the alternatives is often utterly futile by being so controlled and pruned, so watered-down. The world is given only two choices, and both originate from the same source.

Liberal dreamers, abstract thinkers, political theorists who have no practical experience and no aims, are not the sort of people who achieve power; and it is only those who do achieve power who matter historically. It is true, of course, that great spiritual influences, and in the first place Christianity, create a culture and civilization, a way of life, which gives purpose and direction to thought and action, but ultimately it is the practical results which are the substance of history, the fruit, good or bad, of the spiritual and intellectual forces which gave them birth. Even a Christian, who does not practice his faith is but an empty shell.

The rootless and abstract chatterers are either ineffective, or, if used by conscious fighters for real aims, they are useful as a secondary tool. The Liberals and democrats of the more academic kind were among the solvents which weakened and destroyed the fabric of Christian Europe. In Russia, too, the denationalized intelligentzia which stood between the Throne and the people brought about the collapse of the Empire, but they were not the forces which were able, or indeed which seriously intended, to take over power. The ridiculous hot air merchants of the Kerensky Provisional Government, which lasted for only a few months in 1917, after the abdication of the Czar, were incapable of any constructive act. They went through the motions of seriously believing, to all outward appearances, that elections and talkative assemblies were real originators and depositories of effective power. In fact these hotheads merely cleared the paths for the Bolsheviks who, in Lenin's words, found power lying in the gutter. They picked it up and used it.

There was nothing accidental about Lenin and his associates, nothing vague about their aims and actions. They knew exactly what was expected of them. They knew, in the first place, that theirs was a definite and practical problem. It was the seizure of power in Russia and then, with Russia's help, in the whole world, on behalf of the forces which had created them. This was the reason for their existence.

In this connexion we might quote the words of Lenin, the nominal founder of Communism in Russia, and of Comrade Nikita Khrushchev. Lenin said:

"To carry on war for the overthrow of the international bourgeoisie and to reject in advance manœuvring, the making use of contradictions in the interests (if only temporary) between enemies, of pretended agreements and compromises with possible (if only temporary, unstable, shaky conditional) allies, is that not an unboundedly funny thing?"

Khrushchev declared:

"In the West they say that since the Geneva Conference something has changed and the Soviet delegates now smile. If somebody thinks that the Soviet smiles imply the abandonment of the doctrines of Marx, Engels and Stalin, then they greatly deceive themselves. Those who expect this, will have to wait until the lobster whistles in the sea."

In view of the openly expressed opinions of the Communist tyrants, to which many quotations from Stalin and the others could be added, and in view of the utter immorality of the maintenance of "friendly contacts" with these criminals, it can well be imagined what the results must be.

Millions of subtle and false words, volumes of self-deception, innumerable pages of philosophical abstractions, all claim to explain the reasons why Bolshevism was born, why it came to power and what it tried to do when it was in the saddle. And it is true that, if we look back to root causes, we will be involved in a deep and wide problem, the problem of the struggle of good and evil, of the spiritual and the material, but in simple practical terms, on the level on which we can alone consider such matters in practice if we intend to deal with them effectively, we are faced with a conscious plan to take over world power. We are faced with a struggle for global authority, and we now observe its final stages.

Those who may wish to discover in greater detail just how Lenin and Stalin proposed to overwhelm the world, and how in fact they proceeded to do it, can study the writings of these and other leading Communists. They made no secret of their ideas. All methods were used: subversion, sabotage, propaganda, war, trade, dumping, popular fronts, trade union penetration etc. The formal instruments varied: The Third International, foreign Communist parties, the Soviet Secret Police and Diplomatic Service (both now almost entirely one and the same thing), the Comintern, Titoism, fellow travellers, and much else.

The fundamental fact which we must bear in mind is, as has been noted before, that Communism is not of Russian origin. It is only the virus which infected Russia when that country was weakened by internal causes and by war. It follows that the aims and methods of Communism are also not Russian. How could it be otherwise? Despite all slander, despite all the real shortcomings of Russia, it is a Christian country, converted a thousand years ago. The people are tough, but kind. The traditions of Russia are not cruel and, still less, diabolical.

We shall claim without qualification or fear of serious contradiction that Communism is a terrible western disease which has affected Russia because it was so new to it in its essentials, while the West, which always bore some of the virus in its veins, had developed a certain immunity. The fall of the innocent is often more dramatic than the slips of the hardened sinners. But, on the other hand, the process by which Russia is overcoming Communism—the antitoxins and new ideas and approaches which are developing there—will exert a decisive influence on world affairs.

Now here is the key to the possible end of Communism and to the true and effective line of the Christian and patriotic counterattack. We have already noted that the mere echoing of the proposition of Marxist dialectical materialism—that conditions determine outlook—and the resulting proposition that the spread of Communism can only be prevented by raising the standard of living, by investments in under-developed areas of the world, is no answer to the threat. It is merely the repetition of formulae suggested by the coiners and money-lenders, who are ever on the look-out for new markets, new victims of usury. As the bank advertisement says: "Money is our business".

While it would be wrong to be too dogmatic about this, it is very possible that quite soon there could be a Russo-Chinese clash, and not for Marxist, but for national reasons. Russia may have to consider a preventive war, and if that were to come about it would be the end of Communism in both Russia and China.

We have already mentioned that, in part, the differences between the Soviet Communists in Moscow and their former patrons in the West are due to the fact that Bolshevism had been somewhat affected by certain Russian motives. Also the present Soviet tyrants are no longer the pliable instrument of former times. They have their own ambitions, too. On the other hand they must react and struggle with a large number of factors inside Russia, which we have described in general terms as the nation's anti-toxins to Marxism. In short, the Soviet Communist weapon of the circles which are fighting for global power has done its work and, like the Moor, it can now go. Indeed, it is not merely a tool which is worn out, but one which harms the cause since it provokes too much resistance which it is unable to overcome, is not, in itself, the final form of Socialism which the conspirators require and is too largely discredited in the eyes of the world's public opinion.

So the candidates for world rule now come forward in the role of global liberators, and especially as the "democratic" saviours of those who are oppressed by "Russian Communism". This move also helps them to kill two birds with one stone: they are now "fighters for freedom", and they eliminate Russia as such, since that country, if not broken up, will never be reliably manageable.

The general strategy by which the conspirators have fostered Communism as an intermediary weapon, which had, as we have said, been their bulldozer to clear the ground for them, only to come forward, when they think that the job has been done, with their own alternative to the tyranny which they had created, is intended to assure to these conspirators the certainty of world power, and in the form which they require. With all financial, political and other resources at their disposal, they can hope to retain the initiative in the coming phase of the elimination of Soviet Marxism, a phase which has been touched off by them, but which they can no longer stop.

But the Hungarian example has shewn that the true wishes and interests of the nations under the Red yoke, indeed the soul and spirit of these nations, is by no means dead. Communism has not done its job; indeed it never could have done it. The proposition that soulless materialism can really kill the souls of men is fundamentally untrue, and in that fact lies the key to the ultimate failure of the materialistic messianists. That which has happened in Hungary, is latent everywhere. But on the other hand it must not be forgotten that the conspirators are careful to deal with their victims one by one. And they prepare their ground well. Therefore those who value true freedom must also make their own preparations, and of this more will be said below. Only thus will the heroism of the Hungarians be justly rewarded.

The true cause of the Hungarian rising of 1956 is not sufficiently widely known and understood, yet these events are of great and universal importance. In view of the fact that the Soviets had become somewhat unmanageable, those who exercize true power in the West decided to touch off "National-Communist" revolutions in Poland, Hungary and Roumania. The first action was taken in Hungary, in Poland preliminary measures were already in hand, and Roumania was to be last.

In order to make sure that a rising did not become a true counter-revolution, it was natural that leadership was at first given to Communists and the Left-wing elements under the veteran Hugarian Communist Imre Nagy, the companion of Bela Kuhn, and himself soaked in the blood of the victims of the Red terror.

But the whole game misfired. It was not Nagy who was the true political leader of Hungary, but Cardinal Mindszenty; it was not an "improved" Socialism which the nation really wanted, but a return to a Christian dispensation.

As soon as that became clear, the initiative in Poland and Roumania was abandoned and in Hungary the Soviets were given the green light to return in force and crush the rising. This was all the more "urgent" as Soviet troops were going over to the anti-Red Hungarians. This round had been won by the Moscow Reds.

But that is by no means the end of the matter. Either there will be an agreement at one of the coming "Summits", and that is what they are really about, or there will be a modified initiative against the present rulers behind the "Curtain" in order to bring both halves of the world under a unified control under political conditions which suit the candidates for global rule. In view of the Hungarian experience that new attack may have a very "conservative" appearance, and true adherents of the Right will have to be careful in order not to be deceived.

We are now called on by fate to be ready to take over the initiative. To national-Communism or any other form of international Socialism, whatever the false label by which it is camouflaged, we must oppose the Christian and national themes of the countries to which we belong, while also maintaining a common front against the common enemy. And we must also be sure that the bonds of usury Capitalism will be eliminated at the same time as those of its Socialist progeny. We must return to the moral and natural order, we must submit to the laws of God. In the place of the controlled and bogus liberation which the materialists are trying to engineer, we must put the real struggle for freedom. We must reject the materialistic alternative to Marxism, and instead fight for policies which are an expression of real spiritual values. This concerns equally all lands, on both sides of the Iron Curtain. Those peoples who are still free to act, must help those who are enslaved. All are equally threatened by the coming global new Socialism.

20

Russia's Struggle with Communism

What were Russian reactions to the dangerous infection with the Red pestilence? What were the feverish symptoms, the efforts at resistance? Since the fatal days at the end of February and the beginning of March 1917 O.S., when Nicholas II wrote in his diary that he was surrounded by treachery, deception and cowardice, and when apparently isolated and betrayed, he succumbed to the pressure of vain madmen and abdicated his Throne, the whole fifty years have been a constant struggle in various forms. It is true that the act of abdication itself left a dreadful void in the consciousness of the mass of the Russian people, which has not been filled to this day. But, deprived though they are of the natural leadership which had taken them from small beginnings to the highest achievements in all spheres of human effort, the Russians still fought as best they could.

The chain of events which led to the abdication of the Czar can be traced back for two centuries, but there is in all probability one set of circumstances which, more than the others, pre-determined the tragical end of Nicholas II. The forces of revolution were able to come to the surface and engineer very widespread troubles in many parts of the Empire after the Russo-Japanese war, in 1905. But the revolution was then crushed and the mass of the nation was in no way involved. However, the circles which supported subversion were then, though not strong enough to seize power, nevertheless sufficiently able to exploit the situation in order to wrest from the Throne the grant of a Constitution and the partial limitation of the powers of the Crown. This was an admission of defeat, a serious capitulation of the régime, and to forces and ideas known to be anti-Christian and subversive.

Politically and psychologically this broke the back of the old order; its enemies were encouraged and strengthened, its supporters weakened and deprived of full self-confidence. When the next major test came in 1917, the enemies of the Church and of Russia triumphed and the Czar, who had relinquished, if even more symbolically than in fact, his ultimate power as the temporal symbol of Christian truth—which was the only justification of Autocracy—found himself almost alone, with too few to defend the Throne.

This moral and political deflation of the forces of real anti-Communism, which is the greater part of the strength of the Soviets, since they lack any virtue whatever, is still an important factor in the Russian situation. It follows that only under the banners of the Christian Monarchy will the Russian nation be able to throw off the yoke of Red slavery.

From this it does not follow that constitutional forms of government and popular representation are evils in themselves. That is by no means the case. But those political and administrative forms which came into being as the direct result of violent anti-Christian action are certain to be not only poisoned by the virus of godless materialism, but to be its active proponents. The Russian revolutionaries, guided by evil forces abroad were, from their point of view, far-sighted and right in assassinating the Emperor Alexander II, as he had already prepared a constitutional plan and was about to promulgate corresponding new laws, which were to complement his great legal reforms and especially the liberation of the serfs, which had taken place in the 1860s. The crime of 1881 prevented the introduction of constitutional changes on the initiative and by the authority of the Christian sovereign, and made sure that changes would take place under pressure from anti-Christian quarters and for anti-Christian purposes. That Nicholas II reserved for himself ultimate sovereign rights, as, no doubt, his grandfather would also have done, was not enough. The virus of triumphant subversion in the name of materialistic slavery was in the air, camouflaged as democracy and liberalism, and the resulting drama had become almost completely assured. Theoretically it is arguable that, perhaps, a strong policy and the energetic and even ruthless re-assertion of the Imperial régime, which would have been so fully justified in conditions of war, might have prevented the catastrophe, but the faultiness of this assumption would lie in its ignoring the fact that concessions had been made in conditions in which they were bound to do immense harm, and thus it is not possible to assume that in the same conditions the opposite policy could have been pursued.

We emphasize, however, that we may by no means lay the blame at the door of the martyred Nicholas II. Like the whole of Russia, which he both ruled and personified, he was the innocent victim of a terrible spiritual disease, which now threatens the whole world. The suffering and death of the Emperor, his family and many millions of Russians are the seeds of tomorrow's certain resurrection.

Almost as soon as the Soviets were in power, there began the Civil War, which lasted from 1918 until 1920, and in the Far East until 1922. It failed because the Whites suffered from political and moral shock, from a kind of mass inferiority complex, a collective failure of their beliefs. This process had been developing even before the revolution. The intelligentzia lived in an atmosphere in which everything foreign was wonderful and everything Russian secondrate, whereas in fact the opposite was nearer the truth, not only of culture and civilization, but even of the quality of industrial production. But the rootless and empty denationalized and semi-educated tribe of Russia's Bloomsbury had succeeded in spreading this mood sufficiently widely. When the Empire fell, all Russians were affected by this emasculation of the mind and spirit.

So it was that the Civil War, heroic though it was, and necessary though it was psychologically and historically, since without it the honour and self-respect of Russia would have been lost forever—it is not a country which had the right to succumb to Bolshevism without a fight—was lost. The Whites failed because they did not dare to proclaim the aims which all of them had at heart, and all of them knew it. None, with very few exceptions, dared to say openly that the Nation remained Monarchist and Christian. Instead the slogans were in favour of non-predetermination of the future, which was to be settled by a Constituent Assembly. The Whites fought for nothing tangible and their only aim was negative: they were against Communism. In particular they had no answer to the burning questions which the Communists raised and answered: the land which still remained in the hand of the squires, to be given to the peasants and other related matters; also immediate peace.

But no sooner had the Civil War ended, than there was the rising of the sailors in Kronstadt, the great naval island fortress outside the capital, Petrograd. This was suppressed by force of arms; the troops attacked the fortress across the frozen sea. In the years which followed there were peasant and Cossack risings in many parts of the country. The struggle is not at an end.

In the very first years of Soviet rule Lenin tried to introduce extreme Communist economic methods. Money itself was abolished and those who had a worker's passport, a work book, were able to obtain free lodgings, food, travel etc. It is obvious that the system was an utter failure. A great famine spread over the land and all life began to come to a standstill. Lenin, who had always preached flexibility, if other methods failed, did not persevere. He introduced the New Economic Policy (NEP), which meant that for most people normal conditions were reintroduced. It was again possible to buy and sell, to own farms, shops, workshops. Only transport and heavy industry remained in the hands of the state. Soon Russia was again on the way to ordinary prosperity. It was another fight of the nation, of human nature, of common sense, against the evil and unnatural régime.

At the end of the 1920s Stalin decided to bring the reign of the NEP to an end. He was faced not merely by a situation in which Russia was no longer Socialist and in which therefore, there was no relationship at all between foreign activities, which were directed towards the attainment of the world rule of Marxism, and the internal situation, which was not Marxist at all. But that was not in itself the most compelling reason for radical change. Stalin, like Lenin before him, ruled Russia through the Communist party, which was his only support and chief tool. If the party were to weaken or disappear, his rule would have been at an end. Even the Secret Police, the Tcheka, OGPU, NKVD, MVD, KGB, was only a branch of the party. The latter also controlled the army and general administration of the country, by placing its own men in key positions. It was an open conspiracy to maintain power by force. But during the NEP the party was almost entirely unemployed, and it was withering away.

While the terrorist police, under its various names from Tcheka to KGB, was a part of the whole machinery of Communist government from the very beginning, its role in the Soviet State was, also from the start, immense. Owing to the fact that Marxism is unnatural and fundamentally unacceptable to normal people, including the Russians, it was understood by Lenin and his colleagues and mentors that organized terror had to be an integral part of the régime. And to be effective, the machine of terror had to be very powerful. As a result the secret police became, as soon as it was established, a state within the state, and so strong that even Lenin was not able to control it properly. In more than one case, for example, the Tcheka killed men notwithstanding the fact that Lenin had given orders that they were to be spared, or even given important Soviet appointments.

It is believed by some competent observers that it was the thirst for blood of the Tcheka-GPU-NKVD-MVD-KGB which enabled Stalin to use it effectively in his own struggle for power within the Red hierarchy, as he was in full sympathy with the sadistic appetite of the terrorists and willing to give them all they wanted. To the Tcheka and its successors a massive and constant blood-letting was a logical action. On the one hand only criminal and degenerate people were willing to enter the service of such an institution, and only they would be accepted, and on the other hand, once they had made themselves responsible for the most atrocious crimes on the largest possible scale, they well knew that there was no return: they would have to maintain themselves by blood and terror, or be crushed.

That the régime and in particular the terroristic police have repeatedly destroyed their own leaders and members is also inevitable. The mutual suspicions, hates, jealousies and oppositions must, quite naturally, reach the greatest possible intensity. It is for such reasons that the Communist Party government has more than once removed the heads of the secret police, the most recent instance being the liquidation of Beria. The rule of the party is continually endangered by the ambitions of the police, and yet the party cannot remove it.

The ultimate consequences of these strains and complex interrelations, to which the pressure of the Russian nation must be added, cannot be clearly foreseen in detail. All that can be said safely is that, sooner or later, such a situation will have become unbearable and will break. Then the various organized forces in the country, such as the army, the administrative personnel, the professional classes and especially the Church, will each play its role. The living Russia will assuredly emerge from the red cocoon. It is continually struggling to do so.

Yet we must always be on our guard. Recent events in Poland and Hungary have shewn that, on both sides of the "Curtain", encouragement is being given to a bogus political change, to "national-Communism", to an attempt to prove that Socialism is compatible with freedom. These policies must be opposed and those who truly value liberty for themselves and for others must help the true patriots in all subjected lands to assert themselves and save their countries and the world from Socialistic slavery. That struggle concerns all the peoples everywhere.

In part, the NEP lasted as long as it did also because after the death of Lenin in 1924 of the syphilis which had eaten away his evil brain, Stalin had to spend years in consolidating his own position. His struggle with competitors for power within the Communist structure was long and fierce. He had to establish himself sufficiently firmly before he could tackle economic and social changes of great significance the more so as they were to go entirely against the grain of Russia. But, concessions for a time apart, the struggle for global domination had to be resumed. Otherwise the Soviets would have been deprived of the support of their true masters and would have been doomed.

If that struggle for power was largely a fight inside the ranks of the Communists, there were also national factors which played their part in the terrible game. Bolshevism and, perhaps, Stalin himself, were not immune from the influence of the country on which they had fixed themselves as a poisonous parasite. The blood which they sucked in such torrents also influenced them. And, after all, some of them were even Russians.

Then, after 1933, there was also the threat of the approaching war with Germany. Stalin and his associates had no illusions and knew that the Russians would not fight for them or that for which they stood. It became necessary to undertake two measures: to purge the ranks of the military leadership of all those who might be disloyal, and at the same time to make the régime appear to be so national as to encourage the nation to think that it would be defending not Marx, Lenin and Stalin, but eternal Russia. It was necessary to remove true nationalists and replace them with pretended ones; to make the façade more Russian, while making the policy even less so. But again, with the qualification that a great deal of the national will and aspirations had seeped into Communism in Russia. It was a tight rope act, and Stalin succeeded, though with a small margin of safety.

The enforced collectivization of the farms in the countryside, the socialization of agriculture, had been resisted by the whole peasantry. Some millions were artificially starved to death in order to force the rest to accept the virtual end of private ownership of land, one of the most fundamental desires of all those who work on the land. It has also been one of the chief slogans of the Communists at the time of the revolution and Civil War, when they held out the hope of the immediate transfer of the small part of the arable land of Russia, about 10 per cent still in hands of the former big landowners. It was a deliberate deception, as the Bolsheviks at the same time preached doctrines which made private ownership of the means of production, and in the first place of the land, quite impossible under their rule. But the struggle of the régime with the peasantry has never ceased. Here, as in almost all else, the Soviet rulers sit on the crater of a volcano which, sooner or later, will erupt.

But if the desire for ordinary freedom, for the possession of one's land, and much else, were and are the motives of almost all ordinary, normal people, there are in Russia also other motives which lead to the suppressed, but very real, inner tensions within the USSR, indeed within each individual Russian. The revolution did not only bring about social and economic changes, most of which in their ultimate forms went completely against the grain, but the revolution also enforced great political changes. Not only was the old order overthrown in that the Monarchy was abolished and all aspects of the administration, justice, education and so much else were completely altered, but the very name of Russia was almost-entirely abolished; it only remains hidden in the initials RSFSR (the Russian Soviet Federal Socialist Republic), which is one of the administrative divisions of the USSR (the Union of Soviet Socialist Republics). Internationalism and the alleged interests of the working classes of the world, and the ultimate establishment of the global rule of the Socialists, were the new motives of state policy, and not the protection of the legitimate and limited interests of the Russian Empire as such. Indeed the interests of Russia became quite secondary and were sacrificed to the interests of the world-wide criminal conspiracy of the Reds.

In the circumstances there could be only one result: as Russia and the Russians were clearly not dying, Russia would in the end overcome the pestilential red bacillus and parasite. It thus became necessary for the Soviet dictators to make concessions to Russian nationalism, while at the same time trying to attain their ultimate aims before the pressure of Russia overcame them, either by transforming the régime or by throwing it off. This struggle is still in being. It is much complicated by the fact that, of course, over fifty years of Communist terroristic rule have greatly transformed the outward moral and psychological appearance of most Russians. Their true selves are driven underground in each man and woman, and the true Russia, and especially the true Russian Orthodox Church (not the officially tolerated parody of it, fully controlled by the MVD), are in the catacombs. There is even in Russia a well-defined phenomenon of the "internal emigration", of people who have successfully isolated themselves from all Communist influences and live in their own spiritual spheres, having open contacts in this life only with very few trusted friends. But this class is very large.

Even apart from the evidence of Russians who have spent long years under the Soviets, there is that of many foreigners of different nationalities—Poles, Germans, Austrians, Americans—who have been in communist prisons and concentration camps, sometimes for many years. All make a complete distinction between the régime and the people and all confirm that the mass of Russians, and even some who are in positions of responsibility, such as camp guards, display Christian mercy and kindness in their strongest forms. Being themselves starved, Russians nominally free always do all they can to help those in the camps or otherwise in trouble, irrespective of their origins. In fact the spiritual atmosphere of Russia is such that, despite the physical misery, Russians and non-Russians who appear outside the iron curtain are always shocked by the deadly materialism, egoism and spiritual indifference of the still free world. There are Russians who, while hating Communism and the Soviets with every thought and instinct, nevertheless go back, knowing that they will be "punished" for their "treason", for having been abroad without permission, and who yet cannot stand life in the spiritual desert of the West.

Unfortunately it must also be admitted that, inevitably, long years of terror have taught Russians the arts of dissimulation. Nobody reads Soviet papers literally; intelligent people read them between the lines. It is thus that they understand what is really happening. But outwardly they follow the official line and each of its zigzags. They hold themselves in reserve. But even when they escape and reach the West, they still use the acquired arts of chameleonic adaptations to circumstances. If the agents of the US Intelligence ask for their political views, it takes them very little time to discover that the proper answer is that they are in favour of a Republic, and all the rest. And, alas, not a few will also accept paid jobs in political outfits whose objectives are well known to be opposed to all that which Russians hold dear. Luckily such Russians are a small minority. They may seem to be more, as others are silenced by the pressures which money can exert, positively and negatively.

The war played an enormous part in the crystallization of the new, yet essentially old, Russian consciousness. Its approach was felt in Russia, among the rulers and the ruled, from the day when Hitler obtained power in Germany in the beginning of 1933. It cannot be our purpose here to discuss all the details of the events inside Russia in the years which preceded the war, and it must suffice to say that the Soviets had at no time any illusions as to what the Russians would fight for, and what would fail to stimulate their resistance and willingness to attack.

A political parallel to the economic NEP had to be perpetrated; it was necessary to yield much in appearances and even reality, while retaining the essential levers of power and the possibilities of reversing the process in that which was fundamental, as soon as the opportunity came. In many respects this was an easier proposition than the NEP which Lenin had to permit. That had been a reality which transformed the life of all Russia; the Stalinist New Political Policy, as distinct from Lenin's New Economic Policy, was much more a matter of façade. But even symbols have their own powerful reality and educational influence. The effects of the new policies were by no means negligible. In fact they won the war for Stalin, whose huge hoax succeeded. But the seeds which were sown will, in the end, win the struggle for Russia.

In brief, the reforms outwardly concerned such things as the restoration of the old military ranks and uniforms, the creation of new orders and decorations in honour of the Saints, Czars and heroes of prerevolutionary Russia, the renaming of Peoples' Commissars into Ministers and much else. More definitely there were such things as the abolition of legal abortion, which is now permissible not on request, but only if a doctor considers it to be essential, the making of divorce far more difficult, the propaganda in favour of family ties, changes in education, in the writing of history, and so on. Even the positive role of the Russian Church and Russian Rulers in the past was officially recognized. Patriotism became a virtue, though not to the exclusion of Socialist internationalism.

Here we could observe a great duplicity. One hand cautiously gave concessions, while the other hand firmly held on to what are essentials from the Soviet point of view. At the same time, too, Stalin was still completing his struggle for power within the Communist hierarchy. This struggle had little in common with the desires and needs of the Russians; for them a Trotzky was no better than a Stalin. But Stalin had to have an internally unified and stable régime. He also needed an army whose rank and file would fight, as for many centuries past, for Russia, while its commanders would be loyal to the Soviet tyranny. The events which led Marshal Tukhatchevsky and two-thirds of the officers from Colonel upwards into traps laid by agents-provocateurs and to their liquidation, weakened the army by so massive a removal of qualified officers, but it assured the loyalty of the leaders of the armed forces in the coming conflict.

However, when the war began on the eastern front, Russia was at first split. The motives of patriotism and national self-defence mingled with the wish to escape at last from the tentacles of the Red monster and, more, the wish to join those who were assumed to be fighting for the destruction of that monster and were, therefore, thought to be the natural allies of the Russian people.

It was very widely assumed at that time that the Germans would crush the Soviet Union in a matter of six weeks. On the day when the attack began we were commissioned by the London newspaper *Daily Mail* to write three articles on the Russian situation. They were published in the last days of June and the 1st of July, and were thus not an example of being wise after the event. In these articles we forecast correctly that the Germans would enter very deep into Russia, so far, in fact, as to force the Soviet government to transfer the capital temporarily from Moscow further to the East (which, of course, actually took place later), but we also told our readers that, nevertheless, the Germans would leave Russia after being completely defeated. And so it was. It had been known to many Russians abroad, and could not have been fully understood by those in Russia, who were almost completely cut off from true information, that the Germans would come not as anti-Communist liberators, but as anti-Russian would-be conquerors. We had read "Mein Kampf" in the German original, and much else, too.

But the fact remains, as anticipated, that millions of Russians, military and civilians, went over to the Germans. The German Army had in its ranks one million Russians as German soldiers. There was the Russian Liberation Army of General Vlassov, and much else.

Only when the Russians realized without any doubt that the

Nazified Germans, not so much the leaders of the army as the political forces actually in power, despised them and were in all respects their enemies, intent on taking Russian lands, splitting Russia up and eliminating part of its population, while making slaves of the rest, did real resistance begin. Hitler could have had his victory in Russia in a matter of weeks, but only with the help of the Russians. He not only refused his chances, but killed four million Russian prisoners of war by starvation. We cannot help remembering that in 1933 the German Communist party, then having a voting strength of some four millions, was ordered to vote for the Nazis by the Comintern; we cannot help wondering just why Hitler insisted, despite good advice to the contrary, on a suicidal policy from which only Stalin could gain. If it is true that the Russians are like raddishes—red outside and white right through, it may have been true that the Nazis were like roast beef—brown outside and red right through. We do not suggest anything but it is true that Bolshevism was in great danger and was saved, and it is also true that in 1925 Goebbels wrote, in the *Völkischer Beobachter*, the official paper of the NSDAP (Nazis), an "Open Letter to a Young Bolshevik" in which he made comparisons between German National-Socialists and Russian National-Bolsheviks, and he concluded by writing: "Young Bolshevik, we welcome you!" What a welcome.

However, it must not be forgotten that Hitler was not only supported by Communist votes, but by the money of German industrialists and American bankers, in some cases working through German Jewish ones. And it is a fact that the only concrete consequence of the National-Socialist activity was to have given half the world to Communism and to have driven very many Jews to Palestine, thus making Israel independence possible by assuring a sufficient population. The conclusion cannot be escaped that, consciously or not, Hitler was somebody's gigantic agent-provocateur. Did he not write in "Mein Kampf": "I have chosen for my movement the red flag of Socialism." And in German-occupied Russia all the manifestations of Socialism were left intact and used by the Germans. And there is much other evidence which, in many different ways, points in a smilar direction. The Führer was at all times surrounded by spies and traitors.

If the role of Hitler had been complex and not devoid of inner contradictions, some of them in all probability not understood by the Führer himself, the same can be said of the West today in its relations with Soviet Russia. It is true that, despite fundamental errors, Hitler had been in part consistent. In "Mein Kampf" he said: "The German sword must conquer Russian soil for the German plough". This attitude can explain to a great extent his unwillingness even to pretend to be an anti-Communist in Russia, though the true picture is by no means as simple as that.

Similarly it can be said that Western policy during the later part of the last war and after it seemed to start with an active pro-Soviet line, pursued until about the late Summer of 1947, when this policy made way for the Cold War, the Marshall Plan, NATO and so on. But again this apparent anti-Communism is never really effective. We have never been told that Communism is an evil which must be annihilated, as we had been told about National-Socialism.

Of course, it was still possible years ago to think of destroying Hitler, while his armies were of more or less manageable size, and he possessed no nuclear bombs. It is quite another matter to challenge the Communists today, when they can mobilize immense and tough armies and can drop bombs and fire rockets with the most deadly destructive charges.

But fear alone is not the true neutralizer. As we have mentioned elsewhere, there was no hesitation in destroying the Nazis, but there is every inhibition when it comes to eliminating Socialism, whatever its form and location.

And yet it would be rash to claim that the global shadow-boxing which we observe is really completely devoid of any element of true enmity. In the years between 1947 and 1953, when the process came to a head, there had developed in Russia an increasing independence of the Soviet Communist bosses from their former creators and mentors, the Lords of High Finance, the would-be members of a World Government. It is clear that the Soviets are not abandoning the methods and aims of Communism, and we can assume that they want to continue the game of global enslavement, but with the purpose of being masters of the world themselves.

They know not only that the leaders of the West dare not attack them militarily, but also that their opponents are helpless politically, since they also dare not abolish Socialism in Russia and the satellites, which would be its end everywhere. So the Soviets can well afford to humiliate the West at Summit meetings. They know that the men behind them sit on a sinking raft where Capitalism is concerned, and dare not destroy its only alternative, Socialism, which could still assure them continued power. In these spheres we must look for the true theses which are discussed at the "Summit". Here we must search for the proper strategy and tactics of real, not pretended anti-Communism. The situation described offers us great opportunities, but equally a failure to understand all these matters must lead to complete ineffectiveness in the struggle against godlessness and enslavement.

When making a fuller and correct estimate of Russian internationalism and external defence, we must not lose sight of the fact that the Red army was in no sense fully comparable with the Imperial one. It was an army with a split mind and spirit and a correspondingly split command; there were motives of true Russian patriotism and opposed to them were motives of moral and political opposition and defection. At the same time decisions were taken not alone by the military commanders at all levels, but also by parallel and controlling Communist political commissars. This obviously hampered single-mindedness in general attitude and in practical initiative and responsibility. In short there was a tremendous fall in efficiency and effectiveness.

Suffice it to remind ourselves of the fact that, in two campaigns during the period of the last war the whole of the USSR with its huge army and large navy could not defeat, but only exhaust little Finland. It is worse than if France had been unable to defeat Luxemburg in three days, when not engaged on any other front.

In 1914 the Imperial army advanced into Germany to save Paris and France; in 1941 the Red army suffered immediate and immense defeats. During the first three and a half years of the First World War the Central Powers were only very slowly able to take relatively small areas of Russia, and on the Austro-Hungarian and Turkish front it were the Russians who fought on enemy territory; in the Second World War the Germans occupied in several months an area containing half the population of the whole USSR. In 1914–17 Russia provided almost all its own requirements in arms and ammunition for its immense armies, although suffering the consequences of the unwillingness of its Western Allies to deliver certain armaments which had been ordered before the war; in 1941–45 the USSR was catastrophically short of everything, even of food, and was helped by its allies on an immense scale. The performance of the Soviet state and armed forces was very poor indeed.

But the red régime enjoyed one advantage which was partly lacking to sustain the Empire; when war came the leading personnel rallied to the government, and the circumstances that its motives were usually of no higher order than self-defence and self-interest, does not alter the practical facts.

Consequently when the final show-down comes all will depend on the correct estimate of the then condition of the Soviet armed forces, morally and practically, on the mood of the nation and on the political preparations made by the opponents of the Communist block. In a speech Lord Avon wisely suggested the creation of a Western general staff of political warfare. These are the words of a statesman with very long experience as Foreign Secretary and Prime Minister. He has not always been successful, but this proposal deserves the greatest possible attention. On its proper solution depends the fate of the world. Meanwhile we must not allow ourselves to be deluded by any such deceptive appearances as the deliberate "no-win" wars in Korea and Viet-Nam. Such exercises, as also hand-outs to inefficient nations, are needed because usury-Capitalism requires massive monetary wastage to achieve balance, while at the same time these policies provide a false façade of anti-communism and the reality of power.

21

Allied Mistakes Towards Russia

But if the Germans, led by Hitler, threw the Russians who wanted to join him in a fight against Communism back into the murderous and hated embraces of the Soviets, it is a fact that exactly the same policy was pursued by the Western Allies. Before the end of the war some Russians in British hands, who had been taken in France, were forcibly shipped to the USSR. But the worst actions were perpetrated a little later, began soon after the end of the war and continued for three years, until the late Summer of 1947.

Now it must be understood that in the circumstances there has developed in Russia a situation in which the people, both at home and in exile, are divided by two main motives: willingness to serve the hated Soviets, and determination to fight them at all costs. But the latter intention cannot be absolutely unqualified. No man will cure a head-ache by cutting off his head; no Russian wants to overthrow Communism at the cost of the annihilation of Russia. It is not that Communism is in the least acceptable, but merely that the issue must be postponed if the fate of Russia is at stake. It is obvious that this fact gives the enemies of Russia as also the friends of Communism certain opportunities, while it brings them face to face with certain dangers.

At the moment of the collapse of the "Third Reich" Communism was in a position in which it could have been eliminated without the least difficulty. Indeed even earlier, when the German attack began, an attack which all people with their eyes open had anticipated since 1933, and those with even greater foresight since the time when Scheubner-Richter was killed at Hitler's and Ludendorff's side in the streets of Munich during the attempted Nazi Putsch in the 1920s and was replaced by Rosenberg, the renegade, it had been possible to play the anti-Bolshevik card. It was only necessary to let the Russians know that such action was aimed solely at the régime, and not at Russia and that, consequently, all Russians were welcome as allies in the common struggle. To do otherwise was to drive them unwillingly into the arms of the hated régime.

In the early summer of 1945, and for some time after, it would have been easy for the Allies to imply and even to say (however insincerely) that the German attack on Russia had been opposed by them and that it follows that they were not the enemies, but the friends of the Russians, as distinct from the Soviet Communists. But Roosevelt had deliberately rejected the offers of Molotov to alter the whole Soviet policy, with the introduction of free voting and the rest in Russia, thinking it good policy "not to impose conditions on the Russians", but accept them as allies, without strings. Incidentally, it is a part of a deliberate policy of misrepresentation always to confuse "the Russians" with the "Communists", when in fact one is the terroristic tyrant and the other his victim.

Apart from the numerous emigrés who had left Russia after the revolution and Civil War and in the years which followed, in addition to large numbers of members of the Russian minorities in a number of border states, there appeared in the West, predominantly in Germany, Austria and Italy, huge numbers of Russians who had either fled from Russia or had been taken by the Germans as prisoners or "Ostarbeiter". Hardly any of these millions wanted to return to the USSR. To the Soviets the existence of the pre-War exiles had been a great danger, but now the mass of the political emigrés was greatly increased and strengthened by the addition of huge numbers of Russians who had spent most or all their lives under Communist rule and knew Soviet Russian conditions and moods completely.

The Western Allies—Great Britain, the United States of America and France—at the demand of the Soviets, agreed to hand over all Russians other than those who had emigrated before the war, and it was agreed to hand them over forcibly if they proved unwilling to go voluntarily. This was done during three years on the instructions of the governments of the western states. Thousands of Yugoslavs and others were similarly treated.*

Yet on the other hand there are hundreds of thousands of Russians who have for many years, as we have, enjoyed the true liberties, the peace, the well-being, the civilized way of life and the fair-mindedness and kindness of the Britons, the Americans, the French, and all the others. None of us will ever forget this and we shall never be ungrateful. We fully understand that the crimes which our western friends committed were imposed on them. Our hosts of so many years were gravely misled. It is not by chance that the period of such criminal policies also coincided with a spread of Communist rule over half the world's population. Something is gravely wrong. To co-operate with the devil, to become his helper, is a dangerous thing.

In 1945 the West had the atom bomb, and the Soviets did not. The Russian armies and the Communist machine were greatly

---

* "Operation Keelhaul" involved millions of Russians and hundreds of thousands of Yugoslavs. Many thousands were killed in the process and thousands committed suicide. It was a terrible Allied crime.

strained; the West and especially America, was relatively far less exhausted. The USSR was in mortal political danger; the West was not. There was a revolutionary situation behind the iron curtain, but not outside it, and it was of much greater force than it had been in Russia in 1917, because it involved the mass of the nation, and not merely a part of the intelligentzia. All that was needed in 1945 was a call by the western leaders to the people of Russia over the heads of their oppressors, a call backed by the millions of Russian anti--Communists in western hands, all anxious to fight for the liberation of Russia. The excuse that it would not have been right or practicable to "betray" the Soviet ally cannot be sustained as, firstly, this ally had treated the West with the utmost treachery at all times and had been the ally of Hitler during the war, and secondly, because in the First World War the West did not hesitate to give open support to the enemies of the Imperial régime even during the war itself, and also after it. The collapse of the Soviet Socialist tyranny could have been brought about in a matter of weeks, rather than months. But we have already explained that the Russian prisoner has to be transferred from one jail to another, but not allowed to escape. We have also explained that there are enemies in control both in the East and in the West, and the problem of true liberty is not related to that of the present form of the struggle between the "liberty-loving" West and the Soviets. Too much has been done for too many years to save Communism to make this bit of global shadow-boxing in the least convincing to those who know something of the underlying facts.

If there are some who may think that the West has not indulged in shadow-boxing with Communism and that all the various anti-Communist words should be taken seriously, then let them ask themselves whether they can recall any single instance of serious and effective anti-Communist action of the West, which in any way truly endangered the Soviet régime. We can, of course, quote plenty of examples of the opposite, of Soviet Communist expansion and the overthrow of non-Communist states. We could, without difficulty, point out how the West has for years systematically yielded country after country, in Europe and Asia and the Americas, to the Reds, and quite unnecessarily. We can give countless examples of treachery and treason, but we can recall not a single instance of serious counter-attack.

UNO is a glaring example of this line. Founded by a committee whose leading light and secretary-general was Alger Hiss, a convicted Communist agent, UNO is not an organization which even formally pretends to defend and to further virtue. On the contrary, its rules gives the Communists not only equality of standing and influence, but even a veto on all effective action. In the circumstances UNO can help Communism, if only by neutralizing action against it and by legalizing the status quo now and in the future.

But perhaps it could be claimed that such pacts as NATO and SEATO are effective anti-communism in action. It is a truism that only counter-attack is an effective form of defence, and of that there is no sign. We are not suggesting war, but political attack. But what have we seen in practice? The US-sponsored "Voice of America" and "Radio Free Europe" etc. have called on the satellite nations to rise, and when they did so, and Hungary was the most glaring and most heroic example, they (or strictly their patrons) did nothing at all to help those who fought for freedom. Indeed by encouraging rebellion and then failing to support it, these US Intelligence-backed outfits became, willingly or otherwise, effective agents-provocateurs, working in favour of the Soviets. Yet there were no official voices outside the USA which disclaimed this conduct. The fight with Communism has not yet begun in the West.

The war in Korea, officially fought by UNO, was deliberately lost to the Reds. Now the war in Viet-Nam, officially fought by the USA, i.e. by the same overlords, is again not being won deliberately against a Communist opponent, endangering the whole of South-East Asia and a great deal more as well.

And let it be remembered that, by secret agreement when UNO was being set up, the "minister for war" of that subversive organization is always a Soviet nominee.

22

The Motives of the World Struggle

We must consider then what are true motives which underlie the real struggle between what might be described in a simplified way as the Right and the Left. What is the stimulus behind all revolutionary movements? What is it about? Is it liberty, equality, democracy, social justice and so on? Is it a fight for national aspirations? Or is it a struggle for world power by men who use various slogans only to deceive their future victims?

Is it not possible, we ask again, that those who originated Communism as part of a plan of world-subjugation and who conquered Russia, and then other countries, and who now stand on the threshold of world government, must at all costs keep the Russian people out of the game, as also the Poles, the Hungarians, the Chinese and the rest, and, indeed, must keep the Russians in the mass isolated, while a few Russian hirelings do the job? Would it not follow that an active alliance between those in the West, in Britain, America, Germany, France, Spain—and in all the Christian and indeed civilized lands—and the Russians would be the only way in which we could all hope to reverse the trends which now lead us all to godless slavery?

The true motives underlying, on the one hand, the religious traditional, stable and hierarchical way of life, with the acceptance of property in the hands of individuals, and, on the other hand, the revolutionary, egalitarian, socialistic and irreligious ways of life are not those motives which are usually quoted. Fundamentally the Right is religious. It accepts the laws of the Universe, which are the Laws of God. It knows that that which conflicts with the natural law is sinful, and that consequently, sin is harmful. The Right accepts the fact that men are not equal, that they have a right to own that which they need to sustain themselves and their families and maintain their personal independence, which is true freedom. It recognizes that men and women are made as they are and that there are equal numbers of them, and that the complete natural process of rearing children occupies a whole lifetime, and therefore it is the law that marriage should be with one partner and for life. The Right knows that there is a natural authority, both spiritual and temporal, there is a natural and God-given law, and that that authority is thus Divinely ordained. In its highest development the Right is Christian. It knows that the ultimate purpose of life is preparation for the life everlasting and this passing phase is a short preparation and examination. It knows that the salvation of mankind and the Resurrection are the most important facts of human existence and that while we are on earth we should do to others only that which we expect of them, in a spirit of love. The Right thus needs, in moral and political terms, a King, a Prophet and a Priest. The King could be elective for a time, or for life, or hereditary, and he could be called by other than royal names, but he must be a servant and protector of the natural order, accepting Divine guidance and sanctified by the Church. All this would be a part of a statement of the position in its most developed forms. Humanity being imperfect, the full development of this scheme is seldom attained, but these assumptions define the Right. Certain aspects of Big Business are sometimes mistaken for the Right.

In contrast, the Left is irreligious, rationalistic, based not on the acceptance of Divine and natural law, but on the fundamental proposition of the deification of man. This, of course, is a flattering deception, since man is not God, but God's creation. When the Devil tempted Our Lord, he offered Him all the kingdoms of the earth. That is the bait. It is also the story of the fall of man, of the wish to know good and evil, through man's private judgment, of being master of one's fate. It is not merely the recognition of free will, which is well used, in humility, only if used in accordance with the Divine law; it is the postulate of the Left that man's wishes and desires are the law in themselves. But since that is a vain, proud and false delusion, those who accept the theory fall into a fatal trap. Not being able to exercise the ultimate sovereignty which they are tempted to claim, they become the slaves of the Tempter and of his agents.

It is therefore, the first wish of the materialistic false messianists to persuade men that they should by no means retain their faith in God, that they should on no account submit to Divinely ordained spiritual and political authority but that they must claim complete and unlimited sovereignty for themselves, in the persons of their elected representatives. The Left triumphs as soon as the States based on the assumption of Divine sanction and the service of God, and the Churches, are overthrown, and children are brought up laically or even to hate and despise the Faith of their forbears. Here, too, there are many gradations, many stages of degradation, but ultimately that is the process.

It would not be correct to oversimplify the issue so as to make it appear that any elective representatives of the people, who participate in the lawmaking and administration of the country, are, as such, the agents of the Devil. All depends on the assumptions which underlie any given system of government. If the popular assemblies are themselves governed by an unqualified acceptance of Christianity and if they thus realize that their sovereignty is definitely limited, and that, indeed, they are not the supreme Sovereign, but its faithful servants—a legal formula which still holds good in England, though we suspect that its spirit is no longer quite intact—then such a legislature is in the larger and higher sense of the Right. But as soon as the assumption becomes law, and is accepted, that full sovereignty is vested in individuals or assemblies which are not subject to Divine guidance, then whatever may be the temporary political policy of these institutions, they are revolutionary, subversive and of the Left. They then represent a fatal danger to all that which humanity truly holds sacred and dear though most people at some time may be so deceived by false teachings as to fail to recognize the peril.

The definition of "sovereign" man, of the State and of race are closely related ideas and democracy is by no means the opposite of, say, fascism. The only alternative to a materialistic conception of the State and society is a religious one. To ignore this is to contribute to the modern mental and spiritual confusion and helplessness. It is, however, by no means the case that the State must be theocratic to be basically religious. In certain conditions even Communism and Fascism can become a pseudo faith and substitute for a church, with their dogma, prophets and priests, who are also the rulers, yet gross materialism is nevertheless their root characteristic. On the other hand, a technically secular government can be essentially based on Christianity or another great Faith, though such a government might and probably should have some connexion with the Church. It is certain that there must be a higher stimulus than the mere personal and sectional self-interest of the corruptible voters.

Yet it is not false teaching alone which provides the undoubted driving force and practical strength and effectiveness of the Left— be it Liberalism, Socialism, Communism, false democracy, usury-Capitalism and all the many other forms which the Left takes. We have seen the revolutionary movement sweep steadily across the world, all order based on the natural law being gradually undermined. We see many people, mostly so deluded, though having genuinely good intentions, as to serve the cause of the would-be enslavers of mankind. What is the impulse which makes the Left go?

Essentially it is that combination of propositions which include the deification of man, the claim that he must be the full sovereign, that his opinions are the law, that his wishes must be obeyed, that all power and possessions belong to him absolutely, that the millennium will be reached when all the remnants of the old order have been removed and liberated man, the Lord of Creation, will enjoy undisputed mastery of the world.

In practical terms these ideas are profitable. They not only provide a powerful incentive to action, but they are also effective for proselytization. It is easy to point to the actual rulers of nations and to their works, imperfect because human nature is imperfect, and proclaim the intangible and unattained heaven on earth which will follow the final seizure of power by the peoples. That they are not only not entitled to ultimate power by natural law, but quite incapable of really exercising it, and that their supposed power will always pass to unscrupulous adventurers is a fact that becomes often obvious when it is too late.

But in the meantime the practical, material fruits of rationalistic methods, of Capitalism—usury and the capture of the right to coin money, of Liberalism and Socialism and the power and its fruits which they yielded, are a great spur to action and a powerful support for further initiative. The work of the Left is never short of money, because the Left controls its very sources; and each stage of the campaign is profitable. Each seizure of new power and new lands brings in new profits and more power. At the same time the Right withers. To work for or with the Left is to work for a force which is active, aggressive, expanding, rich, successful. It is flattering and it pays. To be on the side of the Right is to be in the company of cranks and dreamers, of failures, is to live in the past, to see one's world wither away.

It can easily be observed almost everywhere that the Left is active, aggressive, expanding, while the Right is more passive, static and almost complacent. It can all too easily be assumed that this fact is, in itself a proof of the greater value of the Left. While it is certainly arguable at a first glance that the energy and activity of the Left may seem to assure its victory, it by no means follows that the moral virtues and ultimate true values of the Left are proved to be superior. Quite the contrary is the case.

All men are made by the Almighty with an immortal Soul and Spirit, and thus all have at the root the same conscience, however much this may be hidden in most people by the results of their sinful lives. In varying degrees we are all under the direct influence of this conscience, this universal and in all men equal measure of right and wrong. But insofar as we all, to varying degrees, depart from the rule laid down by our conscience, we are all, even if we do not know it, to some extent ill at ease with our deepest selves. The Christian Churches have, of course known these problems for two thousand years and know what should be done: the true solution is fasting, confession and communion. Indeed the Churches have known for almost twenty centuries a great deal more than modern psycho-analysts claim to have discovered in a few decades.

When men depart from the healthy urges of their true inner selves, they set up within themselves a struggle, and the resulting tensions can be such as even to affect the health of individuals, or their sanity. But if, for any of very many reasons, a man has been persuaded to follow the wrong paths and depart from Divine natural law, he will usually become restless and continually resolved, consciously and subconsciously, to justify his outlook and his actions by his pronouncements and his work. His inner struggle will lead also to an outward one. The attempt to justify that which is felt, deep down, to be wrong, will lead to a form of aggressive persuasion by the victim of himself and of his fellow men.

Factors such as these lead to the greater activity of the godless and materialistic Left, and even to an often murderous aggressiveness. The Communist Commissar who kills a moral and political opponent is in fact killing, or trying to kill, his own inner voice of God-given conscience. It is not surprising, therefore, that such a Communist truly hates God. But it is the hate of the potentially defeated, the hate of the inferiority complex, to use modern jargon.

On the other hand, as can easily be seen, it is just this same set of reasons which so often makes the Right seem to be passive, unworried, and, alas, sometimes ineffective. What the Right lacks is not the spur of a fight against conscience, but the spur of active and well understood love for good and a justifiable hate of evil, indeed there must be an active love for ones fellow men. A blind complacency is unworthy. But it is widespread.

But does this mean that the cause of the Right is irretrievably lost? Does it mean that in the modern world there must be stagnation, unless one follows the left-hand path? Indeed, is it true that no real movement at all, no progress, is possible unless there is some inspiration from the Left? It is true that outwardly the Right would seem to be the symbol of a static condition and that a passive acceptance of an order sent to us from above must lead to sterile standstill. It could be argued with some semblance of truth that it is the competition, the challenge offered by the Left which has been the cause of much real progress in the world, at least of progress in the material sphere. We shall not take these propositions too far. We are aware of them and we do not hide that fact. We know that these issues are wide and complex. They involve also the definition of human happiness. What do we really need in order to attain that inner calm and satisfaction that bliss, which can be termed happiness? Is it really the possession of the now almost proverbial glossy automobile and refrigerator, the mink and the rest? Or is all that a mere drug, giving an occasional illusion of satisfaction, only to be followed by depression and the demand for even more material satisfactions? And perhaps in such circumstances we are all the more prone to become the victims of the tempters from the Left, ever ready to draw us deeper into the poisonous bog of materialism, where the immortal spirit of man is denied and the soulless slave remains. We assume that most people are not yet so utterly degraded that each in his or her own way could not answer these questions at least in part.

23

The Plan of Counter-Revolution

But there remains the larger problem of how the Right (if it is right) can hope to stop the progress of subversive decay and counter-attack effectively. What are the motives, the effective and active driving force, which the Right could muster? It would, perhaps, not be enough to indulge in mere preaching of moral virtues. We take it for granted that our cause would not flourish unless we invoked and deserved the Divine blessing on our efforts. We must be guided by truly Supreme Law. We must consciously serve God. That would be the greatest spur to action, the best guarantee of success.

However, it may not suffice to ask people to become unpaid crusaders, sacrificing themselves entirely in order to assure the triumph of good. While these motives must operate, there must also be a scheme, a plan of attack, which will make the cause of the Right not only as effective as that of the Left, but even more so. The Right must be able to demonstrate not only that the Left is wrong and that its policies have brought its victims ultimately to starvation and servitude, though in the interval, on the way to total power, those who served the cause were well rewarded. The Right must shew both in general terms and in everyday practice that its policies and activities pay not only morally, but also in effect. That to fight for the cause is possible in all respects and that the final results are an improvement in the state of mankind in every way. We, who are of the Right, must accept the challenge if we are to win, and we must do so at once. The time is very short.

It must always be remembered that there are many people in the camp of the Left who sincerely believe themselves to be of the Right. There are many Conservative and other parties which serve the cause of the Left fully and completely, though their members and even some of their leaders think that this is by no means so and proclaim themselves adherents of the Right. The Left is flexible and subtle, setting its traps and its nets widely, indeed universally. There are organizations, nominally Christian, which are blind agents of the cause of Antichrist such as the World Council of Churches. A proper appraisal of the real issues and of their consequences is essential. It is not an easy task, but it must be undertaken. We need not be excessively dogmatic and we must not be scholastic, but we must certainly be strict with regard to essentials.

If we face a struggle for world power, let us face it with open eyes. It means that we, too, must fight for the same objective. It is useless to try to stem the tide in each separate country, the more so as only the two or three largest really matter in practice. If they are finally overcome, the rest will be mopped up without trouble. But nevertheless we must face the challenge on a universal scale. We, too, must think in international terms, though not with a view to obliterating national independences and cultures, but, on the contrary, in order to protect and restore them. Yet this objective cannot be achieved unless all nations will co-operate. We therefore need a Right International with its doctrine, its strategy and its aims, able to carry out an effective policy in the various stages needed. In this atomic age, when great powers can be used for the destruction of humanity or for its greater well-being, we cannot afford to think in terms of small territorial units alone. True isolationism is suicide, though a mistaken internationalism is also fatal. We will leave a fuller discussion of the outlines of the positive programme of the Right to the end of our notes, sketching meanwhile briefly the strategic plan of counter-revolution.

To succeed in the big practical affairs which we have mentioned, it is necessary to dispose of sufficient means. One must have capable men, sufficient money, adequate power. We will assume that the men and women required for the fight are available. The great Christian culture of Europe, in part transplanted beyond the oceans, is not so finally exhausted that no human forces remain available for the ultimate struggle for survival. We see so much devotion, ability and talent, such great knowledge, energy and initiative applied to so many good causes that it is obvious that we need not fear that the generals and the soldiers are not there, waiting, perhaps unconsciously, for the call.

Money, too, should present no insuperable obstacles. Fortunately all affairs, be it in the realms of trade and industry, art, politics, even crime, are carried out through the ability and initiative of very few people, often even of only a single person. Therefore, that which must be done, need not involve large masses of people and correspondingly exorbitant expenses. On the other hand the still free parts of the world, Europe, Australasia, Africa and especially rich and still so largely sheltered America, the North of which has now inherited such immense responsibilities, can spare much energy and treasure. Everywhere there is an obvious surplus available, much of which is wasted on trivialities and even on harmful pursuits.

Yet the short-sightedness and irresponsibility of the Right must be faced. When the Civil War began in Russia and small numbers of brave men began the fight, they turned, quite naturally, to those who still had large possessions. The reply was usually in effect: "What? In these hard times? After all I have lost already?—Sorry, try someone else." And then the moment came when these men, who could have spared so much, were deprived of all they had, and even of their very lives. They had failed to make the most important investment of their lives, they refused to take out the most vital insurance, and they lost all. Russia was not alone. The same fate has now overtaken other countries. None, in any continent, is immune from one or the other form of the godless pestilential tyranny.

It is to be hoped that soon, before it is too late, men will be found who will have both the ability and the means to start the ball rolling. And great care must be taken to see that the good cause does not fall into the hands of the enemy. Very subtly disguised, he can take control.

Let us face the fact that we were long ago challenged to a fight to the finish. We must accept the challenge fully and with all its implications in mind. All is at stake: life, liberty, country, property, family and faith. We must fight at all the many points of the front. We must achieve power in each of our countries. In some countries this process may take many years as it will require the creation of large organizations and the gradual education of the mass of the people. We must tackle this problem, but we cannot leave it at that. Time is too short. The great spiritual, political and even commercial institutions of the world must understand their duty. We know that most of them are in fetters; they have become too deeply involved in the financial network of the usurer, and they fear foreclosures and other forms of pressure. They must take the required risks and minimize them by announcing in advance the dangers which they anticipate. This will on the one hand put a brake on the efforts of the enemy, and on the other hand the members and followers of these organizations, numbering in some cases untold millions in all lands, will come to the help of their leaders. They must be told. To be silent now is to lose the battle. We can also estimate the effects which could be attained by a sort of financial strike by groups and associations of enterprises; an openly proclaimed challenge to the usurers would put them in a position in which they would have to capitulate and come to terms with those who have lost their illusions. The next stage would call for political reforms.

The main line of attack had been through Russia. That country had been vulnerable, there had existed, together with great and unrecognized virtues, also considerable weaknesses, and the First World

War brought on that revolutionary situation which Lenin correctly diagnosed. Were he alive, he would no doubt recognize that there is still a revolutionary situation in Russia (but he would probably not say so openly). But now the revolutionary situation is due to new reasons, and it is even more explosive and more widely spread. The enemy considered Russia the main support of his further attack. We should be right in making the reverse process a part of our overriding strategy. We must, for the sake of all of us, release Russia from its present bonds and let it establish the régime it really wants. That will assure to all of us a base for further operations. The liberation of Russia is essential for the liberation of the world. Russia has had the fullest experience of the evils of materialism and will provide the most complete answer.

In the immediate task of the elimination of Soviet Communism Russia clearly plays the central role. To cut down the main trunk is to bring down the branches with it; to pull up the roots is to deal with the evil growth forever. On the other hand any reliance on local resistance and liberation is not enough, except as steps in the right direction. In short, there must always be a common front of anti-Communist fighters.

There is also another very important issue. In the light of some of the questions which have been indicated in these pages it will be seen that countries now under the yoke of the Soviets are merely to be transferred to that of a "national-Communism", of "Socialism with freedom and democracy". Yet this would be a great and deliberate deception, a trap, into which those who struggle or hope for true freedom will be invited to fall. Much can be learnt in this connection from the utterances (November, 1956) of Tito. He has tried to please both sides, so as to maintain his true position of deceiver. He has said that Soviet military intervention in Hungary was bad at a certain stage, but in most respects good, since it saved Socialism. In addition we see the West, though full of genuine sympathy for the heroic Hungarians, forced by its present leaders to sit back idly while the Soviets crush "Reaction" and "Fascism". After that the modified Socialistic dispensation will be offered to the Hungarians by both sides. In Poland, in somewhat different circumstances, the same policy is being pursued. While remaining Communist, Poland is to become "an equal and free partner of Moscow". A deliberate deception.

Events in the Near East are similarly deceptive. It is undeniable that there was much to be said for the British and French intervention in Egypt. But there are several factors which are clearly a deliberate deception. Let us leave all the details out of the picture, as we are concerned in these notes with a wider problem which has been developing for centuries, and recent events are but a small part of the picture. But let us note one fact: as the dust of the first clashes in Egypt began to settle, there emerged one practical decision of some importance: for the first time an international police force has been created under UNO, and this, in the light of the Korean precedent, when a UNO army fought the Reds, is a very important step towards a Left-wing world dispensation. And there will be many more clashes.

The former Belgian Congo has provided another pretext for accustoming the world to the employment of an international police force, used to carry out international decisions. Soviet Communist initiative had been checked for a short time, but another Left and international solution is being fostered in its place.

But in general terms the events we have seen in Egypt and in Poland, Hungary and Czechoslovakia are not isolated activities, but the beginnings of a process which cannot be stopped and which will lead to great and lasting changes. All the problems we have mentioned in these pages are now no longer latent, but actively important. Time is becoming shorter. In particular the attempt now being made to establish "National-Communism" behind the iron curtain, and this policy is being prepared for Russia too, is a challenge to us all. Only if we rise to the occasion will the efforts and sacrifices of the heroic Hungarians and all the other fighters for freedom reap their proper rewards. Alternatively, a lack of understanding of the underlying causes of world events will bring about universal enslavement very soon. Let us never forget that there are potential enslavers on both sides of the "curtain" and humanity is the intended victim of both camps.

Today, if the use of A and H bombs means global suicide and if "conventional" war, owing to Communist strength, means Western defeat, a victory for liberty without war can and must be achieved by a moral and political counter-attack on Communism. It is also the only way to avoid economic collapse.

If we consider the plan of attack, i.e. not only the means of overthrowing our enemies, but also the dispensation we want to put in place of present ones, we must formulate the basic essence of the problem.

It is a struggle for power, both within nations and globally. Before the rise of Capitalist States, tribes and families were integrated units, whatever the form of State, be it a Monarchy, a Republic or even a despotism. Of course some forms of State were preferable to others, but they had in common the fact that the rulers and ruled were organically interlinked, even if the dynasty in any given instance had originally been founded on conquest or usurpation. The rulers and the ruled were interdependent, however tyrannical the régime may have been sometimes and however little freedom the mass of the people may have enjoyed. The social organism did approximate to the forms and relations of a family. The policies of the government, even if not subject to popular control, were known and understood and usually the governors and governed spoke the same language, had the same faith and shared the same culture in varying degrees.

But with the rise of usury and money-creating Capitalism there arose a new form of power, whose protagonists had no true links with the nations over whom they had full sway, whose methods and policies were kept secret, and whose interests and aims had nothing in common with those of the various nations and were indeed, opposed to them. There arose a purely parasitical power, internationalist both in form and spirit, both because it cared nothing for the fate of its subjects and because its operations were naturally international and its leading adepts often not members of the nationalities among whom they operated. This form of power no longer had any organic links or common interests with the ruled. In this respect it differed completely from previous forms of power, whatever may have been their legal basis.

Nominally the old State dispensations have largely remained under Capitalism, though the theoretical rulers of the states subjected to the usurers and money-creators are no more than a façade, entirely controlled through finance.

As we have mentioned before, it was Capitalism which created Socialism. This form of power shares with its progenitor the characteristics of being parasitical, not originally a part of the nations it rules, internationalist and operating a policy and pursuing aims which are kept secret and always consciously misrepresented. Socialism and Communism are by no means popular or peoples' régimes, but slavery imposed by force and terror, and nothing else. Under Socialism nothing remains of the old forms of State.

The principle for which we must fight is a return to an integrated and organic State at all levels, where rulers and ruled are in a condition of natural relationship, a part of the same nation, the same culture, and often the same faith and race. The exact legal basis, be it this or that form of Monarchy or Republic, is a matter of each nation's tradition, needs and preference. But it is an essential part of the natural State that its aims and policies are known, understood and approved by the majority of the people, and not enforced by terror or corruption, deceit or subterfuge. The rulers must not be parasitical exploiters, but public servants, devoted to the interests of their nations.

If Capitalism and Socialism had been imposed on all nations by revolution, we are, in this sense, concerned with a progressive counter-revolution, a return to old basic assumptions in present-day forms. Americans should remind themselves that their revolution began as a struggle against the imposition of usurer's money in place of the Colonial currency, but they have not yet achieved their aims; the American revolution must still be completed, the work of Alexander Hamilton must be undone and the Constitution re-asserted.

24

The Russian Émigrés

In this connexion we again draw attention to the potentially *important* role of the Russian political exiles. We have been one of them and have been actively anti-Communist for *over* 40 years. We are left with no illusions, but also we are devoid of destructive cynicism. In part we can derive encouragement from the Jews. They have lived for many generations deprived of their own soil, scattered among all the nations, and yet they have retained their coherence, and their achievements, good and bad, are colossal. They were sustained by their faith, and by the consciousness of a definite *raison d'être*. These things are also not unknown to us.

On the other hand the Russians émigrés suffer from three main evils: treason in favour of Communism, treason in favour of other enemies of Russia, and denationalization. But very many remain steadfast. We can ignore those, especially among the young who abandon interest in Russia and merge into the nation and society in which fate has placed them. These casualties are inevitable.

A far worse enemy is the state of mind which is leading so many Russians to look upon political work not as a duty, requiring much effort and sacrifice, but who see it as a profitable profession. Some, whose corruptibility and cynicism know no limits, have sold themselves, mostly secretly, to the Soviets. Some have fallen into subtle Communist traps, whose essence was the confusion of patriotism and the acceptance of Communism, and have openly declared themselves "Soviet patriots", and some of these have voluntarily returned to Russia. Not knowing it, they have committed suicide, and we are saddened by their fate. But their political importance is slight. There are many people, Russians and others, who serve the Communists openly and secretly in all countries, and a few additional émigrés make no decisive difference. Still less does it matter politically if a few more men and women became the victims of Communist terror or slavery. The revolution has cost Russia some sixty million lives and tens of millions have been and are in the slave camps. We recall the terrible Russian anecdote which divides the people of Russia into three classes: those who were "inside" (in prison or camp), those who are "inside", and those who will be. Even the founders of the régime have mostly not escaped.

In the class of the Russian political "professionals", it is those who serve foreign, non-Russian, countries, who are the most dangerous to the common struggle, with the common enemy. There is quite a class of people who are in the pay of one or more intelligence services and in the paid service of various political organizations. Mostly these renegade Russians work as anti-Russian separatists, ostensibly working for the independence of the Ukraine or other parts of Russia, and they are also mostly, be they separatists or not, working to further Socialism. At the present time it is natural that America provides the greater part of the money for these adventures and adventurers.

There is, alas, quite a long tradition behind this unpleasant phenomenon. A pretended fear of an alleged Russian imperialism mingled with the greedy wish to acquire Russian lands and riches. The true point was to weaken Russia. It is a fact that for many years before the revolution all the groups in opposition to the Imperial régime in Russia were in receipt of foreign subsidies and instructions. The work of Russian revolutionaries and foreign agents was much intertwined. That is not to say that the revolutionary movement was due only to the subsidies of secret services and banks, but there was not a little interdependence. In fact revolutionary work was greatly impregnated in Russia with the mood and tradition of treason. Treason and revolution were very closely related, and they still are among the Russian Left. Though some individuals are quite honourable, they are the exceptions which prove the rule.

We possess enough sense of humour and proportion, enough fair-mindedness, to be able to see a problem from the other man's point of view. Had we been able to contemplate the anti-Russian policies of the past hundred years and seen that they had at least yielded rich fruit to those who pursued them, even though Russia suffered losses, we might have agreed that these policies were wise, these investments were not wasted. If we could see the Ukraine being lustily exploited by Austria-Hungary, or Germany, and other parts of Russia by other candidates for the spoils, with American investments well placed here, there and everywhere, and so on, well, we could see the point. But what is the position in fact? Where are all these starry-eyed and verbose revolutionaries? The few that are left, apart from the Communists, are not in Russia. Where, indeed, is Austria-Hungary? Or Germany? How fares the British Empire? Is America safe? If we are not very much mistaken, each and every anti-Russian investment has been an instance of the sowing of dragon's teeth. The harvest has been one of death, destruction, misery and failure. Japan was backed against the Russians, and what was the harvest of the White race in the Far East? Who, in future, as in the past, will have to stem the Yellow tide? Perhaps Luxemburg? Or will it be Russia? Luckily, Russia still stands, despite all the wars and revolutions. It has a way of outliving its enemies. It will outlive Communism. To be the friend of Russia is profitable; to be its enemy is fatal.

It follows that the time has come when it should be realized that anti-Russian investments and activities are a most dangerous boomerang. They play into the hands of the common enemy of us all. The present plan, whose purpose is to split Russia and socialize its parts while subjecting all, with the rest of the world, to the World Government of the materialistic messianists, is expressed in support for the separatists, among whom the most important are the Ukrainian ones, and for the groups of the Russian Left, chief among whom now are the so-called NTS-Solidarists (the Russian National Labour Union) and others. All receive western, and especially American support and instructions: in fact the NTS would be little or nothing if it were not in effect an integral part of the U.S. special services. In the past, during 40 years, the NTS had served Polish, Japanese, Nazi and other Intelligence Services. A fuller discussion of all these matters would not serve our immediate purpose, which is to point to the healthy and positive factors which should receive support.

Here it must suffice to say that the groups here mentioned are being supported, mostly by the U.S. Intelligence network, for the purpose of being used in the huge political hoax now in preparation, as well as being a reservoir of potential espionage trainees.

The materialistic-messianists are concerned with world power, and it does not matter radically to them whether they attain this power through the medium of Communism in Moscow or that of perverted democracy, with its H.Q. in Washington and New York. But the signs are that the Communist line suits them less and they prefer a solution via the United Nations, rather than the Soviet Communist party. Nevertheless they could still come to terms.

In order to make Russia acceptable to western public opinion, without releasing the country from the grip of the materialists, it may be necessary to bring about a bogus revolution. Alternatively, there must be an arrangement with the present Soviet rulers. It is in the light of this possibility that the whole true character of the "cold war" and western "anti-Communism" and "co-existence" must be seen. So it is that all the chances of overthrowing the Soviet tyranny, which have stared one in the face, during the greater part of recent years, have been deliberately thrown away, while every effort is made to come to an arrangement with the murderers who rule Russia and the other subjected lands.

The groups we have mentioned are being sustained in order to provide the nominal façade for proposed new "free" and "democratic" régimes to be set up in Russia, then split into its alleged parts. It follows naturally that these groups are led by conscious and completely corrupt traitors to their own country, Red Quislings whose treason is but an expression of their willingness to derive a living from this political prostitution, so typical of much that is now done in the name of high ideals. Of course such motives and such methods have little chance of succeeding, and they greatly endanger the still free world. Communist agents, who have always been among the leaders of these groups, know well what they are doing in encourageing this game, which plays into Soviet hands.

It is more than a mere coincidence that the same policies were pursued and the same people were backed during the last war by the Nazi German Eastern Ministry of Herr Alfred Rosenberg. The results we know.

Among Russians the majority were and are Monarchists, though not all are fully conscious ones and some hide their views for opportunistic reasons. The purely reactionary type is now rare, though verbose. Over fifty years have passed since the catastrophe of the old order. And we *have* forgotten a few things, and we also *have* learnt a great deal. Russia has, however, never known a Republican tradition and it has never been a Republic. The present tyranny is certainly not one.

However, the Monarchy is, in present-day Russian conditions, not a régime which can be restored solely by an appeal to the Laws of Succession, nor could the lawful Pretender to the Throne, H.I.H. The Grand Duke Wladimir of Russia, (b. 1917), become effective leader of the struggle for Russia's liberation unless he were to display the necessary qualities of leadership and political perception. This is a problem which the Grand Duke could not solve alone. He would have to be able to rely on the active co-operation of at least a small group of highly competent people. They are available, as are the correct doctrine and strategy, but in the circumstances of practical life there is also a need for a minimum of material assistance.

There are unfortunately complicating circumstances affecting the position and prospects of the Imperial Dynasty. The Basic Laws of Succession demand that all members of the House should marry partners of Royal status, and non-Royal, morganatic, marriages give no rights of succession to their descendants and no titles to the morganatic wives or children. All members of the Dynasty, including the Grand Duke Wladimir, are morganatically married, so that after the death of the present members of the Imperial Family there are no legal claimants to the Throne.

In these circumstances the situation which arises is similar to that which came about in 1613, when, after very serious troubles affecting the State and nation, the senior line of the old Reigning House, established in A.D. 860, became extinct. The National Assembly then called the nearest relation to the Throne in the person of Michael Romanoff.

It could be said that, perhaps, after all that Russia has experienced in the terrible years since 1917, a thorough re-consideration of policies and persons would be appropriate. But this should on no account become a chaotic struggle and manœuvring for sectional power, and this is very unlikely to happen since the end of Communism would be possible only when the nation has become deeply convinced of the need for certain policies which would be morally and politically just and effective, and there are good reasons for believing that that would in fact happen. Tremendous processes are maturing beneath the surface.

Among the expatriates a hard core of effective fighters remains, who are both reliable and capable. To them the iron curtain is not an impenetrable obstacle, nor is Communism a force which cannot be overcome. Here we shall not deal fully with the very large subject of active anti-Communism, its tactics, technique and strategy, so far as Russia is concerned. We must note, however, that this struggle is being undermined not merely by the enemy in Moscow, but also by that in Washington and New York, who is able to spend much money and deploy great forces for the support of activities and organizations whose objectives serve the purposes of the materialistic-messianists. That which is so widely advertised in the world's press as Russian anti-Communism with all its radio "protesters" and the rest of the ballyhoo, is a political trap, set for Russia and for the world. It is by no means a part of the struggle for liberty, but merely a phase in the prosecution of the plans for world enslavement.

The true strength of the émigrés lies in their spiritual links with healthy forces in Russia and in their ability to carry out those aspects of the struggle which are at present out of reach of those who are still under the Soviets.

There should be a generally accepted policy towards Russia and Communism, applying not only to Russian counter-revolutionaries, but to all those opposed to subversion, treason and godlessness.

Such a policy must on no account be based on vengeance or mere hate of persons, however terrible their crimes. On the contrary, after all the suffering and misdeeds of decades, on a scale never yet experienced in all history, there should be efforts at pacification. It does not necessarily follow that all can or must be completely forgiven, but there certainly must be more of a healing generosity than of thoughts of retribution.

Preferably, when the Red tyranny collapses, its perpetrators should be judged more by what they did to bring it to an end, rather than by the crimes they had committed. It should be borne in mind that under Soviet terroristic conditions very many persons had been drawn into actions and even a way of life which they detested and practiced only through weakness, and it took men and women of giant strength fully to resist the temptations and escape the all-engulfing fear.

In any event, critical judgment can only be passed by those who had experienced the worst consequences of Communism, and it is certain that those who have remained or have become ardent Christians will be ready to forgive much.

One of the themes which can reconcile people who had for long been at opposed ends of the Soviet structure is disinterested patriotism. Its potential strength was shewn during the Second World War.

Let those who hold on to power because they fear vengeance for their crimes be assured that they will have every opportunity to earn remission. All should be brought together in a common effort to end the horror of antireligious Communism and to re-establish a Christian State and way of life.

If such changes take place in Russia their beneficial effects will be felt in every corner of the globe.

25

Conclusions

The still free world has now reached the dividing line between the condition in which an effective effort to assure liberty is still possible, and the conditions in which it will be too late and the grip of the enemy, in his Eastern or Western variation, will be such as to make resistance impossible. We must now decide whether we shall stand and fight, or whether we will submit tamely and passively to the yoke which is prepared for our necks. It is surely clear that, having realized the dangers which face us, we shall not submit?

If that is so, then we must define the objectives we have in mind and the plan of attack we shall carry out. Whoever we are—Americans, Britons, French, Germans, Spaniards, Russians—we have all, each in our own ways, known a struggle for freedom and survival. Our forces, spiritual and material, are not exhausted. On the contrary, history teaches us that no individual and no nation is ever really exhausted by efforts and sacrifices. The only thing which does sometimes fail, which does lose its power, like an accumulator run down, is the stimulus of a given idea, need or danger. But if that particular driving force wanes, but is replaced by another, the individual or nation can, after only a very short rest, resume its efforts and its sacrifices. And the greater the stimulus, the greater will be the effort made. Only a man or a country devoid of a driving force is doomed. But the world in general does not run down; it is being re-charged by a dynamo of immense power with a never-ending energy. Fortunate are those who plug in well.

Surely the incentive which the absolute necessity to survive as free men and independent nations provides is enough? Surely, when we see our Faith and culture threatened as never before, we will leave no stone unturned until victory is fully ours? Let us put it, then, like this: we must invest in liberty; in that cause we must invest all we can—our best endeavours, our money, our time, and our prayers. Let us seek Divine guidance and protection, but keep our powder dry. A Faith without deeds is barren. Let those who have the ability set the ball rolling. Start the crusade for freedom!

We need a blue-print of the campaign. In the first place men of known integrity and ability and especially Americans and Britons and representatives of other leading countries of the still free part of the world, should form a not too large and cumbersome Council. Parallel with this there must be a practical expression of a common front between the free Russians, Poles, Chinese, and all the other enslaved nations. There must be put in hand a wide campaign to inform all men of goodwill throughout the world both of the dangers which face them and of the measures which must be taken to meet them, and the help which will be required.

Then there must be carried out, with the help of the free world, an active campaign for the overthrow of the Red tyrannies behind the iron curtain, with the participation only of those who serve the cause of true liberty, with the strict exclusion of all open and secret collaborators of the subversive Left in all its forms, but also with the exclusion of mere dreamers, cranks and blind reactionaries and those who think more of the restoration of their personal losses and less of the fate of mankind and their own countries.

A sustained attack must be begun upon the economic, political and social teachings and practices of the enemy in their Capitalistic and Socialistic forms. It is useless to attack materialism in theory, but leave real power in the hands of its adepts. Bankers, politicians, and many others, must be persuaded to join the campaign and to realize that it is in their own best interests and that, if the enemy finally succeeds, they will all be doomed. They must be brought to understand that only by adopting the new order as their own and playing their proper parts can they serve themselves and the community. This is not a party question. It is far more important than the deliberately deceptive half-truths, and misstatements, which are the stock-in-trade of most political parties.

We can be encouraged by the certainty that the whole plan and foundation of the Left in all its forms is vulnerable in the highest degree. The scheme of the materialistic-messianists is, as we have shewn, based on a hoax, an immense and complex lie. Once this has been exposed it will become quite impossible to maintain it. We must, therefore study the problems which have here been indicated in outline and make our conclusions known to everyone. In their simplest terms they can be made clearly understandable to the majority of decent people. The explanation of the complex lie is simple.

The press, the theatre, the cinema, radio and all the other means of affecting public opinion must gradually be persuaded to change their lines. Businessmen must be brought to understand that it is by no means in their interests to give and withhold advertising as a means of imposing pressure on newspapers, so as to force them to follow a line which is essentially that of the materialists, though often well masked. If the advertisers are themselves pressed, they and the papers, should declare openly just who is pressing and for what purpose. Such a counter-attack would soon end that kind of manipulation of public opinion. Courageous firms and papers would receive the full support of all decent people.

Clearly all these and other actions and their effects are interdependent, and not only within each country, but even internationally. Clearly also the enemy will hit back. He will try to deflect us, to intimidate, to bribe, to infiltrate. He will create and lead competing activities, made to appear to be our allies, but intended to mislead. All this should not deflect us from our course.

In these pages we have not attempted to define an "ism", to formulate a narrow and scholastic doctrine. Such things are foreign to us and we claim that the thesis here set out in outline is far too wide and too deep for such a narrow cast. But, on the other hand, it is bound to occur to some, as it does to us, that if our propositions are true and if they call for action, then that activity can not be effectively carried out unless it eventually acquires some organizational forms and, as would then be inevitable, a name, trade mark or label. Here, at this stage, we are by no means concerned with making definite suggestions of any sort. These, we hope, may emerge in time when other and wiser people will have taken a part in the discussion and any possible action.

However, with all these qualifications in mind we feel that we are here concerned with a proposition which is not unconcerned with the Organic Right in its widest sense. We are by no means afraid of using the word Right, which has the same meaning in all the European languages known to us, for example *das Recht* in German, *le Droit* in French, *Pravo* in Russian. The Right is concerned not merely with a philosophical and political conception, it is also the law, the expression of natural and legitimate rights, the right arm of men. At the Crucifixion it was the sinner on the right who achieved salvation; are we not entitled to take note of this Divine symbolism? Indeed are we not bound to do so?

Yet, it may be well to dot all the i-s. It may be necessary to emphasize not only the differences, but even the basic struggle of the Right with the Left. It would be wise to point to their very different qualities. We have been challenged, and nothing is gained by pretending we cannot understand this or by going through the senile or hypocritical motions of claiming that it is not wise to attempt excessively clear definitions.

While we have stated that the Right is Christian, we have also said that men of other Faiths can also be of the Right. We would feel certain that all those who put the spirit above things material, duty above greed and love above hate and envy are in the camp of the Organic Right.

It would appear to be possible to state a formula by which one can define the Organic Right and its natural adherents, and they are still the huge majority among all nations, potentially as yet unspoilt by the persistent onslaughts of the Left. Humanity is still sound, but it must be helped to organize its best instincts and give them effective practical expression. We must rally all that is best in all its many-sided variety, its depth and strength, separately in each nation, but also within a framework of free collaboration between all, for a struggle for Faith and Liberty.

The Left has shewn, during many years, indeed decades and generations, that it is an integral whole, despite the appearance of variety and even internal oppositions. The reason for that is clear: there is a centralized leadership and an all-embracing doctrine, and a common aim. All this we can also attain. Our aim, our doctrine, our plans and our objectives are interdependent and easily grasped. Until now our weakness has been that our complete case has never been stated as one whole, one single, though naturally somewhat complex problem. And still less have we realized that, personally and nationally, all of us face the same fundamental issues and are threatened by the same dangers. We have allowed ourselves and our just rights and interests to be attacked separately. Let us now, before it is too late, understand the comprehensiveness of the questions which face us and the need for united action. Thus we shall assure the true liberty and brotherhood of mankind under God.

This book is not a party publication, but we feel that it would serve a useful purpose to submit for discussion the programme of a "Right Party".

The Right Party, whatever its name, is proposed as a means of bringing to an end the farce of present day party politics, whose sole object is to give electorates an illusion of choice between Right and Left, when in fact only policies of the Left are allowed to prevail, and will enable true men willing to put the interests of their nations before sectional gain to unite in securing parliamentary majorities under incorruptible and fully informed leadership.

It is suggested that parallel national parties or suitable organizations should be set up everywhere, all these activities being co-ordinated, while adjusted in each country to local traditions and needs. Thus, for example, a republican régime would clearly remain appropriate in America, though fully restored to the aims of the Founding Fathers. Please contact us in this connexion if the idea is accepted.

It is now very widely realised that the forces of Left-wing subversion, in all their forms and guises, centrally controlled and directed towards the establishment of a godless, socialistic World Government through UNO and other means, are close to success. It is also widely sensed in all still free countries that the various Conservative parties of the nominal Right, the political organizations and even the Christian Churches are largely devoid of a true understanding of the aims and methods of the subverters and of the proper positive policies that must be pursued in order to defeat them. It follows therefore that, unless such knowledge rapidly becomes widespread the enslavement of the whole world will take place within a very few years.

It is absolutely necessary that all of us should understand that the struggle for global power in reality represents the ultimate conflict between two fundamentally incompatible doctrines on the purpose of life: one is concerned with the deification of man and rejection of God, with the kingdom of this earth and its material fruit; the other sees life on earth as a spiritual preparation for the Kingdom of God to which purely material considerations must always take second place.

In practical as well as philosophical terms there is no fight between the Capitalist system, based on usury, and Communism, since the former created the latter and gives it every support while pretending to oppose it; both are concerned with the identical aim of founding the materialistic world state. By usurping the power to issue the means of exchange in all forms, once the sovereign right and duty of the heads of states, the money-lenders have succeeded in establishing their rule over every nation in the world. But that rule is unstable, as the ever-growing debt structure and the need to collect interest on all money in circulation puts an intolerable strain on all forms of enterprise, so that it must eventually lead to a collapse of the system, or to war. Therefore, the financiers themselves created Communism as a future substitute whereby to perpetuate their rule through terrorism.

Meanwhile Capitalism must sustain its structure by the imposition of an ever-growing burden of taxation.

It is irrefutable that under a system based on natural law, where the means of production, distribution and exchange remain in private hands, while the government, by being the sole issuer of money, maintains a proper balance between spending power and the true productive wealth of the community, there would be no need whatsoever for such taxes. Were the government to repossess this right and spend money directly, instead of allowing the financiers to lend it into circulation, there would be no National and almost no private debt burden—and no interest charge permanently crippling the public. The State would be truly sovereign in the interest of the nation and not a mere tool of the financiers or their Communist progeny.

Furthermore, the resultant freeing of the economic system and the parallel development of the means of production would lead to reductions in working hours inconceivable now, while ensuring that sufficient money was always in circulation to maintain high wages and enable the people to buy the fruits of their labour. This must lead to greater prosperity for all.

Before coming to a programme proposal, without which the whole discussion would be barren, it is necessary to define the difference between the revolutionary and counter-revolutionary. Action in the interests of an idea and a plan can be subject to completely practical advantages as the true final aim, with the ideological aspects a mere façade, calculated to attract the maximum support, a kind of promotion and salesmanship exercise, or the activity may be completely disinterested, altruistic and possibly sterile.

We recognize that, ambition and self-interest apart, and a measure of both is inevitable in real life, our counter-revolutionary work must be justified solely by a practical, realizable and morally correct idealism. The motives which are dictated by principles must be completely dominant, and other factors merely inevitable in human relations. The sense of duty must be the sole criterion for action. That is the definition of the Right, of the Counter-Revolution.

On the other hand, whatever the pretended ideals or bogus advantages offered to humanity, the fundamental motives of the Revolution, of the Left, are concerned only with the attainment of power and of its fruits in the material sphere. Be it the usury-capitalism of the Golden International, or the communism of the Red International, the ultimate aim of all false democracy, liberalism and "progress", all lead to universal power and almost limitless profits for the intended bosses, who are behind the scenes and are not the leaders of the intermediate phases of the Revolution.

Therefore, phraseology apart, at the roots the revolutionary, whatever his nominal label, from mild bourgeois liberal to murdering communist, is, consciously or not, fighting for profit. Intellectually, emotionally and instinctively he is urged on by materialism, even if he still practises some religion. Thus it is inevitable that the end product of the Revolution must be slavery and misery, except for the intended final beneficiaries, the as yet half-hidden operators of the game.

On the other hand the true Counter-Revolutionary, even if not devoid of some self-interest and ambition, is in all respects a genuine fighter for the best interests of all the people everywhere. His sense of duty and of sacrifice will always dominate over any other considerations.

It follows that our camp should attract only those collaborators who have shewn under severe tests that they are quite incorruptible. They may seem to be rare, but they are very effective, and quality is more important than quantity.

There remains the problem of attracting sufficient monetary support, without which effective action is difficult. Obviously money is easily obtained for propositions which offer quick and large profits, and it is rarely given where the ultimate benefits may seem both somewhat intangible and uncertain. Let those who still have money remember that only if they support the Right will they assure ultimate safety, while "investments" in the framework of Capitalism lead to final slavery. And similarly there are political activities offering short-term advantages, while appearing to be of the Right, but which play fully into the hands of the Revolution. For example, resistance to incompetent "majority rule" as in Rhodesia must not be merely the defence of immediate material advantages, while Capitalism is left intact and potentially in the saddle. Only if the aim of policy is to resist the overall conquest by the subverters and to bring about the ultimate reforms which are essential, can there be any hope of final victory. There must come the break-through to the conditions in which money and politics will understand the issues and support the true liberation.

In broader philosophical and psychological terms it may be said that the difference between the true Right and the Left, between true and constructively progressive Conservatism and Revolution as a step towards slavery, is a matter of faith, tradition and preferences which determine choices. Cynics may claim that the Right is romantic, and that that mood and outlook is outdated. They could assert that today the great majority of people everywhere, on both sides of the Iron Curtain, are confirmed materialists and rationalists, who have no wish to believe in or to serve any cause other than that which dominates the outlook of the so-called Welfare State, which the late Captain Henry Kerby, M.P., always referred to as the "Farewell State", the end of all real and truly worth-while values. Such propositions cannot be denied out of hand.

It is true that the way of life of the Welfare State, while this lasts, is superficially attractive because so easily acquired, but it is also true that once the yoke of "Big Brother" has been accepted life becomes intensely boring, and this boredom leads to drugs, hippies and the rest.

But we shall claim that the spiritual and material attractions of what may seem an irrationally romantic way of life are far stronger if they again become known. After all, the Right life has been dominant during most of human history and until very recent decades. And it may have had its bad pages, since there is no perfection on earth, but it has obviously seen the development of the world's greatest progress and achievements.

A mystical theme may be genuine, or it may be mistaken or even deliberately deceptive. The test must be the past and present performance of any given formula. Tradition must provide much of the guidance. Yet it is undoubtedly true that what we believe, love, support and fight for can be expressed not solely in rationalistic formulae, figures and supposedly exact calculations, but also in religious and national symbols representing a deep and genuine reality.

Therefore our policies and forms of organization must be based on a successful reflection of the whole problem in breadth and depth. We have said much about the, shall we say, scientific side of the problems and solutions which face us, but we also draw attention to the romantic and still very real and very true side of the question. Only when we shall have brought all factors into play shall we acquire the inspiration and strength to defeat our enemies!

AIMS AND PRINCIPLES OF A PROPOSED PARTY OF THE RIGHT

These considerations lead to the following practical proposals of the "Right Party":

(1) That full and true sovereignty should be vested in the Queen in Council, or in an impartial Presidency in Republics; this means that the Monarch or the President should be able to exercise truly sovereign functions when the over-riding interests of the nation require it.

(2) That there be a strengthening of both the Established and the other major Christian Churches so that they can once more exercise their proper influence in all spheres of life.

(3) That one of the basic duties of the State, the issue of money in all forms free of debt or interest and in the right amounts should revert to the Crown.

(4) That the National Debt should be gradually abolished and all private debts be made subject to amortization.

(5) That as a consequence of the foregoing *there should be no longer any Income Tax* and only such indirect taxes as are absolutely necessary to cover the proper expenses of the Government.

(6) That, in view of the great increase in prosperity which will result from the proposed financial and economic reforms, and in view of the consequences of increasing automation, there should be a gradual reduction in the hours per week worked by most employees, making allowance, however, for the effects of new enterprises and diversification of production and services.

(7) That the indirect ownership of business through instruments of perpetual indebtedness should gradually be replaced by direct ownership with full responsibility by individuals, partnerships or co-operatives.

(8) That the representation and influence of individuals and groups in the political and social life of the realm should be governed by their value to the community and their experience and knowledge, expressed directly and not through parties controlled by financiers.

(9) That through education and technical assistance the standards of other races be built up until civilized man has fully discharged his duty to them.

(10) That foreign relations be guided primarily by principles and not expediency; that relations with all Communist states be severed and that encouragement be given to all genuine and effective efforts of liberation. Also that in place of the present subversive efforts to subject mankind to a communist and terrorist slavery through the European Common Market and then World Government through UNO, there should be set up a free association of all nations with non-subversive governments, to co-ordinate policies and actions in the interests of all humanity, not merely in those of the would-be exploiters.

(11) That Integralism be the vanguard of the counter-attack against global subversion in every country.

(12) That the Law of Libel should be extended to include the conception of a Public Libel, to make actionable and/or criminal not only untrue and libellous statements about individuals, but the dissemination through the press, radio, television, etc., of untrue statements which are false deliberately either by commission or omission on any subject of public importance whatsoever.

We do not seek to put ourselves forward: we come forward because no one else with complete knowledge does.

Appendix

Since much of this material first began to be written, there had appeared the "Report of the Royal Commission on Monetary, Banking and Credit Systems", published by the Government of New Zealand in the Summer of 1956.

As this is an official and detailed material concerning a typical, though small "capitalistic" economic system, it would be helpful, by way of corroboration of the statements made concerning these problems, to give some quotations from the Report.

Below will be given named quotations, in most cases with commentaries.

From the main body of the Report, beginning on page 13:
Par. 157: Causes of change in the Money Supply:
"The Volume of Money (on the Reserve Bank definition) is increased:
(a) When a customer of the Reserve Bank or a trading bank lodges, to the credit of his account, foreign exchange received from the sale of goods or services beyond New Zealand, from gifts or legacies from persons overseas, or from the proceeds of a loan raised with an overseas lender.
(b) When the Reserve Bank or a trading bank buys securities or other assets from an individual or firm and the proceeds are lodged to the credit of the seller's account at a bank.
(c) When the Reserve Bank makes a loan to the Government or to marketing authorities. At first, the borrower's deposits at the Reserve Bank are increased, and when this money is spent, the recipients may lodge part of it in their accounts at the trading banks and retain part of it in circulation in the form of notes and coin.
(d) When the customer of a trading bank draws on an overdraft limit granted by the bank and the recipient of his cheque lodges it to the credit of his account at a bank."

Here it will clearly be seen that, apart from the results of foreign trade, it is the banking system as such which is the creator of money in all its forms, such as coin, notes and cheques.

Par. 158:

"Conversely the volume of money (on the Reserve Bank definition) is reduced:
(a) When a customer of the Reserve Bank or a trading bank buys, with a deposit in his name at the bank concerned, foreign exchange to meet obligations overseas.
(b) When the Reserve Bank or a trading bank sells part of its holdings or securities or other assets to persons with credit accounts at a bank.
(c) When the advances of the Reserve Bank are reduced by the lodgment of notes, coin or cheques drawn on credit accounts.
(d) When the advances of Trading Banks are reduced, by the lodgment of notes, coin or cheques drawn on credit accounts."

Again this completely confirms the facts we had set out. Repayment of bank loans reduces the amount of money. This is explicitly and in detail confirmed in subsequent paragraphs of the Report.

Par. 164: Creation of Money by the Trading Banks:

"The fact that a large proportion of our money supply comes into existence as a result of the operations of the trading banks obviously disturbed many witnesses who appeared before us. A number seemed to think that this 'creation of credit' by the banks was a relatively recent phenomenon. In fact, the fundamental principles of our banking system have remained much the same since at least the seventeenth century. Nor is the fact that this 'creation' takes place a very recent discovery, as some witnesses implied. The quotations cited in Appendix D, Part II, show this clearly."

Par. 165:

"Trading banks cannot increase their lending, and thus create money, without limit and at no cost to themselves. Even if there is no control by the Government or by a central bank a trading bank obviously cannot increase its lending if there are insufficient credit-worthy persons seeking loans. But an even more important limitation on the expansion of trading bank lending is the necessity for each bank to keep an adequate reserve of 'banker's cash' (i.e., notes, coin, or balances at the Reserve Bank) and/or of overseas exchange...."

Par. 252: The main Causes of Inflation.

"The main causes of inflation operating in New Zealand during the last twenty years emerge from the historical review contained in Section Three of this Report, as:

(a) Rising overseas prices for New Zealand exports and imports.
(b) High private and Government capital expenditure.
(c) Government expenditure on war and other military requirements.
(d) Inadequacy of voluntary savings to match increased capital investment.
(e) Expansion of the money supply through increases in Reserve Bank and trading-bank advances.
(f) Wage and salary increases.
(g) The comparatively rapid population increase in the post-war years.
(h) Increased Government expenditure on social services and the philosophy and policies commonly associated with the Welfare State."

It will be observed that it is admitted that the expansion of the money supply is one of the factors which lead to inflation. Clearly most of the others follow on this. As regards savings, this matter is also dealt with in our text.

The Report also mentions the importance of the velocity of the circulation of money in affecting its value. Here we should add that the state of mind induced by the Welfare State, when nobody thinks of his future and spends all moneys received at once, is one of the main factors which bring about an increased speed in the movement of money. However, provided the price index is kept stable by a control of the issue of money, or its withdrawal by taxation or other means, an increase in this velocity is harmless in itself.

Par. 428 : The Origin of Creation of Money by Banks.
"The process called 'creation of credit' or 'creation of money' is no new development. Its origin in England in the seventeenth century as a development of the activities of the goldsmiths is described in the following passage from *The Theory of Credit* by Macleod (first published in 1891), Vol. II, at page 520."

There follows a description which is substantially the same as that indicated by us. We naturally assume that anyone wishing to study these matters more fully will turn to all the available sources, and we merely quote this Report as official confirmation of our facts. The witnesses before the Royal Commission include, quite naturally, leading bankers.

Par. 441 :
"The essential ingredients in creation of money by the trading banks are :

(a) Their ability to make additional advances on overdraft.
(b) The fact that they handle the bulk of commercial and industrial business in the country through the cheque system.
(c) The fact that a large proportion of their advances is not withdrawn in cash but is deposited within the trading bank system."

In general the Commission was entirely in favour of retaining the main essentials of the present system. This view is expressed in several paragraphs, such as

Par. 479:
"The Commission is most strongly opposed to meeting the need for extra money in the future through the Government issue of debt-free money."

The argument of the Commission is, in part, that if private banks are eliminated, then the element of competition goes with them, and this will lead to a lowering of efficiency. This is, in part, true, and for that reason we have suggested that even if the issue of money reverts to the State, its distribution should remain in the hands of private bankers, as agents of the Bank of Issue. Another argument of the Commission in favour of a private issue of money is that if it were to pass to the State, then the latter would obtain too much power thereby. But this argument falls to the ground if the functions of the issuing authority are, as we have suggested, limited to an automatic maintenance of the price index.

Appendix C. Section one. Par. 4:
"Accordingly, the Reserve Bank has chosen the following items as the components of the money supply in New Zealand:
(a) The coin in circulation;
(b) The value of notes issued by the Reserve Bank minus those held by the trading banks to pay out to customers who want to convert deposits into notes;
(c) The 'demand liabilities of the Reserve Bank' (excluding the deposits held there as a reserve by the trading banks), which is another way of saying the credit balances of the Government, some of its Departments, and certain statutory marketing organizations which have the privilege of banking with the Reserve Bank; and
(d) The 'demand liabilities of the trading banks', which means the deposits of customers on current account at the trading banks."

As we have already noted, the amount of cheque money created by the banks exceeds the coin and notes held by them to an amount of up to eleven times or more: in New Zealand and some other countries the proportion is lower, being about 5 to 1, but this does not alter the principles which are involved.

Par. 15:
"Until 1934 each trading bank in New Zealand issued its own notes, but from 1 August of that year the Reserve Bank became the sole note-issuing authority. As with coin, the supply of notes varies solely in response to the demands of the public. If their customers want to convert a larger proportion of their deposits than usual into notes, the trading banks and the Post Office Savings Bank must buy the notes from the Reserve Bank at their full nominal value, by drawing on their deposits there...."

In short, as we had stated, it is the banking system as such which determines not only the amount of cheque money to be put into circulation, but also the amount of coin and notes which form the basis of the bank credits. By way of further illustration we quote—

Par. 24:
"The fact that banks 'create money' in this way is not a new discovery, as some witnesses implied. For example, in the *Economic Writings* of *Sir William Petty* (1623-1687), Vol. II, page 446, we find:
Question 26:
What remedy is there if we have too little Money?
Answer:
We must erect a Bank, which well computed, doth almost double the effect of our coined Money.

And Francis Cradocke, a London merchant appointed by Charles II as a member of the Board of Trade, said:
"A Banke is a certain number of sufficient men of Credit joined together in a Stock, as it were, for keeping several men's cash in one Treasury and letting out Imaginary Money (i.e. Credit) at interest for three or more in the hundred per annum, to tradesmen or others that agree with them for the same; and making payment thereof by assignation, passing each man's account from one to another, yet paying little money."
Mr. H. D. Macleod, from whose book *The Theory of Credit*, written in 1894, the above quotation comes, defined a banker as

"A Trader who buys Money and Credits, Debts or Rights of Action payable at a future time by creating and issuing Credits Debts or Rights of action payable on demand." Several other quotations on this subject are given in Part II of Appendix D.

Now, though it is repeatedly stated in the Report that all these matters have been widely known for a long time, this is not, in fact the case. On the contrary, it has been not only often admitted by bankers that the principles of banking are not known, but on many occasions bankers have tried to deny that they create money at all. In Britain, in the inter-war years, it was the Rt. Hon. Reginald MacKenna, chairman of the Midland Bank, who was among those who openly admitted the basic characteristics of banking at shareholders' meetings and on similar occasions.

Par. 62 and 63 (iii). Can Trading Banks Create the Money They Lend Without Needing to Borrow from the Public and Without Cost to Themselves?

"Several witnesses claimed that, unlike other financial institutions which have to borrow money already in existence before they can lend anything at all, the trading banks create the money they lend without cost to themselves. This is a gross exaggeration of the power of the trading banks."

"We have already stressed that, in fact, a trading bank can lend only to the extent that its reserves of banker's cash allow. They must be adequate to meet any conceivable demands by its customers for notes, coin, or foreign exchange, to preserve customers' confidence in its ability to meet their requirements immediately, and to meet the minimum statutory balance which is currently required to keep at the Reserve Bank. The bank can maintain this cash reserve only if people are willing to leave deposits with it. If a much larger number of its depositors than usual suddenly decided to convert their deposits into notes, coin, or foreign exchange, or transfer them to customers of other banks, the bank would be forced to sell some of its investments and call up some of its advances to enable it to meet their demands. Thus a trading bank's ability to lend depends on its ability to induce people to leave deposits with it, and these are clearly debts of the bank to its customers. The trading bank, like other financial institutions, must therefore borrow in order to lend."

Now this apologia of the basis of the banking system is, apparently, the best that could be propounded by a set of experts, whose job clearly was to counter insistent criticism of the system by a large number of groups and individuals in New Zealand. Yet the whole argument is a combination of errors and inner contradictions.

In the first paragraph there is the lame excuse that the adverse criticism of the banking system is an exaggeration. It is not, being quite true. In any event the fact that it is partly true, is indirectly admitted by the Commission.

We have already noted that the amount of cash held by the banks is determined by them. Therefore it is not possible to argue that they are really bound by its amount. Furthermore, we have also noted previously that it is a fact that the banks must maintain confidence in their ability to provide cash on demand, but this by no means proves that they must, therefore, borrow what they lend. The thesis that the bank can maintain its cash reserve only if people are willing to leave deposits with it also does not prove that which it is intended to prove. All it means is that people should be prepared to use cheques for payments many times more often than notes or coin. This is, of course, the basis of the banking system, but it does not prove the abovementioned thesis, since the deposits are themselves in the first place bank loans, i.e. creations of money out of nothing. Then the Commission goes on to say that the ability of a bank to lend depends on its ability to induce people to leave deposits with it. True, since that is again just another way of saying that credit creations should be converted into demands for cash only in a small part, but again this is no proof of money being borrowed before it is lent. But the end part of the sentence suggests that deposits are clearly debts of the bank to its customers. On the contrary, every loan creates a deposit, a loan, however, by the bank to the customer and not vice versa. Thus the whole argument falls to the ground. Finally we may well ask, from whom the bankers borrow that which they lend. Certainly not from their customers, who are holding money most of which came into existence as a bank loan; also not from their shareholders, since the nominal capital of a bank is always but a trifling sum in comparison with the total of deposits; and finally it is neither the State, nor the Central Bank which lend money to the trading banks, since the State is always in debt to the bankers, and the cash which the trading banks get from the Central Bank is only a small fraction of the amounts lent by the banks by means of monetary creations.

It would be fair to conclude that, if the bankers cannot provide a better and more convincing argument in favour of the basis of their system, then it must follow that they know well that the whole scheme is based, as we have stated, on a big hoax, which has survived for many generations. It is true that the hoax was often perpetrated by agreement with others and that the bankers are not alone responsible, but this does not alter the basic facts. The Royal Commission in New Zealand has been quite unable to prove the virtue of the present banking and credit system under Capitalism, despite the fact that the members of the Commission were greatly helped by the ineptitude and incomplete knowledge and understanding of some of those who gave evidence to prove the shortcomings of the system. It is still not so much the positive characteristics of modern banking which are its strength, as the fact that it is still so little known by most people and that the possible alternatives are therefore so often based on incomplete analysis and mistaken views. The sooner these matters are considered by all competent men, the quicker will we approach the establishment of a new dispensation.

* * *

Following on the facts brought to light at the New Zealand enquiry, we have had in 1960 the Radcliffe Committee on the working of the monetary system in the United Kingdom.

We quote from the evidence given by the Bank of England, vol. 1, Memoranda of Evidence,

p.9.,4. *The control of Bank Credit in the United Kingdom:*
1. The commercial banking system in this country is dominated by eleven banks ...
2. Because an entry in the books of a bank has come to be generally acceptable in place of cash it is possible for the banks to create the equivalent of cash (i.e. credit). Thus a bank may pay for a security purchased from a customer merely by making an entry in its books to the credit of that customer's account; or it may make an advance by means of a similar entry. In either case, an increase in its deposits will occur.
3. However, the banks cannot create credit in this way without limit. For their customers will want to exchange some part at least of the additional credit for cash, and cash the banks cannot create ...
4. It has come to be accepted that they should in fact hold an amount close to 8% of their deposits in cash, that is in till money (notes and coin) or balances at the Bank of England ... As a general rule the banks will be very reluctant to see the ratio to their deposits of their cash plus other liquid assets— their "liquidity ratio"—fall below 30% ...
7. ... if the Exchequer borrows by issuing Treasury Bills which are taken up by the banks and spends the proceeds (so that the cash borrowed finds its way back to the banks) the liquid assets and deposits of the banks will be increased and they will be put in a position to increase the supply of bank credit ...

p. 13. 6. *The issue of legal tender*

18. The present position is that the Issue Department (of the **Bank of England**) plays an essentially passive role in the supply of currency. The principal banks draw notes from the Bank as necessary to meet the demands of their customers and to maintain what they consider to be adequate amounts of till money; and the Fiduciary Issue is adjusted as required to meet their drawings ... (End of quotation).

It will thus be seen again that the basic thesis we have set out regarding the capitalistic monetary system is confirmed by the highest authorities. The private banking system has fully usurped the sovereign power of issue of the State and enriches itself by the use of the public credit, which it fully controls to its own advantage.

* * *

The material which can be quoted in support of the contention that in all respects the Russian revolution has either reduced the standard of material well-being of the mass of the Russians, or has at least very considerably retarded the rate of progress and development which had been in evidence prior to 1917, is immense. Only specialists could possibly be induced to study all the available data.

There is ample statistical proof that the purchasing power of wages and salaries of the huge majority of Russians are a fraction of what they had been before the revolution.

Let us give a few details of comparatively recent date, all being inevitably approximate:

The maximum real purchasing power of the Soviet Rouble is approx. 5/- or 25 New Pence (US 60c).

Prices are:

Man's Suit, of low quality	150R.	= £37·00.
Woman's Suit, " "	102R.	= £25·00.
Wool Pullover	40R.	= £10·00.
Cotton Summer Dress	7R.	= £1·75.
Leather Shoes	50R.	= £12·50.

Soviet-type food for family of four for a week:

	Cost:	Working time of male industrial worker to buy it:
Moscow:	32·78R. = £8·20	65 Hours.
London:	£6·42	18¼ "

Paris:	96·36Fr. = £7·10	21½	,,
Munich:	83·98DM. = £9·57	20¾	,,
New York:	$18·43 = £7·68	8	,,

Wages and Salaries:
Legal Minimum 60R. per month = £3·33 per week.
Working-Class family, with more than one member working, appr.: 100R. per month = £5·55 per week.
Middle-Class incomes—doctors, teachers, engineers etc.: 150R.–300R. per month = £8·77–£16·66 per week.
Professor, factory manager, Colonel etc.; average abt.: 500R. per month = £27·77 per week.

A few salaries rise to 2000R. and more, with various additional sources of income, while at the pinnacle of the Soviet power pyramid incomes are unlimited.

Persons employed at the highest levels also have access to special stores at which the quality of the goods is high and the prices moderate, and everything is easily available, while the huge majority of Soviet citizens have great difficulty in finding even basic necessities.

Rents are low, but there is still terrible overcrowding and the buildings are badly built and maintained.

In most cases the money incomes of workers on the collective farms are negligible, though payment is partly made in kind. The workers are not permitted to leave the farms and are thus close to being slaves.

In recent years there has been some improvement in the material conditions of the people, but they are still very low by any normal standards.

We can give some figures from the "Bulletin of the Institute for the Study of the USSR", Vol. III, No 7 of July 1956 (this is published in Munich under US auspices).

Regarding the Russian railways the facts are as follows. In 1913 there were 58 500 kilometres of track; in 1922, 69 600 Km.; in 1928, 76 900 Km.; in 1932, 84 800 Km.; in 1940, 105 300 Km.; in 1955, 120 000 Km.; and in 1960 (plan) 126 500 Km. Soviet sources always take 1913 as a basis for their comparisons, asserting that the network has more than doubled since then. This is not so. Between 1913 and 1918, despite the war, the construction of new railways continued. In 1917 the network totalled 60 500 kilometres. Moreover up to 1928 many sections under construction before the revolution and already partially open to traffic were finished. Thus, between 1922 and 1928, 7 300 Km. of railways were completed.

Between 1929 and 1940 the increase in the Soviet railway network was given as 28 400 Km. It is true that the Soviets did build new lines, but this figure includes the lines of the Baltic countries, Western Ukraine, Western Bielorussia and Bessarabia; the lands were occupied by the Soviets, but most of their railways had been built by the Imperial Russian administration.

Assuming that 7 900 kilometres, including what had been started before the revolution, were brought into service, on the basis of the Soviet figures the increase in the network between 1933 and 1940 would be 20 500 Km. However, from this must be deducted approximately 14 000 Km. acquired from the neighbouring territories, leaving a total of only 6 500 Km. of new lines laid during this period. Shortly, the development has been as follows :

Period	Length in Km.	Annual average (Km.)
1922–28	7 300	1 040
1929–32	7 900	1 970
1933–40	6 500	810
1941–55	14 700	980
1956–60 (plan)	6 500	1 300
Total:	42 900 Km.	1 100 Km.

Now this "Soviet achievement", which is paralleled by a similar scale of "success" in most other spheres, should be compared with the speed at which track was laid before the revolution, when mechanization was virtually non-existent, but when there was also no slave labour as under Communism, with that of the present "Socialist economy". From 1864 to 1873, 12 588 Kilometres of track were laid, an average of 1 250 Km. a year; in 1870, 2 557 Km. were laid; in 1871, 2 856; from 1894 to 1 903, 25 425 Km., an average of 2 500 a year; in 1899, 5 257 Km.

It cannot be said that the Soviets did not envisage increasing the rate of railway construction, since during the Third Five-Year Plan 11 000 Km. were to be laid, an annual average of 2 200 Km. But in actual practice the line laid from 1933 to 1940 was only 6 500 Km., an average of only 810 Km. a year. At the Twentieth Party Congress directives were given for railway construction at the rate of only 1 300 Km. a year.

Yet there are very many people who are genuinely impressed by Communist boasts of immense progress in industrialization, as in all else. In fact, we repeat, the rate of progress everywhere in

Russia has been considerably slower than it had been under the Empire.

Quality, too, has suffered in most directions. This fact is especially striking in the realm of general education. It is true that specialists, such as engineers, are often of the highest quality and competence; here the Russian natural abilities have overcome the handicaps imposed by the régime. But most of these engineers, as also army officers and indeed the large majority of the supposedly educated classes in Soviet Russia cannot spell properly and have a poor grip on grammar, despite the fact that Russian spelling, especially after the orthographical reforms of 1918, is almost completely phonetic and not really difficult. Certainly before the revolution such mass slovenliness was completely unknown. Yet the great majority of the population of Russia were not illiterate.

The flourishing condition of pre-revolutionary Russia and the harm resulting from Communism are well illustrated by an article in the journal "Swoboda" (Freedom), No 52, of October 1956, published by a Left-wing group of Russian émigrés under the auspices of the American authorities, so that this source is far from us politically and its information can be considered, in our work, to be impartial, the more so as the article is seriously and competently written. We take some facts from this material.

Industrial development began in the United States and in Russia in the middle of the last century. By 1913 the speed of industrial development in Russia exceeded that of America and Russian industrial production increased in the half century from 1860 to 1910 by 12.5 times. Development was especially fast after 1908–09 and reached its greatest intensity during the war of 1914–17. In 1913 the number of Russian industrial, building and railway workers was 7 million, i.e. already at that time Russia possessed a huge industry. By the end of 1916 it provided all the supplies required by the huge fronts and that without any foreign help, such as lend-lease in the second world war.

From 1894 to 1914 the population of Russia increased from 122.7 million to 175.1 million, i.e. by 43%, while at the same time the cereal harvest increased in European Russia by 65% and in Siberia even more. It is not surprising that before the revolution Russia was the granary of Europe, while the Soviet Union imports foodstuffs.

By the year 1956 the Soviets had existed for 39 years in Russia. According to the old tempo of development industrial production had increased 12.5 times in fifty years and thus in 39 years it should have grown by 9.75 times. Thus we can make the following comparisons:

Production in 1913–1914		Theoretical Production with normal development by 1955		Production under Socialism 1955	
Cast iron	4.4 Mil. tons.	43.0 Mil. tons.		33.0 Mil. tons.	
Oil	9.0 ,, ,,	87.5 ,,	,,	71.0 ,,	,,
Coal	36.0 ,, ,,	356.0 ,,	,,	391.0 ,,	,,
Sugar	1.88 ,, ,,	18.32 ,,	,,	3.4 ,,	,,

By the time of the revolution the population of Russia reached 180 million. During 39 years, until 1957, in conditions of the normal Russian annual increase of 2.15%, there would have been added another 151 millions. Bearing in mind also the additional increase at the same rate for the same period of 55.26 million inhabitants, we should have seen a total increase of the population of 206.26 million, i.e. in 1956 there should have been in Russia altogether 386.26 million people, but according to the information in "Pravda" of the 7th July 1956 the population of the USSR was 202.2 million. Thus there is a shortage of inhabitants of 184 million, and that is a direct result of the revolution and of Communist rule. In addition the average expectation of life in the USSR has fallen to 46.7 years, while in Europe it is over 60. Among the missing people of Russia one must include those killed by the Communists, those who have died in concentration camps, during collectivization and induced hunger and those who fell in wars, as well as those missing as the result of a lowered birthrate. This is the terrible price of a materialistic policy.

From "The Truth about the Reign of The Emperor Nicholas II" by Al. Messoyedoff.

In order to excuse the Soviet régime for maintaining the living conditions of the mass of the population at such a low level, the Communists have cleverly spread a legend which has disarmed the criticism of those who have not perceived this falsehood. They are willing to admit that the U.S.S.R. has not yet overtaken the Western nations as Khrushchev admitted, as Stalin himself confessed, but they affirm that, nevertheless the Communists deserve praise because before them there was nothing and without them Russia would have remained an underdeveloped country. In the "Economic Problems of Socialism in the U.S.S.R.", the last work published under his name, Stalin wrote: "The work of the Soviets, in view of the absence of even the beginning of a socialist economy was to create, so to speak on virgin soil, the framework of a socialist economy."

This statement is entirely untrue. Certainly, Russia started late on the road to industrialization; it is true that it was only towards the end of the nineteenth century that large industries of a modern type developed. But from 1900 onwards the rate of expansion speeded up in an astonishing fashion. The value of production per head of population rose from less than 9 roubles in 1900 to more than 14 roubles in 1913. A remarkable rate of expansion, all the more so as the population had increased considerably. There can be no doubt that Russia's position in terms of population and economics would be much better today if the revolution had not broken out.

M. Edmond Théry, the distinguished economist, wrote, with good reason, in 1914: "If affairs in the great European nations continue between 1912 and 1950 as they have done between 1900–1912, towards the middle of the present century, Russia will dominate Europe both politically, economically and financially."

POPULATION AND FINANCE

In 1894 at the beginning of the reign of H.I.M. the Emperor Nicholas II, Russia had 125 million inhabitants. Twenty years later, on the eve of the First World War, the population had increased by 50 million and had reached the number of 175 million. It was therefore, increasing at the rate of 2.4 million a year. But the Communist dictatorship has brought Russia a loss in population of a great deal more than 100 million.

Between 1897 and 1913 State receipts rose from 1.400 million gold roubles to 3,471 million. (1 rouble = two shillings gold; 9.40 rouble = £1). This was an increase of more than two thousand million in sixteen years. These receipts covered all the expenses of the State and in 1914 had allowed an excess of 512 million, without any increase in taxes. Moreover, before the First World War, the latter were the lowest in the world.

In spite of the Russo-Japanese war of 1904–1905, which cost Russia two and half thousand million gold Roubles, the gold reserves of the Russian Empire had risen from 694 million (gold Roubles) in 1894 to 2,257 million in 1914. This reserve covered by more than 100% in gold the bank notes in circulation. During the same twenty years the deposits in savings banks rose by 1,876 million (gold Roubles) from 360 million in 1894 to 2,236 million in 1914.

INDUSTRY AND ECONOMY

Between 1890 and 1913, Russian industry quadrupled production. Not only did its revenue almost equal that of agriculture, but output already covered four-fifths of the internal demand for manufactured goods. This is the more remarkable as until the end of the nineteenth century Russian industry was backward in comparison with the industries of England and Germany. Moreover, Russian industry developed very early what one might call an

American pattern, in the sense that it was very concentrated and that large concerns—employing more than a thousand workers— were in 1914 relatively more numerous than in any other country.

Here are some figures which will enable the reader to judge the development of Russian industry during the last decades of the nineteenth century and the opening years of the twentieth.

CAST IRON
Production rose from 25 million poods in 1890 to 378 million in 1913. (1 pood = 16.38 Kg.)

COAL
Production rose from 259 million poods in 1885 to 2,159 million in 1913.

PETROLEUM
In spite of the fire in the Bakou oil wells in 1905, production rose by 65% and in 1913 reached 600 million poods.

COPPER
An increase of 375%.

MANGANESE
An increase of 364%.

On the eve of the revolution Russian agriculture was booming. During the two decades which preceded the 1914–1918 war, output had doubled. In 1913 Russian production of the principal cereals was one-third greater than that of the Argentine, Canada and the United States together. Russia had 37.5 million horses, more than half of all those in the world. She was supplying 50% of the world's imports of eggs.

CORN
Production in 1894: 2 thousand million poods. In 1913: 4 thousand million.

SUGAR
An increase of 24.5%. During the same period the consumption of sugar per head of population rose from 4 to 9 Kg. a year.

TEA
Consumption in 1890: 40 million kilos. In 1913: 75 million.

FLAX

On the eve of the First World War Russia was producing 80% of the world's flax.

COTTON

An increase of 388%. As a result of the great irrigation works in Turkestan begun during the reign of Alexander III cotton production was, in 1913, sufficient to cover the annual needs of the Russian textile industry. The latter had doubled its production between 1894 and 1911.

LEGISLATION FOR THE WORKING CLASSES

The industrial development of the Russian Empire caused a great influx of workers into the factories. It would be untrue to represent the condition of workers in Russia before the revolution as idyllic. Their life was hard and difficult as in England, Germany, and France, but it was certainly better than that known by workers in the Soviet Union to-day.

It must be observed first of all that it was in Russia in the eighteenth century (during the reign of the Empress Catherine II) that for the first time in the world, laws were made governing conditions of work, e.g. the prohibition of night work for women and children, a ten-hour day in factories, etc.

In 1882, a law regulated the work of children between twelve and fifteen years. In 1903 came the creation of workers' delegates who were chosen by the employees of industrial concerns. Syndical rights were recognised by an act of 1906. But above all, superiority over the present Marxist system came from the opportunity that workers had to defend themselves by means of the classic weapon of the working classes. One could strike in the Russia of the Tsars, but a strike is impossible in the Russia of today, as it was in that of Stalin and Lenin. In factories controlled by the inspectorate of Labour—one existed in Tsarist Russia—there were 68 strikes in 1895, 118 in 1896, 145 in 1897, 145 in 1898, 189 in 1899, and 125 in 1900. As for "Social Insurance" it was introduced in 1912!

THE AGRARIAN QUESTION

One need only say that the history of the Russian peasants since the revolution has been one long Calvary.

We confine ourselves to quoting a few lines from the pen of M. François de Romainville:

"The peasants resisted collectivisation sullenly. The first result was the great destruction of livestock. It fell from 270.2 million heads in 1929 to 118 million in 1933. Even more serious was the number of human victims. Peasants were deported with their families to the icy regions of the north and to the steppes of Asia. Between 1928 and 1937, five million homes, that is the homes of twenty million people, were destroyed.

During the reign of Nicholas II a happy solution and one which could have been final had been found for the agrarian problem, which is the chief preoccupation of many governments.

In 1861, after serfdom had been abolished by the Emperor Alexander II, the Russian peasants received, for a small sum, the land ceded voluntarily by the landed proprietors who formed the majority of the nobility. The peasants, however, did not own the land individually because the latter belonged to the village communes, which distributed it to the members of the community. In following this agricultural policy the government had adhered to the custom usual in Old Russia known as the 'Mir'—and had sought to protect the peasant from the temptation to sell the land granted to him. If the latter had been able to turn what he had received into cash, he would, without doubt, have left the land to join the urban proletariat. Communally owned property on the other hand, guaranteed him a means of existence for himself and his family.

But in spite of many advantages this agrarian policy also had many grave defects. The peasant did not feel himself to be master of the soil, and, not being certain of receiving the same plot at the next distribution, he was neglecting his work and losing his sense of responsibility. On the other hand, not having any property to defend he did not respect that of others. Finally, the increase in the rural population in European Russia was decreasing the size of holdings at each distribution. Towards the end of the nineteenth century, the dearth of land made itself seriously felt in the most highly populated provinces.

The revolutionary movements exploited this situation to the full, and made a purely economic question into a political one. Profiting by the discontent of the peasants, the Marxists excited the rural masses and urged them to demand the expropriation of the private proprietors.

Faced with this problem which was becoming more acute every day, the President of the Council, Stolypin, did not hesitate to take some extremely important measures which would have cut short all Marxist propaganda if they could have been carried to completion.

In the first place he decided to encourage the rural population of European Russia to emigrate to Siberia. The peasant who agreed to go was freed of all taxes for a long period, was aided financially by the State and received free ownership of a holding of 15 hectares (1 hectare = approx. 2½ acres). This measure had great success. Siberian agriculture expanded rapidly and this progress soon made possible the export abroad of large quantities of agricultural products.

In the second place the Stolypin government authorised the Peasants' State Bank (created under the Emperor Alexander III) to buy land on the free market from the rich proprietors in order to resell it to the peasants on particularly easy terms (a long period of credit amounting to almost 90% of the value of the land, a very low rate of interest, etc.) *The result of this measure was that in 1914 more than 80% of the arable land in European Russia was in the hands of the peasants.* The Peasants' State Bank, justly called the greatest and most socially beneficient institution of land credit in the world, had agreed to loans which had risen from 222 million roubles in 1901 to 1,168 million in 1912!

Lastly, the law of November 9th, 1906, (known as the Stolypin Act) allowed the peasant to leave the collective ownership of the Commune and to become the individual and hereditary owner of the land which he cultivated. The success of this law was tremendous. More than two and a half million requests from the heads of the families were at once presented to the 463 special commissions which were engaged on the reform. By 1913, two million families had already received their land. A veritable army (more than 7 000 persons) of land surveyors was mobilised to direct the work of division. A few months before the war 13% of the land of the Communes had become the individual property of the peasants. On the eve of the revolution Russia was on the road to transforming herself into a country of small landed proprietors who were rapidly increasing their wealth.

CONCLUSION

The Emperor Nicholas II was the initiator of all these economic, social and political reforms. The greatest landowner in Siberia, the Emperor did not hesitate to *give freely* the 40 million hectares of land which he possessed beyond the Urals. Everything had to be created in this immense region : roads, schools, hospitals, churches, etc. The Emperor Nicholas II spent without stint for this work. It was on his personal initiative that the system of travelling clergy was instituted in Siberia.

"Russia needs thirty years of tranquillity and peace to become the richest and most prosperous country in the world", said

Krivoshein, the minister of agriculture, to the German professor Seering when he came to Moscow in 1912 at the head of a commission to study the famous "Stolypin farms".

Alas! the first world war and the revolution did not allow the Russian Empire these years of tranquillity. The tyranny of the red seducers reduced the Russian people to slavery. The millions of people in concentration camps are testimony that happiness does not exist under the Communist régime.

We hope that those guiding Western policies will not forget these unhappy people and will not allow themselves to be deceived by Soviet propaganda!

We have mentioned, in the course of this material,* the fact that unemployment or alternatively inflation cannot be avoided under the present capitalistic debt-money system. If the prices of almost all goods and services must include a fraction to cover the interest obligations, direct and indirect, of the firms providing them, and if the mass of the consumers are not in receipt of usury incomes in any forms, then it follows that there is a shortage of purchasing power, which expresses itself as unemployment, unless there is artificially induced inflation. This then serves to bolster up the total purchasing power and thus reduces or excludes unemployment. But, as we have also pointed out, this perpetual reduction of the value of the money, accompanied by a perpetual increase in the debt and interest burdens on the economy, must lead to an ever-increasing average rate of interest and an ever-increasing rate of growth of inflation.

On the other hand if, basically, money is not created as an interest-bearing debt and if it is spent by the State and not lent into circulation, thereby immensely reducing taxation, then there is certain to exist a natural balance of the economic system, with the total of all prices being equal automatically to the total of all wages and salaries, as they would in effect both be the same thing, profits being the variable salary of the entrepreneur.

But we cannot entirely eliminate either taxes or interest on loans; the State may have to have income in addition to the sums annually to be created as new money (in amounts which maintain a steady purchasing power of the means of exchange), and the capitalization of business expansion, even in conditions of the prohibition of perpetual debts, would not be easily attained unless savings etc. can earn interest if lent for useful purposes.

Therefore we have potentially a situation in which the bad phenomena of usury-capitalism we have mentioned could be produced, even if on a much smaller scale than at present. Yet this

*See page 67.

danger can be completely averted without in any way putting a brake on investment, providing the average rate of interest on debts outstanding, not counting amortization or insurance against loss, is not higher than the average rate of the creation of new moneys in all forms, i.e. the total volume of interest paid in a given period is equal to the total volume of new money issued, though certain other factors may vary the proportion.

And there is every justification for the assumption that that rate of the periodic increase in the turnover of the economies in healthy countries would be quite high enough to make possible a volume of capitalization adequate for the needs of the growing economy.

Thus one can visualize a monetary and economic system in which there would be balance, growth, stability, full employment for all who want to work and minimal taxation. Any interest or any taxes, such as a value added tax, which firms would have to add to their prices, would have no harmful consequences either economically, socially or politically.

It should be obvious that in conditions of a freely competitive system, where all can find work or start a business, there would seldom, if ever, be any need for strikes. But if the present mismanagement continues then the European and the World Communist dictatorships, now being prepared, will become inevitable, and very soon.

Index

A.E.G. (Allgemeine Elektrizitäts Gesellschaft), also G.E.C. (General Electric Company), 19
Alaska, 154
Alexander I, Emperor of Russia, 1801–25, 156
Alexander II, Emperor of Russia, 1855–81, 139, 168, 229
Alexander III, Emperor of Russia, 1881–94, 228
Alexander the Great, King of Macedonia, 23
Alexeieff, General, Chief of Imperial Russian General Staff in First World War, 130
American Intelligence, 199
American Civil War, 158
Arabs, 120
Armenia, 155
Aschberg, Olaf. Director of Nya Bank, Stockholm, 11
Austro-Hungarian Empire, 131, 136, 178, 198
Avon, Lord (Sir Anthony Eden). British Foreign Secretary and Prime Minister, 178

Bank of England, founded 1694, British Central Bank, 21, 91
Banks, 32 et seq.
Baruch, Bernard M. Powerful American financier and politician, 19
Beaconsfield, Earl of. (See Disraeli), 18
Ben-Gurion, David. Top-level Zionist and first Premier of Israel, 21
Beria, Lavrentii. One-time chief of the Soviet secret terroristic Police —KGB, 171
Bielorussia. (See White Russia), 138
Black Sea, 154
Bordeaux, Duc de. (See Chambord), 123

British Empire, 160, 198
Brussiloff. Commanding General of the Russian Imperial Army in the First World War, 131
Buddists, 139

Caesar, Julius. Roman Emperor, 43
Campbell. Large US landowner, 48
Capital and Capitalism, 40 et seq.
Catherine II, the Great. Empress of Russia, 228
Caucasus, 154
Chambord, Comte de. De jure Henri V, King of France, 123
Charles I, King of England and Scotland, pseudo-judicially murdered by Oliver Cromwell and his party, 24, 37
Chiang Kai-Shek, Marshal, Head of State and leader of Free China, 115
Chile, 126
China, 50, 57, 114, 160, 164
Churchill, Sir Winston Spencer, KG. British political leader and Premier, 130, 133
Cochrane, Sir Charles. British Theatrical leader, 105
"Cold War", 177
Comintern (Communist International), 163
Congo, 194
Constitution of the United States, 94, 123
Counter-Revolution, 208
Cromwell, Oliver. Traitor and regicide; Revolutionary misleader, 24, 37
Cuba, 126
Cyprus, 156
Czechoslovakia, 194

"Daily Mail", 175
"Daily Telegraph", 133

Daly, Jerome. American patriotic lawyer noted for telling legal attacks on the unconstitutional money of the USA, 92, 93

"Decembrists", leaders of Russian revolutionary plot of 1825, 149

Democracy, 84 and others

Dialectical Materialism, 32

Disraeli, Benjamin (Earl of Beaconsfield). British Conservative leader and Premier, 18, 19

Dividends, 65

Dolgoroukoff, Prince Paul. Chairman of the Central Committee of the Russian Kadet (Constitutional Democrat) Party at the time of the revolution, 134

Dubcek, A. Son of a life-long Communist and himself a leader of the Czechoslovak Communist Party. Was the chief figure in the events which were intended to prove the impossible, i.e. that Communism can be combined with liberty, 17

Duma. The Russian Parliament in the years before the revolution of 1917, 131

Eccles, Marriner. One-time chairman of the US Federal Reserve System, 94

Elizabeth I, Queen of England, 148

Elizabeth II, Queen of Great Britain, 93

Engels, Friedrich. Collaborator and backer of Karl Marx, 47, 162

Eskimos, 139

Ethiopia (Abyssinia). Ancient Christian Empire in North-East Africa, 102, 117

Faisal, King of Saudi Arabia, 120

Fascism, 186

F.B.I. (Federal Bureau of Investigation) USA, 129

Fiat (Fabbrica Italiana de Automobile de Torino), 48

Finland, 136, 178

Ford, Henry, Sr. Great US Car Manufacturer and political writer, 44, 48, 123

France, 153, 155, 178

Freedman, Benjamin H. Eminent Christian-Jewish American writer, 22

Freemasonry, 38, 98, 123, 150

French Revolution, began 1789, 38

Georgia, Ancient Caucasian country, 155

Germany, 198

Glubb Pasha, Lt. General Sir John Glubb, former Commander of the Arab Legion in Jordan, 120

Göbbels, Josef. Nazi German Minister of Information, 176

"Golden International". Leadership of High Finance, 208

Goldmann, Nahum. Zionist Leader and President of World Jewish Congress, 20

Goldsmiths. Became early bankers in later Middle Ages, 30, 31

Goldstein, David. Roman-Catholic American Jew, 22

Gomberg, Moritz. Writer on World Unification, 57

Goschen, Donald. Member of distinguished banking family. Rhodesian farmer. Important expert on the truth about Money and Finance, 118

Graham, Lord. (Duke of Montrose). Farmer in Rhodesia, former Rhodesian Minister of Agriculture, External Affairs and Defence. Top expert on Money, Finance and subversion, 118

"The Great War", book by Winston Churchill on the First World War, 130

Greece, 155

Hegel, Georg W. F. German Philosopher, 33

Henry VIII, King of England, 37

Hiss, Alger. American politician. High office in State Department. Close adviser to President Roosevelt. Convicted Soviet Communist agent. Chairman of committee which set up United Nations, 182

Hitler, Adolf. Leader of German Nazi Party, head of Government and State as "Führer" from 1933

until death in 1945. Financed on way to power by International banks, 13, 115, 116, 157, 174, 180
Holland, 153
Hungary, 165, 171, 193
Income Tax. First proposed by Marx, 62, 210

Indo-China (Viet Nam), 57
International Court of Justice at The Hague, 110, 117, 158
Israel. Jewish Zionist State in Palestine, 120, 176
Italy, 115

Jacobites. Supporters of the Stuart Dynasty, 95
James II, King of England and Scotland, 24, 37
Japan, 110, 115, 116
Jerusalem, 22, 120
Jesuits. Catholic Religious Order, 18
Jesus Christ, 43
Jews, 18, 139, 144
John IV the Terrible, Grand Duke of Moscow and Czar of Russia, 148
St. John, the Revelation of, 120

"Kadet Party". Russian Constitutional Democrats until the revolution, 134
Kenyatta. Formerly chief of Mau-Mau in Kenya; now head of state, 118
Kerby, Captain Henry B. British Member of Parliament. Expert on questions of Money and subversion, 4, 92, 93, 209
Kerensky, Alexander. Minister of Justice and Premier in Russian Provisional Government in 1917, lawyer and socialist, 134, 162
Khrushcheff, Nikita S. Former head of Soviet Government. Close collaborator of Stalin. Responsible for millions of deaths, 162, 225
Kiev. Capital of Ukraine (Little Russia), first capital of All Russia over 1000 years ago, 125, 138, 147
Koltchak, Admiral. Commander of the Baltic Fleet in the First World War. In the Russian Civil War against the Bolsheviks after the revolution head of all the "White" Armies as "Supreme Ruler of Russia". Murdered by the Communists, 130
Korea, 57, 179, 183
Kronstadt. Island fortress in the Baltic at the approaches to Petrograd (Leningrad), 169
Krupp. Great German industrial firm. Last sole owner Alfried Krupp von Bohlen und Halbach; the business is now controlled by finance, 53
Kuhn, Bela. Head of short-lived murderous Hungarian Communist government shortly after the First World War, 165
Kuhn, Loeb & Co. Famous New York bank, top-level member of constellation of leading International banks. In the period before and after the First World War the senior partner was Jacob Schiff and the Warburg founder and first chairman of the Federal Reserve System, was a partner and a brother-in-law. They led the consortium of international bankers which financed the Russian Communists, 11, 21

Law of Libel, 211
Lenin. Vladimir Il'itch Ulianoff. Of nominally good family and of mixed Russian, Kalmuk, German and Jewish origin. Leader of the Bolshevik Communist party and head of the Soviet government, 17, 33, 34, 103, 128, 162, 170, 174
Liberalism, 95, 98, 150
Limited Liability, 73
Lincoln, Abraham. President of the United States of America. A great patriot. Issued constitutionally legal money and was assassinated, 158
Lloyd George, David. Liberal Premier of Britain in the First World War, 25
Louis XVI, King of France, mur-

dered by the revolutionaries, as was his Heir, nominally Louis XVII, 157

Louis XVIII, King of France after the fall of Napoleon. Brother of Louis XVI, 157

"Lublin Committee". Bogus Polish government set up by the Soviets in the Second World War as preparation for the communist forcible take-over, 115

Ludendorff, E. General. Chief of the Imperial German General Staff in the First World War. Later for a short time collaborator of Hitler, 130, 136, 180

Lvov, Prince. First Premier of Russian Provisional government before Kerensky, 150

Mahoney, Judge. Patriotic American in Minnesota. Gave a judgment in a lawsuit in defence of constitutionally lawful US money. Died soon afterwards, 92

Malaya, 57

Manchuria, 115

Marshall, General George C. Chief of US General Staff in Second World War. Later Ambassador to China and Secretary of State, 115, 177

Marx, Karl, 32, 33, 47, 150, 162, 172

Mary II, Queen of England. (See William III), 24, 94

Mau-Mau. Semi-secret organization of the Kikuyu African tribe in Kenya, having most obscene and filthy ceremonials. Led by Mr. Kenyatta, now President of Kenya, 118

"Mein Kampf". Hitler's Memoirs and Political Testament, the false "Bible" of the Nazis, 175

Mexico, 125, 158

Mikolajczyk, V. Polish Premier during Second World War. Deceived and abandoned by Allies, 115

Miliukoff, P. N. Leader of Russian "Kadet" Party in the Duma, Foreign Minister of Provisional government, journalist in exile, 134

Mindczenty, Cardinal. Primate of Hungary, 165

Mohammedanism (Muslims), 41, 139, 155

Molotoff, Viacheslav Skriabin. (See also Ribbentrop). Criminal black sheep of a respectable military family of the minor nobility. Relation of the composer Skriabin. Bolshevik since before the First World War. One-time Soviet foreign minister, 19, 181

Montrose, Angus Duke of. Known in Rhodesia by one of his lesser titles as Lord Graham, 118

Morris, William. (See Lord Nuffield), 53

Moscow, 154

McCarthy, Senator Joseph. US anti-communist, 112

McFadden, Louis T. US Congressman. Protagonist of Sound Money and Finance, 20

McKenna, Reginald. British banker and Chancellor of the Exchequer, 20, 94

MacMillan, Harold. Former British Prime Minister, 117

Nagy, Imre. Long-time Hungarian Communist leader. Was used in 1956 in the attempted "national-communist" coup, 165

Napoleon I. French Emperor, 38, 124, 156

Napoleon III. French Emperor, 158

"National Communism". Agent-provocateur stunt to deceive people and create a trap, 165, 193

National Debt, 44, 62, 71, 73, 79, 210

NATO (North Atlantic Treaty Organization), 177, 183

Nazis. Members of the German National-Socialist Party, Nationalsozialistische Deutsche Arbeiterpartei—NSDAP. Led by Hitler. Fascist in style. Doomed from the start, but had the support of most Germans, despite its serious shortcomings, 34, 157, 176

"New Economic Policy"—NEP. Introduced by Lenin when full Communism led to all-round failure. Largely restored a normal free economy. Ended by Stalin on the introduction of collectivization and increased terror, 169, 174

"New Deal". Semi-Socialist policies introduced under Roosevelt as the supposed answer to the great crisis after 1929–30, 49

New York, 21–158, 201

New Zealand Royal Commission on money, 21, 213

Nicholas II, Emperor of Russia, murdered 1918, 25, 131, 158, 167, 230

Nilson, Ralph. Chairman of the Rhodesia Front Party, 118

NTS (Solidarists), Russian National Labour Union. Allegedly anti-communist émigré organization, collaborating since its foundation in 1929–30 with various intelligence services, 199

Nuffield, Lord. (William Morris). Great British car manufacturer and philantropist, 53

Nüremberg. City in Southern Germany. Important Nazi centre. After the war scene of the "trials" of the Nazi political and military leaders, some of whom were guilty of serious crimes. But *ex post facto* laws and the seating of Soviet criminal thugs (who are by any standard far worse than any Nazis) on the bench of judges and among the prosecutors, brought Western jurisprudence to the level of gangsterism, 157

Okhrana. Imperial Russian Police department, similar to French Sureté or British Special Branch of Scotland Yard, 129

"Open Market Operations". One of the major methods by which, in centres such as London and New York, the private banks obtain cash for money-out-of-nothing, 43

"Operation Keelhaul". Major Allied War Crime. In accordance with treaties with the Soviets millions of anti-communist Russians were forcibly handed over to Stalin and killed, except the many who preferred suicide. Men, women and children shared this fate, 181

Orthodox Church, 100, 122, 139, 150, 155, 156, 173

Palestine, 20, 57

Paris, 157, 178

Pasternak, B. Soviet Russian novelist. Forced to participate in policy game whose purpose was to persuade Western people that Communism can be combined with liberty, 17

Paterson, William. Founder and first chairman of the Bank of England, 91

Pearl Harbor. Naval harbour in Hawaii, scene of destruction of large part of US Navy by Japanese aircraft, which was deliberately provoked in order to bring the USA into the war. The naval and military authorities were not warned, 116

P.E.P. Political and Economic Planning. Founded before the war for the furthering of hidden Socialism. Most of the time the chairman was Israel Moses Sieff, now Lord Sieff, of Marks & Spencer multiple stores, 49

Persia (Iran), 155

Peter I, the Great. Czar of Moscow and Emperor of Russia, 149

Peter II, King of Yugoslavia, 115

St. Petersburg (Petrograd), at present Leningrad, Capital of the Russian Empire, 150, 169

Portugal, 118, 153

Poland, 50, 115, 154, 165, 170, 193

Provisional Government. Set up in Russia in March 1917 after the abdication of the Czar. Mildly Socialistic. Replaced by the Communists in November of the same year, 150, 162

Radcliffe Committee. Study of Money and Finance, 21, 220
"Radio Free Europe". US-controlled, in Germany. Stunted anti-communism, 183
Rapallo, Treaty of. Soviet-German agreement, 19
Rarick, John. US Congressman from Louisiana. Sound fighter for correct Money, 92
Rathenau, Walter. German financier and politician, 19
"Red International". Leadership of communist subversion, 208
Reed, Douglas. Outstanding British writer, deeply aware of issues of key importance, 56
Rhodesia, 118, 209
Rhodesian Front Party. Politically dominant, 118
Ribbentrop, Joachim von. Nazi German Foreign Minister. Co-signatory with Molotoff of Treaty of 1939, 19
The Right. Intellectual, political and moral state of mind opposed to subversion, 205
"Right Party". Proposed trend to mobilize the Counter-Revolution, 77
Romanoff, Michael. Chosen by the Russian National Assembly in 1613 to become Czar, 201
Roosevelt, Franklin Delano. President of the USA. Rendered great assistance to subversion throughout the world, 21, 53, 54, 56, 115, 181
Rosenberg, Alfred. Minister for Eastern Affairs of the Nazis. Ideologue of the Nazi Party. Of Russian Baltic origin. Russian officer in the First World War. Introduced a violently anti-Russian policy into the Nazi programme, thus assuring defeat in the war. A sinister figure, 180, 200
Rothschild. Famous banking family. Played immensely important role since late 18th century, 18, 38, 39
Roumania, 165
Rousseau, Jean Jacques. French revolutionary writer, 149
R.S.F.S.R. Russian Soviet Federal Socialist Republic. The Great-Russian part of the USSR, 138, 172
Russian Civil War. Followed the take-over of power by the Communists, 168, 172
Russo-Japanese War. Japanese attack on Russia without previous declaration. Japan was backed by Britain and America. When about to collapse, it was saved by Anglo-American ultimatum to Russia to conclude peace, 167
"Russian Liberation Army". Led by Soviet General A. Vlassoff, formed mostly from PoWs in Germany, against the orders of Hitler. Did not become effective, 175
"Russkoye Vosskressenie". Russian émigré newspaper in Paris, published after last war, 134

San Francisco. Californian city in which the committee creating UNO worked, 158
Sarolea, Professor Charles. Edinburgh University. Great authority on Russia, 139
Scheubner-Richter. Nazi ideologue and expert on Russia before Rosenberg. Also of Russian-Baltic origin, but pro-Russian and Monarchist. Killed in the abortive Nazi Putsch in Munich, 180
Schiff, Jacob. Head of Kuhn, Loeb & Co., New York bank. Chief financier of the Russian revolution. He admitted having given $22 Mill, 11
SEATO, South Atlantic Treaty Organization, parallel to NATO, 183
Serfdom. Law by which some of the Russian peasants were tied to certain lands, to assure military

mobilization. Far outlived its usefulness, 139, 168, 229
Siam (Thailand), 57
Siberia, 128, 154
Smith, Ian. Prime Minister of Rhodesia, 118
Solidarists. (See NTS), 199
South Africa, 114
Soviet. Meaning Council (or advice). Supposed "democratic" form of communist government, 47, 48, 116
Spain, 153
Special Branch of Scotland Yard, 129
Stalin, Josif Vissarionovitch Djugashvilli. Georgian-Russian communist tyrant, 48, 54, 115, 161, 170, 225
Stock Exchange, 39, 70
Stolypin, P. Russian Prime Minister. Great Reformer of conditions of peasantry. Outstanding administrator, 145, 229
Struve, Peter B. Former Russian Communist, 129
Subasitch. Yugoslav Premier under the King, 115
Sureté Générale. Parallel in France to the Special Branch of Scotland Yard, 129

Taft, William Howard. President of the USA, 142
Tammany Hall. US Political Club, notoriously corrupt, 125
Tcheka, OGPU, NKVD, MVD, KGB. Various initials for the different names of the Soviet secret terroristic police, 170
Théry, Edmond. French economist, 226
Third International. Marxist organisation. At one time nominally above the Soviet government, 163
Third Republic. French régime after 1871 until 1939, 123
Tito. Real name unknown, but supposed to be Josip Broz. Communist dictator of Yugoslavia, helped to power both by Stalin and the Allies, 115, 193
Tolstoy, Count Leo. Outstanding Russian novelist, but very faulty philosopher, excommunicated from the Orthodox Church for blasphemy, 149
Tories. British Conservatives in their early years, 95
Transjordan, now the Kingdom of Jordan, 57
Treasury Bill. Governmental IOU, promissory note, given to lenders of money to the State, mostly to banks. They often exchange the Bills for cash, which they thus receive for money they created out of nothing, 96
Trotzky, Leo. One of the founders of Bolshevism in Russia. Headed the Red Army in the Civil War. Later expelled from Russia by Stalin. Proponent of the Permanent Revolution, 136, 175
Tukhatchevsky, Soviet Marshal one time C in C, 175
"Tunnage Act". Law founding the Bank of England, 1694, 92
Turkey, 136, 155, 178
Turkomans. Inhabitants of Russian Turkestan, 138

Ukraine. Little Russia (Malorossia). Southern part of European Russia. The original medieval Russia. Has never been independent, 125, 138, 160, 198
UNESCO. United Nations branch, 108
"United States of Europe". One of the plans for the creation of a European State, centrally controlled, as a major step to World Government, 57, 118, 211
U.N.O. United Nations Organization. Successor to the pre-war League of Nations. A godless and subversive scheme. Intended to prepare ground for World Govt, 58, 108, 112, 182, 211
U.S.A. United States of America, 57, 116, 120, 123, 160
U.S.S.R. Union of Soviet Socialist Republics. Soviet Russia. Intended to be the world state, 48, 104, 120, 138, 172

Usury. Money-lending at interest, 31

del Valle, General Pedro A. United States Marines, Ret. The generally recognized top leader of the American true Right Conservatives. Chairman of the Defenders of the American Constitution etc, 93
Vennard, Wickliffe B., Sr. Outstanding US writer on economic and political subjects. Active leader, 20, 93
Viet Nam. Former French Indo-China, 179, 183
Vlassoff, General A. A. Soviet General, PoW in Germany. Tried, with others, to organize a Russian Liberation Army, despite Nazi opposition. Handed over to the Soviets and hanged, 175
"Voice of America". Radio Station in Germany. Attuned to the line of Finance "democracy", 183
"Völkischer Beobachter". Newspaper of the Nazi Party, 176

Warburg. Famous German and American Banking family. Also a branch in London. During the First World War two brothers in the USA and Germany worked together to finance Communism even when America and Germany were at war, 11, 21
Ward, Harvey G. Head of the News Department of Rhodesian Radio and Television. Very well informed on questions of basic importance, 118
Warsaw, 154
Weitzmann, Chaim. Zionist leader and first President of Israel, 20
Welfare State. Socialism by stealth, 89, 209
Whigs. Early British Liberals, proponents of "Dutch Finance", 95
White Russia (Bielorussia). Western Part of Russia, 138
"White Russians". Opponents of Communism, 168
William III, of Orange. King of England with Mary II, 24, 37, 94
Wladimir, Grand Duke of Russia, Pretender to the Throne, 200
Worker's, Council of Deputies. Communist revolutionary method for mobilizing and organizing, 134
World Bank. Paralleled by Bank of International Settlements etc. Centralization of global control, 58
World Council of Churches. Subversively controlled, 190
World Government, 21, 58, 72, 73, 80, 108, 112, 126, 177, 211
Wrathall, John. Rhodesian Minister of Finance and Vice-Premier, 118

Zionism. Jewish movement towards creating State of Israel and converting it into centre of world power, 120